T0248164

DREAMWORK

DREAMWORK

Why All Work Is Imaginary

Steven Connor

REAKTION BOOKS

Published by
REAKTION BOOKS LTD
Unit 32, Waterside
44–48 Wharf Road
London N1 7UX, UK

www.reaktionbooks.co.uk

First published 2023

Printed and bound in Great Britain
by TJ Books Ltd, Padstow, Cornwall

A catalogue record for this book is available from
the British Library

ISBN 978 1 78914 756 8

Contents

1

Dreamworks

One can often tell interesting things about a topic of concern by taking note of who is thought to be in charge of it. In the case of the puzzling activity known as work, for example, one might judge it to be a concern primarily for philosophers and political economists, understood in the sort of broad terms that would allow for religious speculations to be regarded as a kind of philosophy and political economy to subsume any number of different kinds of purposive reflection on the nature and needs of society. Reflecting on work, in the form of questions such as 'how should work be understood?', 'what forms has work taken in the past?' and 'how should work be organized?', tends to be regarded as a serious and weighty business, one, in other words, that itself deserves and demands to be worked at. To take something seriously is in fact to see it as requiring to be worked at, meaning that to take work seriously is to be drawn into a reverberantly issueless tautology: work embodies seriousness, which means requiring work. While there are plenty of people whose business it is to take work seriously, the ranks of economists, social scientists and policy-makers being swelled daily by managers, superintendents, administrators, coaches and commentators of all kinds, all of them constituting not just what used to be called a workforce, but an army of workers pledged to the upkeep of the force of work, it is not immediately clear whose job it might be to ask how and why work came to be the sort of serious business, and perhaps even the principle of seriousness itself, that it is. I will try in this book to make it my business to demonstrate that the meaning of work lies in large part in the craving for seriousness of which it seems to be, if far from the unique, then assuredly the supreme form.

It is sometimes said that culture and civilization depend upon leisure, considered as a kind of surplus gained through work-efficiency, such as the use of tools, or the subjugation of other creatures, or other humans, to make them perform the office of tools. At that point, we are sometimes informed, the necessity for work recedes sufficiently to allow for detached and non-instrumental forms of contemplation, the creation of useless entertainment and artifice, and so on. The truth must surely be the inverse of this. When human beings are wholly taken up in a hand-to-mouth and unreckoning way with the life-and-death matters of seeing off rivals, building dwellings or foraging for roots and beetles, their blest condition is identical with that of the bee or beaver, who, because they work all the time, never work at all. It is only when one has the opportunity for reflection, or a time of remission from getting a living into which reflection must seep, that the condition known as work can start to stand out as work from the immanence that had previously characterized it. Art does not arise from the remission of work: rather work is invented through the intervention into existence of art, revealed as a sort of purposeless work, but which really has the purpose of demonstrating the apotheosis of work into magical absoluteness.

I am by profession and repute a professor of English Literature, a profession in which the act of professing, in the sense of avowing, declaring, confessing or even pretending, remains surprisingly alive, if not exactly wide awake.[1] However, the area in which I largely lay waste my powers nowadays is that of lay or amateur literature, as it is to be found in the exercise of rhetoric, romance, performance and other ways of making things up and spreading them about, throughout the non-book story-world. In the academic world in which I used to have my being before retirement, these topics would be the ones I 'worked on', as in the answer I might be expected to give to the question: 'what do you work on?' A very considerable advance in status is guaranteed by progressing from an occupation in which one works as, or works at, something, to one in which one works *on* things – as composers, architects, writers and other workers who define their objects and occupations for themselves are believed to. Such a self-appointed specialism in verbally made-up things might involve the kind of word-centred expertise that a linguistician ought or might be thought to have, though in fact much of what concerns a literary scholar or critic is the kind of higher-level forms of organization into which verbal artefacts like poems, plays and stories tend to resolve themselves, and which share many of their features and dynamics with artistic objects like paintings, plays and films, and their social counterparts such as legends, scandals, projects, rumours, romances, movements and conflicts. The kinds of organized comportment and behaviours of imagination with which I have been concerning myself for a number of years now might be regarded therefore as a sort of literature in the wild, or amateur dramatics.

Freud suggested that dreams were not the arbitrary and chaotic products of an unsupervised mind running in neutral, but rather the outcome of a specific set of mental operations, consisting in intricate but unconscious processes in which raw daytime thoughts and memories are subject to various kinds of transformation and encryption. Once their rules of construction are understood, they can be reverse-engineered by the psychoanalyst to identify the latent dream-thoughts of which the manifest content of the dream is the codified translation. Freud called this night-shift undertaken in the mind, if not self-consciously by it, 'dreamwork' (*Traumarbeit*).[2] The title of this book partially inverts this idea, to allow for a condensation of the work done in dreams, and the dreams that we engineer about the nature of work. Just as Freud proposed the idea of dreamwork for the way in which dreams are formed, so one might postulate the existence of a vast domain, almost large enough to extend over the whole panorama of social life as such, of organized oneiromatics, though I promise that is the last that will be heard, in this book at least, of that term. It is precisely because there is no such thing as society, in any sort of natural, raw or unreflective state, that social life can be understood, and very likely cannot be otherwise understood, as what the one-time surrealist turned sociologist Charles Madge called 'social eidos' or 'society in the mind', borrowing the term *eidos* from Gregory Bateson.[3] Given how actively we are all concerned, as both actors and audience, in the work of upkeep of this apparitional play, I prefer to see it as a kind of dream theatre. The sense in which representations of work, and, through it, of social life itself, may be seen as theatrical rather than simply propositional – in other words things we must put on show, to and through each other, rather than just things we assume or notice – will emerge, with any luck, through this book. In previous ages, those less generously provided with means of representation, or organized around means of representation coded in ways that made them inaccessible to most, such as writing, the audience for this theatre was highly constrained and stratified. In a media-saturated society, however, more and more people are, as we say, in on the act, and involved in a myriad of different capacities in keeping the show on the road.

The oxymoron contained in Freud's notion of dreamwork invites us to see the serious psychic graft that goes into the formation of the dreams that are often regarded as the opposite of serious business. It also allows us to put a case that the ways in which we comport ourselves in relation to the thing we think of as daylight or workaday work may themselves be the application of a kind of dreamwork. Like those peculiar dreams in which we dream that we cannot get off to sleep then wake to realize we have woken from slumber, there may be a large quotient of dreamwork in the ways in which we understand work.

Work is one of those concepts that veils itself in its apparent availability. There is no easy way, for example, to collect discussions of the philosophy of work, because so much philosophical discussion is conducted through reference to different kinds of work, especially, of course, philosophical works. There are dozens of texts that purport to tell you how various kinds of thing work – *How Fascism Works, Why Civil Resistance Works* – but vanishingly, and for me encouragingly, little about how work works. Dreams, desires and what in other contexts is called ideation are so busily at work in our thinking, about almost anything, that it is hard to get a fix on it. This, however, is just the offer that Joanne B. Ciulla makes at the beginning of her valuable and suggestive book *The Working Life*:

> I invite the reader to explore the meaning of work with me. By examining the historical and cultural presuppositions behind the meaning of work, I hope to give readers a place to stand so that they can examine their own ideas and expectations about work and the choices they have made about work and life.[4]

In my own case I do not hope or expect whatever truth I may be able to intimate to make anyone free, or make their lives or work work any better than they currently do, or don't. I am interested in no more than unfolding some of the ways in which, in Ciulla's offhand but raking phrase, 'work works for us'.[5] Though my interest in the workings of work extends no further than this, it is of a very intense kind, which persuades me to hope that there will be some who prove susceptible to infection by it. Whether it will itself do any further work beyond this work of infection I do not know for sure, but I rather doubt it.

Some Enlightenment philosophers, unable to believe that sensate and intelligent persons of the past could seriously have believed in the myths and religious doctrines that prevailed in their times, developed the idea of the double doctrine – that there was a sort of popular, everyday truth, made up of foolish fictions, ludicrously feeble consolations and superstitious prejudices, the purpose of which was to keep the mass of ordinary, uneducated people stunned, amused, docile, apprehensive and, when required, up for a fight. Meanwhile, the priesthood and their equivalents kept to themselves the secrets of how things really were, reserving for their own use the prerogative of being able to contemplate these higher truths. It may be that my readers will take me to be espousing a similar kind of elitist or conspiratorial double doctrine about the nature of work. If so, it will probably do no good for me to say that though I think that understanding work really means making out the ways it works for us, I do not offer, let alone secretly harbour, any dream of enlightenment coming from this. I do not imagine that being offered understanding, or even the sensation of it, in the things I have it in mind to articulate about the phantasmatics of work will either make it work better for us or, alternatively, sweep away the ectoplasmic floss of dreams and fantasies to open up some new, radiantly sober prospect of things as in themselves they really are, leaving the world lying all before us. *Dreamwork* will likely not make you free, or bring you loss, or leave you very much happier than before. And so, and yet, with gloomy prudence thus forewarned, to work.

Necessity

If work always has some serious meaning, in the sense of a meaning-to-do – some decision, intentness, commitment – it is another kind of seriousness which we must be concerned with in thinking of work. This is the seriousness of the idea of work – the work, so to speak, which the idea of work does, the reflexive seriousness with which we take the different kinds of serious business constituted by work.

The seriousness of work is a given: work performed unseriously is not a different kind of work, but a different kind of thing altogether from work. It is obvious from the way we feel and think about the things that are not work that they are nonserious variations, reprieves or distractions from what we tend to think of as the serious business of work. As I was writing another book about the styles of seriousness, I began to suspect that the necessity for work, in the somewhat mysterious sense of the necessity of the kind of necessity that work seems to stand for, might be the secret, seriousness-imparting ingredient in all the other styles of seriousness that were considered in the book, all of which require the work of shaping and styling, verily the oldest profession. To live seriously, I began to think, is to undertake the hard work of making over mere being into active doing, making living into a transitive verb, with a subject, the one doing the living, and an object, the life that they thereby contrive to live, or, as more often seems to be the important thing, have lived. Trivially, human beings seem to need to have something to do. Less trivially, and in fact rather mysteriously, that something to do needs to be something to be done, something, in other words, that needs to be done. This is to say that human beings of the kind we have become – for possibly there have been, or may yet be, other kinds – need the sense of the pressure of need.

Work is the vastly complex precipitate of this vague but supersaturated need for need. The need for need is a convergence of the two sides of the immensely intricate development of the verb *need* in English, the active sense of needing something, in the sense of having need of it, work, money, rest and so on, and the impersonal sense, usually coupled with a passive infinitive, in which we say that something needs to be done. Need brings together the ideas of lack and of coercion: my need for something is both the fact that it is lacking to me, and the force that that lack seems to exercise upon me towards the making good of the lack, though perhaps I exercise it upon myself through the idea that 'needs must'. We assume that we work because we are coerced into action in order to reduce lack: hunger, comfort, anonymity, sexual gratification. If I am right, we are also subject to coercion by the sense of the need for coercion itself.

Work seems to concern the necessary, and therefore the imperative. Animals work at the things that are necessary to their survival – stalking, hunting, grooming, nest-building, mating display, rearing young, food-gathering, excretion – and many animals also play in what seems like purposeless activity or activity that is only indirectly purposeful, concerned perhaps with the development of skills and capacity, or perhaps sometimes not purposeful at all. But it seems unlikely that they are serious about the serious business of work, or are therefore entirely serious about their play either (how curious it is that only serious play can be really playful). Because the actions and behaviours animals undertake are such obviously serious and necessary matters, to say that they 'take them' seriously would have no intelligible meaning, for this would imply that they had a choice in the matter. And this is perhaps why it also sounds somewhat forced or factitious to call animal actions or behaviour work, except by metaphorical transference in cases where animal activity resembles human activity sufficiently to look like human work, as in the architectural endeavours performed by birds, bees and beavers, which tend to result in the production of the kinds of constructions that, when effected by humans, we would call works. Work, as opposed to action or behaviour, does not simply occur but is performed, and so involves what, following Aristotle, Giorgio Agamben calls impotential, meaning that no matter how necessary work may be to one's well-being or survival, one can always fail or forget or decline, or indeed not even be required, to do it.[6] Breathing is not work, unless or until one conceives it as a form of action voluntarily exercised, in some particular fashion, to some end, and so therefore able to be voluntarily abated. This capacity to avoid, defer, refuse or refrain from work – to be or stay 'off work' in the nice, widely implicating English phrase – is a necessary part of its constitution.

Why do we need to work? It is not any more just because of the proximate necessities of needing money, or needing the products of work for food, shelter or clothing, because we scarcely need to work to supply ourselves with ample quantities of these things. The Christian myth of the first man and woman construes work as necessary to existence as such: in the fourteenth-century *Cursor mundi*, the curse of work is coeval with the course of the world: 'Sore he swanke & Eve his wif/ Vp on þe erþe to wynne her lyf'.[7] We need to work because we need the necessity that work embodies. Why do we need necessity? This seems nonsensical. All of our actions, and all of our ideas about those actions, suggest that what we need and seem most earnestly to crave is freedom from necessity. But perhaps we need necessity precisely because we prove on inspection to be so unnervingly free of it, or perhaps, we had better say, short of it: what need five and twenty, five, what need one? This is the sense in which work is unnecessary necessity, the necessity it is unnecessary that we accept, and so derives its necessity from that.

The chummy first person plural is salient here. We work largely because working requires and produces the solidarity of the 'we', so that whatever the particular aim may be of what we may be doing, overseeing recruitment and retirement arrangements, emptying dustbins, painting walls, we are really working at keeping the project of work working. This is why, as work grows steadily less corporeal, depending less on aggregated physical effort, the institution of the meeting has grown in significance, producing entire classes of workers whose job is to hold meetings or to service them. Such meetings give themselves the work of deliberation or reaching agreement, but their real work is achieved through meeting the requirement to meet. It is telling that the verb 'to work' has come to mean not only to strive, or to effect some action through exertion, but to 'go', or function, a usage that comes into being in the seventeenth century in relation principally to machinery. It is through the fact of working as exerting or effecting that societies 'work', in the sense that they remain functioning. The fundamental necessity of this work is as reflexive as the work itself, for the only operative necessity for a society is that it persists in being. Small, tightly knit traditional societies are perhaps able to hold themselves together through well-understood customs and practices running through the fabric of ordinary life, which perform in a much less urgent and highly charged way the work of performing the society's identity, literally its capacity to remain *idem*, the same, from day to day, and to recognize itself as such in ceremonial self-presentations. As human collectivities grow larger and more pluralized, and have to cope with the effects of competitive rivalries within and between sub-groups, systems of self-recognition and self-synchronization are required that are at once more abstract and involve more orchestrated exertion than in less differentiated societies. As we will see elsewhere in this book, work does much of the work of war, but must always be distinguished from it, since war always involves the all-or-nothing possibility of defeat. If all work is war-work, that is because work is the optimized alternative to war. Only when it becomes possible to lose without losing everything can war be routinized as work.

Organized work, and the customs, practices and institutions, along with the tightly woven affective fabric of wishes, dreads and ambitions, that sustain it, provides the means for societies to maintain themselves continuously in being, maintaining themselves through the maintenance of exertion itself. Societies may project aims for themselves through five-year plans and vaguer ambitions for ever-greater dominion over the natural and human world, but this imperial expansiveness is not really projective in that it must in fact remain open and incomplete, since completion of a society's aim would produce exhaustion, inertia and dissipation. Societies bound by the *mythos* of work as collective striving grow in order to remain the same, or not to decay and disappear. By the same token, they remain in being through exerting themselves. Work always aims at some kind of completion, cessation or remission: keeping a society 'working' in the way that projects of work do aims at ongoing incompletion, or the work only of keeping itself at work in being.

There is another aspect to the necessity of work, which relates more to the question, to which this book will frequently return, of what is necessary for work to be or count as work – for there is no being of work aside from this counting-as-work. There is something necessary to work that need not be necessary to any part of its action, in the way that aprons or gumboots, or obedience or alacrity, or accomplishment may be said to be. Though this complement of counting-as-work will never be a necessary part of the work itself, as practised or enacted, it will nevertheless be the thing, and, heavens, the only thing, that makes it work. The only real thing about work is the fact that it is taken to be, or in the strong sense, imagined as, work. Having one's work recognized has recently itself come to be recognized as a major component in the recognition by others that seems to be so important a part of one's social and personal being.[8] But the necessity of having one's work recognized, as useful, honest, honourable, authentic and so on, is an accessory to a more fundamental and yet more elusive kind of recognition that is necessary for one's work to be work at all, or indeed for there to be such a thing as work in the world. This is the necessity, entirely unnecessary to any part of the performance of one's work, for it to be recognizable and so acknowledged as a kind of work. The essence of work, that which is essential for it to be work, is no part of the work itself. So not only is work action that it is unnecessary to perform in any absolute sense, it is also action that, in order to be known, shown and lived as work, depends on a necessity entirely exterior to itself.

Alternatively, one might say that work is necessary, but its necessity is ritual rather than practical, where ritual implies belief delegated to, or downloaded into, practical action rather than the more abstract action of believing. For this reason, ritual is in fact enacted belief in the efficacy of one's action itself in forming and maintaining belief. The belief in the idea of work, the idea of practical action rather than its actuality, has sometimes seemed crazy, but its very craziness is also surely part of its efficacy. This is on the Tertullianic principle of *credo quia absurdum*: any idiot can believe in gravity, but to rely seriously on the Holy Ghost requires real gumption.

Somewhat surprisingly, therefore, work embodies the necessity of action that it is not strictly necessary to perform, in the way that, say, breathing or eating are supposed to be. Almost everything that is important about work funnels back to this principle: that it is the necessity of the unnecessary. This is true even of the many kinds of coerced labour that might instantly be brought forward as an exception to this rule, and constantly are, from out-and-out slavery to the many different kinds of social and economic necessity that might require people to engage in different kinds of labour. But none of these is necessary in the sense that it is not possible to sustain existence without them. Slavery could only be an exception to the rule of the non-necessity of work for one who believed that it was ordained by nature or God that work should be performed in this manner. Slavery is an enormity not because it is coercion, but because it substitutes a false, heteronomous coercion by another person for a genuine, autonomous act of willing self-coercion, or a willing subjection to what would otherwise be coercive. The words 'false' and 'genuine' in the previous sentence might well be epauletted with quotation marks, since I mean to imply by them 'assumed to be false' and 'assumed to be genuine': the determination of quite where the coercive force comes from in either case is much more difficult to make than to imagine.

Indeed, the very existence of coerced labour, as though this were some kind of scandalous affront to a natural order of things, is an indication of the fact that work is always an effect of forcing, urging or coercion against a background of resistance, inertia or indifference. Even where work is voluntary, it must, to be considered as work, always seem to be the product of some impulsion, or itself exert some force towards some end. What we mean by coerced labour is labour coerced in certain unacceptable ways, since, though labour can certainly be freely or voluntarily performed, there can be no labour free of coercion. So, whenever I say 'I have to work on Wednesdays,' or 'I think I need to do a bit more work on the Introduction,' I must be pointing to or painting in some kind of requirement to which I am not in fact absolutely required to submit. It is the imaginary self-coercion that makes it work, that makes it work as 'work'. So even sleeping can be work if it forms part of a regime of training, for an athletic event, say, or as a form of spiritual discipline, or some other project that, *qua* project, I take seriously enough to subject myself to. Even breathing, which a moment ago I characterized as a simple and absolute necessity for life, can become the kind of unnecessary necessity I am calling work if I subject it to some supplementary regulation, through training myself to breathe at a certain rate per minute, or through alternate nostrils, as part of some spiritual or anthropotechnic project. Every action that may be thought of as work, as opposed to a simple, accidental, involuntary or gratuitous action, divides the worker into master and slave, the one who sets to work and the one who thereby sets themselves to work. It is this commission or commitment that constitutes the seriousness of work.

There are many who will genuinely believe that they disagree with this. Some may believe that the exercise of force, even over oneself, cannot coexist with the kinds of free, spontaneous, expressive or creative activities that represent for them the ideal of work (an impossible ideal, in my view) performed without compulsion or constraint. They may point to the pure, self-fulfilling joy of vegetable gardening, lace-making, dog-walking, car maintenance or any other of a host of activities that human beings may undertake in what we call their spare time, once free from the necessity of work. But such a view arises from a careless understanding of the nature of coercion. A freely chosen activity is nevertheless the exercise of a coercion insofar as it necessarily excludes other kinds of activity. The devotion to macramé or amateur entomology could only be free if it were not in fact the result of any choice or pleasure-seeking predilection, but entirely random or unwilling. Whether or not there can in fact be such a thing as a free choice, the making of any choice and, more importantly, the exercising of it must always constitute a reduction of freedom, a forcing of things into one channel rather than another, or than none. It is the limitation involved in devotion that constitutes its coercion. That is its point, coming to a point always being the result of some coercive act of contraction.

So, on the one hand, forced labour cannot really exist, since you cannot in fact really be labouring if you are simply being forced to, but only pretending to. Forced labour is false labour, labour under these circumstances being just a joke name for forcing people to perform actions that, if voluntarily performed by others, would count as work. On the other hand, there is no labour that does not involve some kind of force, either through self-coercion or consent to the coercion of another, since coercion is what distinguishes just doing things from doing work, or doing things workwise. This is a very disconcerting state of affairs, and accounts for the ways in which the idea of work reaches so far into our conceptions of what it might ever mean to act freely. What we mean by work, or do our best to mean, so hard is it to keep tabs on what we really do mean, is some reflexive relation, usually of a rather slippery or occult kind, between choice and coercion – coercion chosen, or the coercion of choice. Merely performing actions that look like work – lifting pails, toting barges – just does not count, unless this kind of relation, which must always involve or invoke some entity believed to be able to perform the action known as choosing or consenting, is in force. Machines, animals and slaves can appear to be performing work only through a sort of feint or pathetic fallacy. If you really think that the wind performs work in turning a windmill then it ought to be paid, or at least thanked, and nobody really thinks that. Slavery is manifestly an atrocity, but the manifestness of the atrocity has much to do with the fact that it is also an absurdity, like cheating in sport.[9] It may sound atrocious to say that slavery is a pantomime, but that is just what is most atrocious about it.

Phantasmatics

An astute reader will be beginning to suspect already that this will not be a book about work, but rather about our ideas about work. And it will indeed be taken up much less with the understanding of work that such ideas might seem to provide than with the effort to understand the work that they themselves do. 'Ideas' is really far too strong, though. For I will be concerned not with conceptions and representations of work that we simply and recognizably have, but with the inflections and modulations of those ideas that carry our feelings about them – most notably as ideal notions that we would like to be thought to have, and flatter ourselves that we do, and repellent, appalling ideas that we dare not entertain, and yet do, if only by means of what English sadly no longer allows us to call our appalment. The word I propose to use for these affectively inflected ideas is *phantasmatics*.

Work is characterized by an insuperable difficulty. Human beings feel, and transmit to each other, an unmasterable compulsion to work. But it is not clear to them what work is. Aristotle insists that all virtue or excellence comes about from fulfilling one's function, understood as its *ergon*, or the work that it is to do:

> excellence has a twofold effect on the thing to which it belongs: it not only renders the thing itself good, but it also causes it to perform its function well . . . excellence or virtue in a man will be the disposition which renders him a good man and also which will cause him to perform his function well.[10]

But difficulties crowd pressingly and persistently in on the question of what one's proper work is. These difficulties of definition blend with the difficulty of performance that must always be a feature of work: and indeed perhaps the greatest difficulty attached to work is the question of whether work that poses no difficulty can in fact be work.

It is clear that the eye is for seeing and, for Aristotle at least, that a horse is for galloping and carrying its rider.[11] Aristotle's general principle is that 'the virtue [ἀρετὴ] of a faculty is related to the special function [ἔργον] which that faculty performs.'[12] But what, in the case of a human, is that *ergon*: what is a human for? If that human is a slave, the answer is clear(ish): it is to perform the functions required of a slave. Yet if a human is not a slave, if a human has the right to self-indenture to one project or another, without the necessity of doing so, what then is a human for? What is a human's proper work? Perhaps we are not quite ready to say that it may be to make difficulties for himself or herself, even if that conclusion may be progressively more difficult to avoid.

Work is the action of work supplemented by the idea of work, where the idea of work is none other than the idea that work can transform action into idea. There is no easy end to this circle of recursion. The principle of the Gospel of Work was articulated by Thomas Carlyle: 'properly speaking, all true Work is Religion.'[13]

Carlyle has usually been taken to mean that work is the means to a life devoted to the principles of Christian morality. But his words may be taken in a much stronger, stranger sense – that work is identical with something like a religious, even perhaps a positively mystical principle. Work is a devotional principle that is identical with transcendentality. One devotes oneself to the devotional action that work is.

Most sociological accounts of the value of work assume that work is instrumental, that it is undertaken for the sake of some purpose separate from the act of working itself. But if work is work for a purpose, what is this purpose? Of course, there are many possible answers to such a question – to earn money, to manufacture items or to effect changes in one's environment that will be useful or desirable, to attain or maintain social standing, to keep boredom at bay. Indeed the bottomless multiplicity of the things that work might be thought to be for may be a clue that such instrumental ends may themselves only be instrumental means, accessory ways of convincing us of the necessity of our work. The fact that there are so many different reasons to work might seem like a voluble hint that they are in fact excuses or pretexts for work, ways for us to experience the work as necessary or purposive. The suggestion of this present book is just this: that the purpose of work is to give us, and give us to, this necessity, which is not really necessary, since we are not in fact impelled to it in order to remain alive. Work is therefore the necessity of the unnecessary action it is.

This is never more apparent than at times when the necessity of work seems in danger of receding. Though it is true that in some cases the performing of work does involve something like a blueprint projection, for I may indeed follow a pattern in tiling my bathroom, this need not always be the case. Sometimes I simply intend to perform some action continuously and repeatedly, with no end in view other than finishing a task, or getting to the end of the day. One might see this as a perverse or parodically diminished form of labour, compared with the grand designs of the poet, architect or political theorist. But it does seem nevertheless that labour must always accommodate or allow some idea of itself, some doubling of pure action, that it is a kind of work. I would prefer, however, not to imagine the architect having the outcome of his labours in his imagination as the destined aim of his work, but rather having that aim in order to allow and animate the necessity of the work required to erect it. Phenomenologically, the working is for the sake of the work that it is intended to bring about; phantasmatically, the work is for the sake of the working.

We can dramatize some of the difficulties involved in defining the act of working by reference to an example that J. L. Austin gives in the course of his 1958 essay 'Pretending':

> That chap over there, he's all right I suppose, he's cleaning the windows, eh?
>
> Ah, *him*, he's *pretending* to be cleaning the windows right enough, cleaning 'em a treat too: but I seen him taking note of the valuables through 'em all the time.[14]

So, in this set-up, the burglar, whether actual or aspirant, for this might well be his inaugural temptation, is obscuring his real intent by his pretence of being a window-cleaner. Austin invites us to wonder what pretending to clean windows means here: whether the simulation involved in using window-cleaning as a cover for some other purpose is different, for example, from the kind of pretending that might be involved for an actor performing a window-cleaning scene for the benefit of a long-range camera out of view, or indeed, as one might imagine, a philosophically disposed performance artist mounting a real-life demonstration of Austin's example. To mention only these possibilities: he could also be a burglar by vocation, conviction and settled practice, or, come to think of it, even a fully paid-up member of the Guild of

Window-Cleaners, who is cleaning windows in his spare time, like John Cleese in the Monty Python 'Argument' sketch. Austin's example is not meant to open up labyrinths of perplexity (this being Austin, I am not quite decided on this point, but I do not think so), since his concern is really to distinguish the different kinds of thing we seem to mean when we say that somebody is pretending to do something. It is true that he does semi-seriously suggest at the end of 'Pretending' that this kind of philosophical exercise might be regarded as part of the larger ground-clearing project of surveying the whole field of 'not exactly doing things' in order to get clear about what really doing things might mean; but it is not clear that this is in fact what Austin is doing in 'Pretending', not exactly.[15]

Still, I think it can be helpful in making clearer some of the converse difficulties involved in deciding what conditions will need to be satisfied for us to conclude that the subject of the example is really performing the work of window-cleaning, as opposed to deceptively 'performing' the work of 'window-cleaning'. None of said difficulties has anything to do with getting wet, tired or giddy. They are made more exacting, and therefore, for somebody semi-professionally committed, as I am, to making work for myself and my readers on such matters, exciting, by the following consideration. It might well be thought that cleaning the windows of a house one is intending to burgle, while undoubtedly doubling as a cover for one's inspection of the rooms to establish the most likely location of valuables, could be a very useful preliminary to that inspection, if performed in earnest, in procuring a view of the interior unimpeded by cobwebs and grime. Pleasingly, what might be a kind of screen in one sense is the removal of a screen in another. One might even imagine that, if cleaning the windows of a house were to become a conventional preliminary to assaying its potential for burglary (perhaps because our putative window-cleaning burglar or burgling window-cleaner might sometimes actually be a photographer who has been commissioned to take photographs with a concealed camera for more leisurely private perusal by an offsite team of burglars), the exotic but still existent offence of 'going equipped to steal' might very well begin to extend to the carrying of buckets and chamois leathers as well as jemmies, which latter items I earnestly hope still exist.

Among other things, it seems to be the case that we can only ever be sure that the act of window-cleaning is also to be regarded as real window-cleaning work conditionally, and as far as it goes. It is not just that new considerations can enter the picture to change the observer's understanding of what might really be going on. It is also that new considerations can arise that can change everybody's understanding of what has been occurring, as it were, all along in this no-longer-very-primal scene of window-cleaning. Say, for example, the burglar were to return to his den, or lair, or wherever burglars resort to, bursting with plans for the burglary to come and ways of spending the ill-gotten, but then begins to find himself strangely fixated on his memories of the pleasures of the window-cleaning in which he engaged. Although his intention throughout the masquerade has been firmly and unambiguously to use it as an accessory to his projected act of breaking and entering, he may nevertheless have made himself vulnerable to any number of contingencies that can modify that intent. For example, his honest window-cleaning friend (from whom, let us say, he may have had to borrow his amateur-dramatic apparatus) may call him, distraught at the loss of his real-life partner following a fall from a ladder and imploring him to fill in for the interim. It is only at this point that the burglar realizes how genuinely pleasant and fulfilling it would be to throw over the risky and uncertain profession of burglar for the honest, open-air work of window-cleaning. Looking back, he might even come to see the episode of crooked window-cleaning as a genuine apprenticeship in the straight-and-narrow work to which he has hereafter devoted his life. If so, what at one moment was not work, but pretence, will have been transformed by later circumstances into the beginning of real work, which is to say, *real* work.

Work is never merely executive, in other words, since it must always also be performative, must always involve a formal acting out of the action of which it consists. Austin's playacting burglar is evoked to suggest the difference between really cleaning windows and only pretending to clean them. But if somebody, let us say a window-cleaner, for example, though they would not need this professional accreditation, is cleaning windows for real, they are also performing, only in a different way, in the sense in which we say that we perform a task. What the burglar is doing is pretending to be engaged in the complex kind of real pretending that the work of cleaning windows involves. The real difference is between the shower of rain that accidentally and with no kind of benefice prepense washes the windows clean and the man who arrives with all the properties incident to his salutary office, ladder, bucket, chamois. Both actions render the windows clean, but only the latter performs the kind of work known as window-cleaning. This may seem like a confirmation of the suggestion just made that the work of window-cleaning must conjoin an action to an intention that it enacts. The cloudburst does not mean to clean the windows, so does not do the work of window-cleaning that a window-cleaner does, except through a metaphorical transference that confirms the difference between them.

And what if the windows are already gleaming, perhaps because they have been the subject of assiduous attention by an aspirant burglar for an hour or so before the arrival of the actual or official window-cleaner? If the window-cleaner decides to go ahead with the work of cleaning the windows nevertheless, or is instructed to do so by their foreman, even if their professional judgement tells them that there is no prospect of getting them any cleaner, so glitteringly thorough has the pretence of the burglar been, does this mean that, when they set nevertheless to the superfluous work of sopping and wiping, they are not really working, but, like the burglar, who by this time is doubtless already inside rummaging through drawers, only pretending to work? Assuredly not, since the work known as cleaning windows does not require there to be windows dirty enough to require cleaning. Doing work does not require there to be work to do, only, as noted above, that there be work to be done. Indeed, I have hopes of making good the suggestion that work requires there to be no absolute requirement that the work in question be done. The work of the window-cleaner is governed by the intention, not of making windows clean, or at least in some discernible measure cleaner than before, but of performing the work known as window-cleaning. An obsessive-compulsive window-cleaner who insisted on cleaning the windows of his house hourly might very well be performing unnecessary or supererogatory work, but it would be surpassing strange to say that they were not, for that reason, actually cleaning windows at all.

Work, or the philosophically exalted form of it known as 'labour', has been mightily bound up with questions of value and reward. Marx proposed, in the formalization he gave to traditional ideas of work, which has become known as the labour theory of value, that the value of an object is measurable, and indeed only measurable, in terms of the amount of labour put into it. Labour thereby becomes an ultimate measure of value. This appears to put labour into the world of absolute and external quantities, alongside the quantities of energy measured in the thermodynamic theory of Clausius. Its principal intention and effect has been to make work a foundation, a measure of value that is absolutely independent of price.

Given the amount of destruction wrought in its name, the number of people who have perished to secure it and the social arrangements that are believed to be predicated upon it, the labour theory of value may be regarded as the most igneous of fatuities.

The masquerading window-cleaners can be summoned to the scene again. A plausible reading of their action might be that they are indeed working, just not for their putative employer. They are at work on their own account, pursuing the business of planning a burglary. This might appear to remove the idea of work savingly from the realm of pantomime, where it seems like to cause so much difficulty for the mind, and perhaps for other things besides, to the realm of measurable and exchangeable actuality. In pretending to work as a window-cleaner, the burglar is now revealed to be assiduously engaged in a work of imposture that is part of the stock-in-trade of the ancient and honourable profession of housebreaker. Like the beggar who assiduously displays their idleness, he or she is going, if not exactly hammer-and-tongs then chamois-and-bucket, at manufacturing the spectacle of work. As a self-employed burglar, he or she is in fact operating as a part-time actor. On this account, their imposture of work actually seems to clear the idea of work of the charge of imposture.

It is easy to multiply examples of actions that similarly seem to be identical with actions of work, but are not. There are many kinds of work – playing sport, driving, writing literary criticism, cooking – that cease to be work if performed by amateurs for fun. Indeed, there is no kind of work, however arduous, dreary or apparently soul-destroying, that is immune in principle from being performed in such a way, or in such a context (being acted out on a stage, for example, or some other performative setting, including the internal theatre of one's fantasy) as not to count as work at all.

So, in the case of the burglar/window-cleaners, much seems to depend on what we, or they, make of whatever it is we take them to be up to in their lathery charade, rather than on what it is in itself. If one were really trying to determine the value of their 'labour', one would have to include in it some preconception of the value of that labour, not as a certain or ascertainable amount of 'toil and trouble' but as a sort of projection or preconception. So the labour that is supposed to provide a measure of the value of their work will in fact be dependent on the idea of labour, or the degree to which it will seem to count as work.

Indeed, one might say that this is in large part wrapped up in the occult operations of the word *labour* itself. As so often in English, the Latinate word does some extra symbolic-affective lifting, and so appears culturally more 'cooked' than the primary Germanic word, *work*. The charge exerted by the words *labour* and *work* form a complex chiasmus. *Labour* signifies, first of all, a lower, less dignified and ennobling form of work. According to the distinction made by Hannah Arendt, labour belongs to the sphere of unproductive work, driven by necessity rather than the free exercise of power involved in work. Labour is typically much more exacting than mere work. Hard labour is the name given to arduous work imposed as punishment. There is no easy or straightforward equivalent to the term 'laborious' derived from work, since 'working' or 'workaday' do not focus on the suffering associated with work. As Arendt notices, *labour* cannot be used to refer to the product of labour, as *work* can.[16]

And yet, *labour* also has an elevated status compared with *work*. The labour of childbirth enacts just this passage between ignoble striving and dignified work. *Labour* is used by economic and political theorists to signify the concept of work as well as the exercise of it. The use of the word *labour* to signify the class of those who work, mostly in manual occupations, and their interests, would lead to the formation of the Labour Party in the United Kingdom in 1900. The name of the Socialist Workers Party, formed in 1950, offered a desublimation of labour back into the immediacy and honesty of work, even as it borrowed the sublimation effect of the word 'worker' in socialist discourse. The transition is oddly evidenced in the rapid evolution of the party's paper, formed in 1961, from *Industrial Worker* to *Labour Worker*, and then to *Socialist Worker*.

Although other languages make similar kinds of distinction between different styles of work, and different attitudes towards them, labour and work derive much of their force from the double-column accounting system provided by the co-presence of words of Latin and Germanic origin in English. The chiasmatic force of *labour*, which means arduous and sometimes-unproductive toil, and yet also embodies an abstract understanding of that process, represents a coming together of the ideal and actual that are often split between the Latin and the Germanic. Much of the charisma of *labour* derives from its use in the King James Bible, in which there is a tendency (though a very uneven one) for labour to signify dutiful struggle and work to signify accomplishment. The earliest appearance of the word *work* is in Genesis, which affirms, 'And on the seventh day God ended his work which he had made; and he rested on the seventh day from all his work which he had made' (Genesis 2:2). God is never said to labour in the King James Bible, and the division between labour and work is perhaps best codified as the division between human and divine modes of working.

The range of different words picking out different aspects of work, and centring especially on the contrast between the ideas assumed by English work and labour, has attracted the attention of linguists, economists, sociologists and political theorists. It is strange, both that there should be so much variation in the words used for work, and also that the strangeness of this fact should itself be so rarely remarked on. Given the centrality of work in so many societies, one might have expected it to have generated some core designations, like the words for the primary though equally various actions of doing, making, going and so on. Olivier Fraysse's schematics of the metonymic associations of work, which he distributes between the process, the subjects and the outcomes of work, suggest not just that work is thought about in different ways but, more significantly, that there may be no one way in which to think of work, and that this very plurality may be part of its nature.[17] Work is nameable only through misnaming – stand-in, surrogate and catachresis, the 'figure of abuse', according to George Puttenham.[18] This may suggest that work, which has commonly been regarded as a core activity for human societies, defining what human societies are through the ways in which they do what they do, has evasion and obliquity at, and in fact as, its core. If work has a heart of darkness, it may imply that working consists in large part of the work of representing it, if only (only!) to oneself. Perhaps then work might consist in the kind of work of which Freud found the evidence in dreams, jokes and processes like mourning. If so, it may not be too extravagant to posit a kind of 'labour-work', or work of displacement, that makes it impossible to know and name clearly and steadily what work is *eo ipso*, or when it seems to be at home.

One might decide to be satisfied with the idea that the different understandings of work do no more than gesture towards a family resemblance between things that we should not expect to aggregate into a whole and do not need to have some essential, cohering thread running through, to borrow Wittgenstein's expression.[19] But this analogy between the plural behaviours signified by work and by language conceals a disparity. For even if all the things that may count as language form an open and incompletable set, the behaviours picked by terms like stating, promising and complaining are things with their own conditions, subject to some degree to the modes of their ascription and description but independent of them too. However, the actions of labour, work, service, toil and so on are much more dependent on the evaluation of them. This means that whether or not something will count as work will depend not just on shared conventions as to what they are, but also on interpretations of those conventions. The difference lies in the capacity for error. If I deny making a promise and my husband tells me that my actions imply or amount to a promise, he would quite simply be wrong to say that I have made a promise because my actions have implied it, since implied promises are simply that: promises that have not met the conditions for having actually been made, which might typically include being meant and uttered. But if I am sentenced to ten years hard labour, it will be necessary for me to experience it as laborious for it to have been. It will do no good for me to protest to the governor that I have been promised labour, if only in the negative form of promise constituted by a penal sentence, but have not got it, finding, as I have, the daily breaking of stones or digging of ditches health-giving and rewarding: for the experience and expectations of the judicial authorities will reasonably lead them to think that prisoners will experience those activities as 'hard labour'.

This is a case in which what qualifies indisputably as hard labour from one point of view is disqualified from another. The governor can do no more than shrug and say, well, most people would find the prison regime pretty arduous: it would be perverse though understandable for her to tell me that I am plain wrong about the matter, because there are actually no shared frames of reference, only a kind of guesswork, if admittedly of quite a predictable kind, as to what will count as hard labour. The point becomes clearer and more familiar with the opposite case, in which I seem, from an external point of view, to be doing work while from my own point of view I emphatically am not. This case is, if anything, even more enigmatic, even if it is much more familiar. The intervention of communicative-representational media allows for actions that I do not experience as any kind of work, like searching the Internet for videos of talking dogs, to be taken as what is called data, and for that data to be captured and exploited – put to work, in other words, for different kinds of purposes, most innocently, for the purposes of selling me this kind of video, less innocently, perhaps for inferring my voting intentions, variations in my blood pressure, the likelihood of my carrying out high-school massacres and so on. That profits can be made from the attention paid to my attention produces a swelling sense of outrage in some commentators at the idea that, because some process has made my activity look like work, from which profits might be made, I must in fact be regarded as working without meaning to, such that what must now start to be called my 'labour' must greedily and unjustly be appropriated in such a process.

In fact, strange and exotic as this may seem, the fact that I can retroactively be thought of as having performed some kind of work by means of some work being performed on my actions, meaning in turn that I am worked on involuntarily in such a way as to transform me into a worker, is a very common state of affairs in nature. The use of sails to propel a boat, grind corn or generate electricity extracts work from the wind by performing work on it, but only in a metaphorical sense can it be said to make the wind perform work, even if this idea remains an important part of the phantasmatics of the idea of work.

Labour is not a different kind of activity from work, but a specific ideation or act of recognition with regard to an activity that might otherwise be taken to be something else, for example work, toil, service or even play. In fact, the exchangeability of work with idleness is one of the most powerfully recurrent apprehensions in the phantasmatics of work, especially in contemporary experience. The different modulations of work, labour, travail, toil and trouble are not simple objects in the world, like daffodils, DNA and demonstratives, but intentional objects, like wars, weeds and wives.

What makes work different from weeds and wives as a category is the fact that the idea of work performs a secondary function of what might be called *quasi-ontological insistence* – by which I mean acting as a proof of absolute and non-falsifiable existence in itself. The QUOI, which makes for a particular friction of actuality and category, even if in reality it is founded on a principle of *je ne sais quoi*, is what makes work seem more like war than weeds or wives. The phrase 'don't you know there's a war on' is a hint at how non-self-evident a war actually is, since war, like work, is of necessity something more than the blood, sweat and tears.

The gap between desire and definition is filled by the substitutive or compensatory work of phantasmatics. Phantasmatics consists largely of the formation of projects, enterprises and undertakings, possibilities that we bend our lives to making actual, in the hope that possibly they will turn out to be, or be able at least at length to be taken to be, the fulfilment of our ownmost *ergon*. The long and successfully sustained work of these phantasmatics is aimed at having fulfilled the condition of freely chosen coercion.

We will see in Chapter Two that it matters that work should be what is called 'real work'. The German *Wirklichkeit* means 'reality', signalling the *wirklich* as that which *wirkt*, works. The concern with the reality of our work is one of its leading features, a little as romantic love is always supposed to be qualifiable as 'true love'. We can never simply do our work, for we must always do something supplementary in or to or through that doing, or whatever the work consists of, sweeping, sorting, fetching, carrying or commanding, to have it qualify as work. Work performs an indispensable work of definition, defining us severally as tinker, tailor, soldier, sailor, solicitor, and yet work itself can never be self-evident, self-defining or self-underwriting. This accounts for much of the conspicuous theatricality involved in work – the apparatus of costume, posture, gesture, rhythm and locution as well as the changes of pace and place that belong to work and serve to mark it off from non-working activity. Hence probably all of those expressions that imply some transitional state or action, required for one to move from a condition of not-working to working: setting someone to work, getting to work on something. As we will see in Chapter Three, to work is to be 'at work', as though working were not just an action but an action of attendance, or being in some particular place. And yet exactly what it is about these symbolic supplementations that serve to turn the actions of work into actual work is often hard to determine. We may observe, however, that the features that make actions qualify as 'real work' resemble the kind of framing, setting-up or setting-off conditions that make actions that might otherwise be taken to be real the kind of merely enacted, or not-exactly-real, acts we recognize as theatrical. So the very things that make actions less than real on the stage are what make them ultra-real on the stage of work.

This complexity is the inverse of the principle articulated by Nicholas H. Smith and Jean-Philippe Deranty as part of the movement of ideas that has become known in social theory as the 'psychodynamics of work':

> There is always a gap between the prescribed aspects of the working activity, the way the engineers and managers define the task (in terms of procedures and outputs), and the reality of the activity. Real work, even the apparently most mechanical or simple kind of work, always involves some creative intervention by the worker, simply because it is impossible for the organization of work to foresee and pre-empt all the obstacles that get in the way of the realization of the task. The reality of work, as a result, resides in the bridging of this gap.[20]

The principle that work consists largely of what have come expressively to be called 'work-arounds' certainly accords well with many aspects of working experience. But it is also the case and, when it comes to accounting for what work is rather than how it is performed, more fundamentally so, that work must always be 'realized' by bridging the gap in the opposite direction, from the performing to the to-be-performed, or, in the terms I once tendered, the *performans* to the *performandum* of work.[21] The prescription of a task can exist independently of the fudges, fiddles and forcings by which it actually gets accomplished, but the work-around must always work around some work prescribed for it. A work-around for the task of building a brick wall that consisted in taking oneself off to watch cricket instead would not normally be regarded as just an unorthodox way of getting the job done, since it would sever this relation between the task and its manner of accomplishment completely. For 'the reality of work' must always include some form of assignment, as some work to-be-realized. The form of this realization will always differ, in some degree or another, from the model, but its very differing maintains a relation, however apparently irresponsible, to its assignment that is absolute – at least, whenever one is talking about something that will seem to count as work – for the relation between an exaction and its enactment is essential for something to count as work. Even if the way in which a given task is to be performed seems entirely unprescribed, as in some programmatic work of performance art ('Spend the next five minutes performing some action that might otherwise be unlikely to occur to you to do'), it must be assigned, programmed or underwritten as a task to be done if it is to count as work, or the realization of 'a work'. *Task* is probably from Latin *taxare*, to touch sharply, censure, rate, reckon or judge: to undertake a task is to submit oneself to this process of estimation, whereby something will be accounted as having been work, whether through the process of payment or reward or more generally through acknowledgement that the work performed could indeed count as work, or the specific work that has been commissioned.

When it comes to work, being real means qualifying as work, meeting the conditions for being taken to be work. We may suspect that much of the work we do consists of efforts aimed at meeting these qualifying conditions. A large part of the purpose and even practice of work is not in order to realize the ostensible aims of the work, but rather to have succeeded in being acknowledged to have been at work, and in the specific way required.

Establishing this relation between action and getting that action to count as work is a large part of the phantasmatics of work. Phantasmatics refers to fantasy, defined not as fiction or fable but as representations of things invested with value, whether positive or aversive. Fantasy, in my usage, is characterized not by falsity but by force: not by whether something is true or not, but by the pressure of wanting it to be true, whatever we may suspect or believe about that truth. The rhyme of 'phantasmatic' with words like 'automatic', 'symptomatic' and 'systematic' seems to lead the psychoanalysts who use the term to reserve it for what can be thought of as organized systems of fantasy. Daniel Lagache writes that 'fantasies are not scattered and incoherent: they have their own logic which is certainly not that of scientific knowledge; we might call this kind of systematization of fantasy "phantasmatic" and this phantasmatic system is the true object of psycho-analytic investigation.'[22] The pull of a word like 'problematic' participates with this idea of systematic fantasy to make the adjective into a noun: 'The fantasy system (phantasmatic) is a structural notion, the organization of dominant fantasies.'[23] Jean Laplanche and Jean-Bertrand Pontalis propose a similar usage of 'phantasmatic' as a noun meaning the structured form of fantasy:

> the psycho-analyst must endeavour in the course of the treatment to unearth the phantasies which lie behind such products of the unconscious as dreams, symptoms, acting out, repetitive behaviour, etc. As the investigation progresses, even aspects of behaviour that are far removed from imaginative activity, and which appear at first glance to be governed solely by the demands of reality, emerge as emanations, as 'derivatives' of unconscious phantasy. In the light of this evidence, it is the subject's life as a whole which is seen to be shaped and ordered by what might be called,

> in order to stress this structuring action, 'a phantasmatic' (*une fantasmatique*).[24]

Didier Anzieu uses the word to describe the way in which the life and work of Goethe struck the young Freud: 'Freud was guided not so much by Goethe himself, a learned and inventive man with an encyclopaedic mind, as by a mythology of Nature, which, although only a pastiche of Goethe, struck a chord in his personal "phantasmatic".'[25] The phrase 'transcendental phantasmatic' has been proposed to designate 'the idea of an archaic inheritance involving both symbolism and also the set of Urphantasien which reflect humanity's past and have become constitutive of the mind'.[26]

There are many points of overlap between what I represent here as the phantasmatics of work and the movement to which I have already alluded, centred on the work of Christophe Dejours and others from the 1980s onward, that has come to be designated the 'psychodynamics of work'.[27] There are indeed overlaps between the two attitudes to the question of work, most particularly in the shared understanding that the meaning of work is as much phenomenological as economic or political. For the psychodynamics of work, as for the phantasmatics that I make out here, what matters about work is as much the way in which it subjectively matters to the worker as the ways in which it is organized and the outcomes it may be intended to have in the world.

The difference between the psychodynamics of work and my phantasmatics of work lies in the normative dimension of work associated with the former term. Christophe Dejours focused in his earlier writings on the psychopathology of work, aiming to identify and help to alleviate the characteristic psychological maladies to which working gave rise.[28] Even though Dejours' focus has broadened beyond those whom work may be thought to have made ill, to the psychological motives and processes centred on the experience of work, the psychodynamics of work is still essentially a form of critical theory, which concerns itself with the relief and remedy of work conditions. One might say that where psychopathology considers the illness to which work can give rise, psychodynamics considers work itself to be ill, and in need of healing. Psychodynamics is in essence an ethics of work, a theory of the forms that work should take in order to maximize individual and collective well-being. As such, it might also be understood as a kind of ethical engineering of work, an organized, even organizational work of analytic enhancement practised on it. It will become apparent in Chapter Five that I believe much of what we think of as work can be regarded as this kind of working to remedy or redeem work itself.

From my point of view, this implies that the psychodynamics of work is not so much an opponent to the phantasmatics of work as a component of it, for its hopes and fears for work are part of the phantasmatic territory it sets out to map. The phantasmatics of work concern the ways in which work is lived out, or exists, without reference to any ideal horizon or duty of critique. The psychodynamics of work asks: how should we work and what should work be and mean? What work should work do for us? The phantasmatics of work asks: what do we imagine work to be, and what do we want from it? What work is done by the ways in which we imagine work? The psychodynamics of work aims to improve it and so is part of the work of work; the phantasmatics of work aims to understand what it means to us, and consequently stands apart from its necessity. It is part of the phenomenology of work, or the conditions under which we live our relation to it, that work should tend to become a recursive work-in-the-making, such that, in part, we work in order to work at the idea and imago of our work. But for an approach based around the phantasmatics of work, this ideal horizon, or more properly, horizon of ideality, which seems to promise the necessity of the ideal work situation to correspond to the 'ideal speech situation' that Jürgen Habermas saw implied in every actual speech situation, is part of the landscape being surveyed, not part of its necessary future.[29]

Psychodynamics suggests a view of work as a kind of physics of competing forces and energies, in which the psyche is conceived not only as impacted by the physical demands of work, and acting reciprocally upon them, but as itself a dynamic field or system of forces. The markedly mechanical, hydraulic or otherwise kinetic systems favoured by Freudian psychoanalysis exert a strong influence on the construing of these psychodynamic relations and processes. Phantasmatics concerns itself rather with the projection of dreams, illusions, phantoms, fancyings and fantasies. Psychodynamics promises to show the workings of work, as they essentially are, beneath or running across the play of appearances. Phantasmatics focuses on this play of appearances, or rather the work of making them appear in the theatrics of work, the ways in which we represent work to ourselves and invest it with various kinds of symbolic value. It is in this sense, too, that the semiotic scenery of the psychodynamic, as an essentially imaginary physics, is part of what a phantasmatics of work will be likely to concern itself with. Psychodynamics, in short, focuses on functions, while phantasmatic analysis focuses on fictions (including, it will be conceded, not only the fiction of function, but the function of that fiction).

Psychodynamics is a systematic modification of psychoanalysis, in which the concept of work is a central, determining principle, even if it only intermittently comes into the analytic foreground. Psychoanalysis depends so much on the idea of work for the work it wants to do that it is difficult for it to constitute work as something that might be thought about.

Different idioms and occasions of work feature strongly and definingly in the way in which work is treated in psychoanalysis. Rodrigo Ventura suggests that work is fundamental to the constitution of the 'psychic apparatus':

> As constant force and stimulus for the psychic, the drive is an intensity that obliges the psyche – to avoid displeasure and helplessness – to work into finding a way to express this energy in the material and psychic world. Considering the psychic apparatus a device that captures instinctual forces, the psychic work is a response to its own demand of satisfaction that the drive does to this device.[30]

Ventura then distinguishes a number of the different applications of the concept of work in Freud's German text, through terms such as *Trauerarbeit*, the 'work of mourning', *Traumarbeit*, the 'dreamwork', and the different inflections that German allows in words like *Bearbeitung* (working out or working on, sometimes rendered as 'elaboration'), *Verarbeitung* (working over) and, most notably, *Durcharbeitung*, or working through. Ventura himself proposes that 'the psychoanalytic experience makes the subject responsible for an erotic work that, by enabling the instinctual trend, widens its scope of existential freedom and allows the experimentation of new ways of being.'[31] Although the prefixes seem to be minor variations of the process of working, they seem to be doing the real work in these terms, establishing the process of work in each case as a specific vector.

One might say that the call that animates psychoanalysis to invest the process of one's self-understanding with seriousness and significance – to cathect the process of self-understanding – involves a secondary cathexis of that very process, construing it through the investment as a kind of work, less process than project. The work of self-investment in projects of remedy or transformation crystallizes into the investment, at once more abstract and more mighty, in the idea of work itself, the largest, emptiest passion.

In all the accounts of psychological work brought forward in psychoanalytic writing, work is defined as doing something difficult. Only Ives Hendrick seems to offer a positive account of the content of work, in what he describes as the instinct to mastery.[32] Even here, there is something circular in the definition of work, since mastery is a matter not just of shaping or subduing objects in the world but also of the pleasure in one's own executant functions: a pleasure in one's work, and the desire for that pleasure. This might seem like a recourse to a notion of the laborative or operative faculty in work, in parallel to the *virtus dormitiva* of opium according to Molière. Everywhere, it seems, work is understood as the imperiously real set or surging up against the imaginary, even as it seems itself to gather thereby magical force, as the *virtú* which suffuses the idea of work with moral force. It is as the real, the serious and the intractable that the idea of work is most magical. The psychoanalytic idea of work seems to be closely allied to the magical workings of psychoanalysis itself, a magic disguised by its imaginary practices of dispelling and disenchantment.

In most of the work that is supposed to take place, either in the psychological processes unearthed by psychoanalysis or in the process of psychoanalytic treatment itself, we may be confronted with something like imaginary work, where the projecting of the different kinds of psychological work-project – thinking, speaking and writing about them, for instance – nevertheless seems undeniably to involve what is recognizable as work. The question here is whether the work of imagination is in fact an imaginary work. And if all work requires not just the recognizable actions of different kinds of work but the recognition itself, then we may perhaps have leave to wonder whether all work must be, if not exactly imaginary, then certainly imagined. In order to work, I have to imagine that I am working, and thereby accede to a work-imaginary.

This work of imagination is in a curious way both active and passive. Imagining earns the name of work because it really does feel that it requires effort, primarily at the beginning of the exercise.

Work is brought into existence by the ways in which one makes a transition from not-working – sleeping, say, or eating (provided one is not taking part in a business breakfast) – to working, often accompanied by some vestimentary action, like putting on uniform or overalls, showering or going to the works or office. The experience of working from home that became common in many occupations during the COVID-19 pandemic, which consisted mostly of writing and speaking rather than lifting, fetching and carrying, nevertheless seemed to require of many of its practitioners a more or less elaborate ritual of kinetic scene-setting, perhaps by going to a work room, or, for those inhabiting a single apartment, a different part of the room set apart as a workplace. Working involves going or getting to work. Children who do not readily and reliably perform the action known as going to sleep, an action which is largely synchronized with the requirements of work – if not their own, then that of others – can usually be helped by a rather similar routine of mise-en-scène, including the change of clothing and location.

The effort of making a change is reduplicated during the process of working by the rhythms of suspension and resumption of which it must always consist, whether that involves wiping one's brow and stretching one's cramped muscles, or simply jerking one's wayward thoughts back to whatever matter must be thought to be in hand. The force exerted by this artificial and arbitrary self-government is at once a kind of work in its own right and the work of maintaining the work-imaginary.

Luckily, however, most forms of work allow for the remission of effort, not just through breaks for tea or reverie but through the remission of effort provided by the work itself. This is the sense in which work consists of a kind of willed passivity. Every kind of work requires and authorizes, if only intermittently, forms of drudgery, or automatized effort – effort into which we do not have to put much effort, so that we can tune out of it by tuning in to it.

Although none of us is likely to want such occupations, it is surprising how many forms of recreation in fact involve these kinds of hypnotically repetitive actions, many of which turn out to require some form of counting or numerization, a symphony of striving which expresses and diffuses stress. And it is part of the work of imagining oneself at work, or, let us say, into it, that one surrenders to these mechanical routines, in which the very mechanism therefore becomes a kind of idling. There is certainly torment in any kind of mechanized labour which is actually not mechanical enough to allow one to float free into daydream. This is the sense in which the work-imaginary is both active and passive, in that one projects oneself into a condition in which one is voluntarily subjected to the work one is 'doing'.

This work of getting oneself to work and then of giving oneself over to it is both actual and a way of imagining oneself into the condition that will persuade us that we are, or have been, working. That we may have polished a grate, or deleted a dozen emails, will give the extra confirmation that our work has resulted in a work, or some visible outcome.

It is not clear whether we take work as seriously as we do because it is an intrinsically serious matter, or, on the contrary, devote so much time and attention to work because it furnishes a convincing way of being serious. At some times the former predominates, at other times the latter, and most of the time, work and seriousness form a reciprocating engine, each summoning and confirming the other.

Work is the evidence of our concern for things, and capacity to take them seriously, but is also the subject of concern in itself. In fact, perhaps the characteristic tonality of the phantasmatics of work is not fear, longing, disgust or any other of the primary-colour affects, but worry. We worry about our work – getting the opportunity to do it, doing it well, losing a job, working out how to get out of it, being admired for it – even as worrying is itself a kind of work, a worry-work that Freud might with justice have set alongside the psychoergonomics of dreamwork and the work of mourning. 'Worrying' derives from the Old English *wyrgan*, part of a family of Germanic verbs meaning to strangle or throttle to death, a usage which survives in references to the worrying of sheep by dogs. To worry at something is to strive to subdue or destroy it, typically in modern usage in a metaphorical sense, meaning that one worries at a problem by working to solve it. But there is something about the action of worrying that prolongs and so defers the action of subjection and subduing, and in the process turns it against itself, worrying about losing the object of the worry as well as worrying about not being able to negate it. Worrying is commonly reflexive, meaning that one often worries at or about one's worry, as well as about its object: typically, we worry that we may not be working hard enough at our worry, pulling ourselves up with alarm when we recognize that we have forgotten to worry for a few moments before returning to the cockpit. In a sense, the passage from serious concern to worry involves a reversal, in which the one doing the worrying – which never seems like something one is exactly doing, though it is no less exhausting for that, and probably all the more – starts to worry the worrier, as we seem to make clear when we express the fact that we are worrying about something with a phrase like 'something is worrying me'. 'In headaches and in worry/ Vaguely life leaks away,' W. H. Auden writes, pointing us to the mixture of suffering and vagueness that is part of worry, worry being the attempt to relieve the ague it itself is.[33] Worrying about work, as we seem to do systematically, is the principal way in which we try to work through or work over our relation to our work. But worry itself is a work that is not work, or a work that somehow works on us, rather than a work that we ourselves straightforwardly do, this being part of what is worrying in work, and in worrying about it.

The central importance of phantasmatics in thinking about work is clearly suggested by a fact that should strike us as stranger than it does. That is, in much of what we say and think about work, the most important question is not whether it is necessary, productive, valuable or fulfilling, but whether it is real, or, as we oddly sometimes say, honest. The Mark Knopfler song 'Money for Nothing' articulates the suspicion that may be felt about, and derision directed at, any kind of work that does not seem to require enough work, and so looks like imposture: for example the work of singing songs like 'Money for Nothing'.

This is another clue to why work calls for an understanding in phantasmatic terms, as consisting essentially in operations designed to make the existence of work not effective or productive but actual and credible. Work is phantasmatic because we work so hard to prove that our work goes beyond the working of fantasy. Honest labour might be taken to refer to honourable, in the sense of legal and approvable, activities, as opposed to burglary and drug-smuggling. But the principal reference of the idea of honest labour is that one *means* the work one does (along with the vague but powerful idea that dishonourable activities are all in fact a kind of legerdemain, however strenuous the work of drilling into the vault might be). The phantasmatics of work are never more intricately and intensely in play than in the effort to mean one's work. Indeed, it may increasingly appear that this project of realization is what we work hardest at when we work. It matters much less what we accomplish in a given period of work than that it provides the warrant that we have been at work during the period required to accomplish it. Again, the products of the work are there to produce the work.

The early experience of children seems to offer extensive verification of this tendency. For what children seem to play at most earnestly – the play of children being a notably grave affair – are various kinds of work-operation. The toddler who demands to push their own buggy is both supplying themselves with a walking aid and demonstrating their nascent understanding that walking itself may be turned into a task or operation. Indeed the mirroring of parental occupations in the play of children, cooking, cleaning, feeding, caring for children, indicates that they have understood the nature of play as training for work. It is not just action or acting out, therefore, but the enactment of the sense of imperative action to-be-done.

We often oppose real work to the mere appearance of work. There are two principal forms of this counterfeit. First of all there is the simple pretence of work, the thriller slipped in behind the primer, the burglars pretending to be window-cleaners so wearisomely earlier, and so on. But then, more surprisingly, there is the kind of deception exemplified by drudgery or menial toil. Drudgery undoubtedly consists of real work but it is not, we tell ourselves, authentic, since it does not allow for any kind of subjective fulfilment, the fulfilment of work that ceases to be work. So drudgery is a kind of work that falls short of being work in the full and proper sense, namely work that goes beyond itself. Only work that has ceased to be work is work in the fullest and most authentic sense. Work that is nothing more than work, or merely work through and through, is not really work at all. This is part of the reason why, as already noted, slavery or forms of coerced labour are such an outrage, since they not only take away the slave's freedom but, in the process, take away their possibility of working. The slave is both forced to work and, even worse, forced to pretend that what they are doing is work. It will do no good to protest that the work of the slave is too cruel and exhausting to be simulation, since it is the very fact of being pure arduousness that takes away its reality as work, substituting for it mere pointless suffering. Work is never more phantasmal than when it is supplying the various kinds of proof it is held to (in both senses, believed to be and forced to adhere to). We may with justice say of work what Bertrand Russell said of mathematics, that it is 'the subject in which we never know what we are talking about'.[34]

And yet, even though drudgery can never be authentic work, there can be no work without some measure of drudgery, otherwise work will risk becoming mere play. I have read surveys which report that many people regard the most desirable job as that of a writer. This is presumably in part because writing appears to be a work of pure and effortless invention, a kind of systematized and salaried daydreaming. But even here there is something in the disciplining of the daydream that provides the element of the subordination of the mental to the demands of the mechanical that seems to be necessary to sustain the fiction of work involved in the work of fiction. There must always be some drudgery to prove the reality of work, a fact sufficiently exhibited in the assiduousness of the burglar window-cleaner.

I was once in a seminar which became mightily and merrily preoccupied with the question of how proponents of egalitarian ideas and Enlightenment values could nevertheless have kept slaves. Understanding this problem, it seems to me, entails understanding the coercion that must form part of all work. One who regards participation in slavery as unthinkable must assume the possibility and moral necessity of freely chosen work. But this possibility has not existed for most human beings in history, for whom the choice has been work or starvation, and for whom work has always required some form of indenture. Contracts of employment, even ones into which one may be said to have entered freely, contract one's capacities for free choice. This is not at all to say that all work is reducible to slavery, but rather that it is hard to imagine any work that is free of any taint or tincture of it, since the choice of how, when and how long to work is never in any transpicuous or uncomplicated sense free. There is supposed to be a clear and absolute cleavage between the labour one is forced, by threats or customary relations, to perform and the labour that one freely agrees, or freely wills oneself, to perform. But in neither case can there be work without coercion and the overcoming of reluctance. Though it is assumed to be impossible for me to coerce myself unjustly in free work, one may at the same time readily imagine examples of just this kind of compulsive or self-destructive self-coercion. The workaholic is assumed to be in the grip of a compulsion which means that they have not in fact freely chosen to work all hours, but this example makes it much harder to know for sure what choosing without any form of this compulsion – choosing to be compelled without any kind of compulsion in the choice – could possibly be like.

At the same time, the absolute condition known as working, required for the idea that the slave has been made fully identical with the action of their work, with no margin of freedom left over, is hard to imagine, though the figure of the slave is perhaps designed in part to make it imaginable for us. The value of what I have taken as a kind of primal scene of work, in J. L. Austin's window-cleaning burglars, is as an illustration not of something to do with pretending but of something to do with working, namely that whenever we are confronted with the question of whether what somebody is doing is work, we will require a great deal more than immediate and external evidence to decide, and we may never in any case be able to decide for a certainty, once and for all. Even slaves, and perhaps especially slaves, will often be under the necessity of pretending to work at least some of the time, even setting aside my argument that slavery might be defined through the requirement in it to pretend to be working all the time.

To imagine work is to create plausible pictures, for ourselves and each other, of what it looks like. This is not just a matter of imagining the forms that work can or should take, it is also a matter of imagining our relation to work, and therefore what we feel about it. It may be harder to think of feelings as things we imagine rather than things we have. We might, for example, have a feeling that our work, or the work of others, is futile, or undemanding, or not real work at all. Under these circumstances it really does not feel as if our feelings are themselves imaginary. But our feelings about work are not feelings we simply have, or that simply and spontaneously arise in us. Feelings about work, like most of the things we think we feel about anything, are collective, in a sense that is more complex than a matter simply of having the same feelings as others do.

The most important feature of the phantasmatics of work is that they are projective representations. Projective representations are things that we believe or expect to be true, or wish were true. They are not just feelings about work but metafeelings, feelings we feel in various ways, and for various reasons, impelled to want to have, feelings that stand at each other's shoulder. Though these feelings are organized relationally, and even, it sometimes seems, systematically, they are constantly in production, so we are more likely to be able to recognize them than to be able to collect and enumerate them in their entirety. In *The Madness of Knowledge*, I argued for the existence of systems of what I called epistemopathy, the systematic feelings that we have in relation to knowledge.[35] The phantasmatics of work might be similarly thought of as fulfilling an ergopathic function.

A projective feeling is a feeling that we do not merely experience but also posit, purpose or suppose. Projective feelings are usually feelings that we do not simply and immediately have, since we also have a relation to them, and the most pressing thing about them may be that relation. Of course there are many kinds of relation to feeling where the relation is not an essential part of the feeling – wondering in advance whether we are going to be nervous giving a speech, or reflecting that we no longer know why we got so upset about dropping service in the second set. Projective feelings are those which, while unarguably being my own, are nevertheless held at an internal distance, allowing for and insisting on the fact that I can recognize that I am experiencing them, or, what can be oddly equivalent, even come to wonder whether, in fact, I am: 'Goodness, is this what people mean when they say they feel "offended" or "distraught"?' Borrowing the rather formal expression one may come upon in eighteenth- or nineteenth-century romantic novels, we may say that collective feelings are 'entertained' rather than experienced, or experienced by being entertained. To entertain is from the Latin *inter* + *tenire*, to hold between, and many of the feelings to which we lay claim, especially about moot or highly mediated subjects like work or love or belief, we seem really to host, or give house-room to, rather than to have and to hold. Having feelings about such topics is often a matter of making a temporary withdrawal from some collective fund of things we assume other people may feel or may expect us to feel. This is like a fund in more than the obvious respect, since funds consist of symbols that we are confident others will have confidence in. To say that we draw on a shared assumption as we draw on a fund is to say that we draw on something that is itself nothing other than a shared assumption, making the vehicle of the metaphor its tenor.

Projective feelings will tend to be social feelings, feelings which are currently nobody else's but mine, but nevertheless could well be those entertained by others. Many of these feelings belong to what may be called the honour register, in that they concern my feelings about my likely standing in the eyes of others. Projective feelings by no means always have this uncertain character, and it may well be that the feelings we feel most blisteringly convinced about – feelings that we have been slighted or subject to disrespect, for example – are the ones we most mean, or wish, to feel, or wish others to believe we do, perhaps in order to help us be sure we do in fact feel them. I have never forgotten hearing Christopher Ricks remark during a TV interview that we think we do not know what we think but know for sure what we feel, whereas the opposite is more likely to be true: we know perfectly well what we think, but do not know what we feel.

Work is not the only matter of human concern to generate a phantasmatics, or system of projective sentiments. I use the slightly dainty word 'sentiment' here to intimate by assonance the kind of feeling that is apt or able to give rise to the kind of thing we can call a sentence. Indeed, a feeling that one has to posit in order actually to have it may be said for that reason to be a quasi-proposition, a supposition or putting-case. But in the case of our projective sentiments about work, we will often come upon an intriguing doubling, since the projection of sentiments entails a kind of work being performed on them. In such cases, we find ourselves needing to work on our feelings of work, in the process I will persist in calling, unless and until I can think of something better, labour-work (though the awkwardness is part of the discovery I mean to make with it). None of this should imply that projective feelings are merely pretended, or, if they are, it would have to be in the earlier meaning of pretending as maintaining rather than dissimulating (the Young Pretender really was not kidding about his claim to the throne). For this reason, though the operation of phantasmatics may include the kind of suspensive or subjunctive feelings characteristic of fantasy, it is not coextensive with it. What is characteristic of phantasmatics is the work of maintaining the projective sentiments it involves, work of which we may not be fully conscious.

Phantasmatic feelings about work are not only projective, but are typically obsessive, which is to say that they consist of fears and desires that exercise demands on us. It is not just euphonious felicity that has suggested the term 'workaholic', formed in 1947 when the *Toronto Daily Star* wrote satirically, 'If you are cursed with an unconquerable craving for work, call Workaholics Synonymous [*sic*], and a reformed worker will aid you back to happy idleness.'[36] For the addictive nature of work, an addiction being something to which one has been assigned, devoted or made over – from *addicere*, part of the family of words that includes prediction, jurisdiction and contradiction – is doubled by the demanding and even frankly laborious nature of every addiction, which only earns its name when there is a limit or impediment to the realization of one's desire which one must struggle to overcome. We do not speak of an addiction to eating, breathing or sleeping until these have been formed into a compulsion, rather than a simple reflex or attraction, and have thereby become a kind of project demanding work. In addiction, one's wanting is not quite in one's possession: one wants what one wants without exactly wanting to.

The demand exercised by an obsession can be neither fully articulated nor fully accounted for, which is what leads to its characteristically phantasmatic effects of projective rather than straightforwardly experienced feelings. This surplus to representation, making the representation at once excessive to and deficient in what it represents, also means that the obsession cannot fully be satisfied. The iterative aspect of the obsession may have some connection to the mechanical iterability that is itself so recurrent a feature of all work. Our understanding of work is linked to the idea of production, and thought to result in completed productions: so work can refer to both our working and the work done as a result of it. One might even say that, in a phrase like 'my work here is done,' the action of work tends to be self-objectifying, being directed not just at the making of objects but also at making an object of itself. This characteristic seems to be shared in other examples of processes that are conceived as work-like endeavours: 'my love for you will last for ever.' But it is equally of the nature of work to require resumption and repetition, as though its satisfactions could only ever be temporary, or as if it were striving to satisfy itself through us. No carpenter could content himself with the production of a unique, radiantly Platonic table, and the author of a single text may not reasonably be thought of as a writer unless they have at least set to work on another. Anyone can make a shoe, of some description, under the pressure of curiosity or need, but a shoemaker has to have surrendered in some degree to an obsessional demand, an internalized demand from outside, to keep making shoes. The frequentative nature of work means that we are haunted by it, even if it does not take the incubus-like form of the 'toad work' that squats on Philip Larkin's life.[37]

It may have occurred to my reader, for it has certainly occurred to me, that what I am calling phantasmatics I might just as well call ideology and be done with it. I cannot deny that many of the projective sentiments we have about work could easily be ingredients in what others are content to call the ideology of work. I decline this tender, however, largely because, despite how it may be characterized, ideology tends in most uses to suggest something more finished and formalized than the projective sentiments I see at work in phantasmatics. Projective work may sometimes have in common with ideology something that might be called 'false consciousness', as we used to call it in the 1970s, to cheer ourselves up, but it is much less fixed and formulated than the ways in which ideologies tend to be conceived, even in their most supersubtilized conceptions. Ideologies tend to be explicated as systems of ideas, rather than processes of sentiment-experiment and sentiment-prospecting. This is part of what I mean by saying that the phantasmatics of work are projective rather than conclusive, suppositions rather than settled propositions.

Most importantly of all, ideologies tend, if not to consist of, then certainly to be regarded as reducible to, what people think. The sphere of phantasmatics as I conceive it consists rather more of how people think, or, as we might say, what they feel about what they think, as well as what they want to feel that they know. Phantasmatics are performative rather than definitive or declarative, belonging therefore to the considerable repertoire of ways in which people stage, try out or 'put on' (a phrase that nicely conjoins pretending and producing, as for the stage) ideas, stories, identifications and other projections of what they would like to think they are up to in their lives. This is a large part of the reason I prefer a term like phantasmatics, for all its possible wispiness, to the cut-and-dried, straight-up-and-down address of ideology.

When I say that work is phantasmal, I do not mean to imply that we are not in fact doing the things, toting pails and taking temperatures, that we take ourselves to be. These actions are really being performed and we are really enacting them. What I mean to say is that the idea we may or may not have of what those actions amount to or count as, is always, for it can only ever be, in part the work of fantasy. I will likely need to keep reminding my reader at intervals, as I have to remind myself, that, despite the promise seemingly embodied in the word 'fantasy', which is used almost always to indicate projections of unreal yet desirable states, fantasy also involves the dark, the dreaded or the undesired. This is maybe because, following Freud's suggestion in *Beyond the Pleasure Principle*, to project or replay in symbol or imagination some duress or disaster is to subject it to a kind of 'binding'.[38] I explore in Chapter Five the philosophical fantasies we forge about the redemption of work from every form of arduousness or misery, the systematization of the 'dream job' that all of us may individually crave. But fantasy may also enter into the hardness of work, as the very thing that may make intolerable work tolerable, or half-way so. For the phantasmatics of work are no mere idle fantasy, or empty reverie. There is always work involved in fantasy, always a phantasmatic component, as the labour of the negative, even and especially in the negativity of labour.

Books that aim to convince their readers that various things are phantasmal rather than real – ideology, error, deception, myth – commonly present themselves as a means of dispelling fantasy and awakening to some acknowledgement or other of the reality principle. Such works represent themselves as reforming or sanative. That is not the case with this book, which assumes that the need for work is an ailment with little prospect of relief. If religious belief may be seen as a compensatory reification of human helplessness, work is an overestimation of the capacity to change one's environment, local efficacy inflated into omnipotence. Work serves ideally as the mediation of power and powerlessness, for it can seem to guarantee omnipotence even as it is also used to explain the inevitable failure of many human projects, as owing to idleness or perverse unwillingness to obey the imperative to work, or to work as hard as we should have. Not many of us nowadays feel that work is satisfactorily to be explained as the consequence of original sin, as maintained in some strains of Christian doctrine, but such doctrines formalize the twin sense of human power and unrealized potential that seem to be an essential condition of the human, born with prodigious powers of projecting its needs but with almost complete limitations on realizing its projections. Occupying the abyss between projection and realization, work comes to embody the sense not so much of the real as of the actual.

This explains why there can be no final remedy for the work imperative. Since it is itself dreamed as the sovereign remedy for the essential incapacity or infirmity of the human, the operation in us of the idea of work is inoperable. Work is not just the will to power, which might very well remain merely and ineffectually willed, in melancholy or resentment, but also the power to execute one's will, or put it to work.

Writing of the relation between temporality and technology, Bernard Stiegler finds the invention of the human in the reciprocally constituting encounter of subjects with objects, or the *who* with the *what*:

> Différance is neither the *who* nor the *what*, but their co-possibility, the movement of their mutual coming-to-be, of their coming into convention. The *who* is nothing without

> the *what*, and conversely. Différance is below and beyond the *who* and the *what*; it poses them together, a composition engendering the illusion of an opposition. The passage is a mirage: the passage of the cortex into flint, like a mirror proto-stage.[39]

Stiegler does not seem to realize what he is saying here, or rather perhaps the reverse: his argument seems to realize all too well something that he himself does not quite come to the point of saying. For it is not just the encounter between the *who* and the *what* that counts in this constitution of subjects through objects, but the *how* of this encounter, in the fact that it is a matter of work, rather than some accidental and inconsequent convergence:

> This proto-mirage is the paradoxical and aporetic beginning of 'exteriorization.' It is accomplished between the Zinjanthropian and the Neanthropian, for hundreds of thousands of years in the course of which the work in flint begins, the meeting of matter whereby the cortex reflects itself. Reflecting itself, like a mirrored psyche, an archaeo- or paleontological mode of reflexivity, somber, buried, freeing itself slowly from the shadows like a statue out of a block of marble.[40]

When Stiegler concludes that 'The paradox is to have to speak of an exteriorization without a preceding interior: the interior is constituted in exteriorization,' it is not the paradox of technology that he characterizes so much as the paradox of work, as the healing that keeps open the wound of lack it heals.[41]

So the QED of this book, that which will have been to-be-demonstrated, is that all work is imaginary. This does not mean, I will say again – likely in vain – that work does not exist, is a footling kind of hallucination or diabolical deception. To say that work is imaginary is to say that in order to occur, in order to do the work of work, work always has to be imagined. One might in fact say that, like my projected argument, it seems that it is itself a *demonstrandum*, a to-be-demonstrated. Work is subject to demonstration inasmuch as demonstration can be regarded as a defence against the charge of being imaginary, since demonstrating something is meant to be a conclusive rebuff to the charge that we have simply made it up. And that 'having to be imagined' indicates that there is a work-like effort or imperative in the process of imagining work. Imagining work – making it out rather than just making it up – really does seem to require quite a lot of what feels like work (writing this book, for example). The last thing we should ever seek to affirm of fantasy is that it is idle.

So to say that all work is imaginary does not mean that it is merely or entirely imaginary. There are always real actions involved in work, or recruited to its cause: blood, sweat, tears, boredom, striving, every kind of toil and trouble. But those actions can easily, and do readily, occur without being regarded as work (in exactly equivalent actions performed by animals, for example), because those actions must be imagined, by which one will often mean demonstrated (shown, proven) to be work, to *be* work. For reasons that, at the mooted end of all this, may continue to be obscure, or more simply, if that is what it is really, because there may not be anything like reasons impelling them, the task we give ourselves of imagining work does not seem at all easy to dispense with. But what kind of imagination is this then, so labour-laden? A kind of its own.

Inevitably, there have been many who believe that we are needlessly enslaved by work, or by the idea of it. The writers associated with various kinds of anti-work project often set out to demystify work in order to loosen the illusory hold that it might have on us. It might be expected that an argument like my own, that work must always imply a work of imagination, might have a similar aim, of freeing us from the squatting succubus that the compulsion to work may be revealed to be. This is in fact so far from being my aim that I am going to devote quite a few pages to the part that the dream of release from work plays in its coerciveness. My aim is, if anything, not to demystify but rather, as one might say, to remysticate work (as opposed to remystifying it) by making detectible its stubbornly ineradicable mystical components.

It is not just that I think we are unlikely ever to achieve a clear-eyed understanding of work, or escape from myth into reality, though I have certainly come to that view. It is that I think that illusion is intrinsic to work, and to the work that work does on, to and for us. Not every living organism which evolved the elaborate cognitive-symbolic supplements that humans have would be bound to come up with a practice of work that demands such devotion and to which we are so bound by our history. This is why it seems to me to be appropriate to understand the phantasmatics of work as a mysticism rather than an imperfect understanding. Mysticism may be characterized not just as a pledging of oneself to the service or exploration of the unknown, but more specifically as a cathexis, even a consecration, of unknowability as such: a rapt devotion to making known its permanent unknowability, and bearing witness to its inexplicability. The need for work includes the need for it to remain esoteric, veiled from understanding or the possibility of daylit exposition. Mysticism concerns not so much the unknown as the keeping secret from oneself of some knowledge – to the point, possibly, of keeping secret the fact that there is in fact no secret to keep (except that).[42] It may even be that the reputation work has for being precisely the opposite of mystical – routine, self-evident, wanly workaday – is part of its deliberately maintained mystery, a word that was used from the fourteenth to the eighteenth centuries to mean a craft, trade or form of work.

2

Hard Work

As I have mentioned already, we seem to care much less about whether work is successful or effective – whether and how well it works, in the sense that it actually achieves the ends assumed to be projected for it – than about whether the work is real, which is to say whether it works in the alternative sense that it counts for us as work. Work, to be real, or at least realistic, must be what we call hard. This is a strange conception, though it jumps together vigorously with other, even more general assumptions, like the bracing and repeatedly cited claim made by Fredric Jameson that 'History is what hurts, it is what refuses desire and sets inexorable limits.'[1] This is, if not exactly nonsense on stilts, then at least in teetering heels. Why on earth would history be thought to exclude circuses, panettone and the frolics of cultural theory? We can certainly admit that limit, extremity and other phenomena of improbable ultimacy do tend to be regarded as more essential and defining than average or highly probable conditions, but it is hard to think of convincing reasons for this predilection. We must suspect that an excitable thumb is pressing on the scale, a thumb impelled by a need for excitement. To believe that History is what hurts amounts to believing that history is whatever you see on the news. The idea that history, or rather real History, as opposed perhaps to mere history, should hurt is of a piece with the idea that realism will characteristically be gritty, rather than, say, gooey.

The hardness of hard work is obviously metaphorical, though it is a metaphor that draws deeply on certain kinds of non-metaphorical experience that might be characteristic both of work and of suffering. In fact we are going to see that work is not just accidentally characterized by hardness, since hardness would need to be defined as the need for work. Oh dear. It will neither be the first nor the last of the tautologies that will characterize work by the time I have done here.

Hardness has a certain reputation for embodying indubitability, as in James Boswell's account of Samuel Johnson's response to being told that Bishop Berkeley's theory of the pure ideality of matter, though evidently untrue, was very hard to refute: 'I never shall forget the alacrity with which Johnson answered, striking his foot with mighty force against a large stone, till he rebounded from it, "I refute it *thus*."'[2] The fact that Boswell might very well have performed precisely the same action in defence of the proposition of which Johnson performs his defiance is an indication of the shiftily elusive quality of hardness under close inspection.

Johnson's contemporary, Thomas Reid, for example, is struck by the fact that the sensation of hardness seems to have nothing in common with what qualifies the objects that we feel to be hard as hard, namely, a condition in which 'the parts of a body adhere so firmly, that it cannot easily be made to change its figure'.[3] We are so used to attending to what the sensation seems to evidence or allow us to infer about the object of which it is the sensation that we find it very hard to pay attention to the nature of the sensation itself:

> There is, no doubt, a sensation by which we perceive a body to be hard or soft. This sensation of hardness may easily be had, by pressing one's hand against the table, and attending to the feeling that ensues, setting aside, as much as possible, all thought of the table and its qualities, or of any external thing. But it is one thing to have the sensation, and another

> to attend to it, and make it a distinct object of reflection. The first is very easy; the last, in most cases, extremely difficult.[4]

Reid goes on to claim that it is so difficult to attend to this sensation that nobody, least of all, perhaps, the philosophers whose business it might be thought to be, has even attempted it:

> It is indeed strange, that a sensation which we have every time we feel a body hard, and which, consequently, we can command as often, and continue as long as we please, a sensation as distinct and determinate as any other, should yet be so much unknown, as never to have been made the object of any thought and reflection, nor to have been honoured with a name in any language: that philosophers, as well as the vulgar, should have entirely overlooked it, or confounded it with that quality of bodies which we call *hardness*, to which it has not the least similitude.[5]

We know that things are hard, and we know what hardness consists of in such objects: pleasingly, perhaps, hardness consists in a certain principle of what we call consistency. What we do not know, Reid insists, is how the sensation we call hardness permits us to infer that hardness. This is a more general difficulty than Reid seems at this point to allow. For it is in fact generally the case that sensations need not, and usually do not, have any resemblance or natural relation to the qualities of which they are sensings: the auditory sensation of a high note does not feel like an accelerated vibration, unless transmitted buzzingly through the reed of a clarinet, say. Reid does not doubt that there is a connection between feeling things to be hard and their having the qualities of hardness, but he cannot account for it, beyond the frankly rather flimsy suggestion that there may just be a natural relation between the two:

> I see nothing left, but to conclude that, by an original principle of our constitution, a certain sensation of touch both suggests to the mind the conception of hardness, and creates the belief of it; or, in other words, this sensation is a natural sign of hardness.[6]

When it comes to work, we are not directly concerned with physical sensation, though it seems very likely that something to do with what we think of as hardness in the objects of sense is powerfully operative in the idea of hard work. But some of the same difficulties seem to arise in accounting for what might be meant by the kind of hardness that we seem to feel is the essential and defining condition of work as such. We know that work is hard when it seems hard, by which we seem to mean, when we feel we cannot deny its hardness, or that there can be no argument about it. But I hope what has been said so far has softened my reader up sufficiently to recognize that we may not know as well as we suppose what that hardness is. The work performed by the idea of hardness is to seem to refute that unknowing through some means other than thought or representation.

As may be suggested by the attention paid by recent philosophers to the conundrum of hardness for Reid, hardness is not just one quality among others, but one that has a generally representative status.[7] This representative status comes not from a quality inhering in the kind of hard object for which Johnson's stone is taken to be paradigmatic, but an assumed or projected relation between the stone and its perceiver. I think we can assume that the reason why hardness seems to have the representative quality it does is that it seems to resist us in a way that other qualities, like figure and colour, do not. We do not have to do any work to understand immediately that lifting a heavy weight, or attempting to drop-kick an embedded stone, will entail a lot of work – 'mighty force', in Boswell's description. Reid affirms that his idea of hardness in a body is 'the conception of such a cohesion of its parts as requires great force to displace them'.[8] In other words, the hardness of something is the measure of what we call, confusingly, perhaps, the hardness of the work required to change its position or disposition. The primary conception of the hard is that of something that is intractable or that will not easily yield: Boswell's manuscript makes it clear that the stone against which Johnson launched his foot was in fact 'one of the large projecting stones of the Building' from which they had just emerged, a church in Helvoetsluys in the Netherlands.[9] But by not yielding easily to work, hardness yields it up, or delivers it to awareness. Something hard stands out, stands up for itself.

Let us recall the question of why realism might seem more obviously gritty than, say, gooey, or gaseous. It cannot be because grit is any more material than gloop or gossamer, though something in the way we think of matter, or the relation between ourselves and it, seems unrestingly and irresistibly to weight us towards this view. I surmise that it is because we have inherited an ergological view of matter, as that against which we must strive, and it is therefore primarily characterized in modes of tractability or yieldingness. Hardness is not an absolute indwelling condition of things, for something that is hard for a finger may be soft as butter for a tungsten blade. Hardness is therefore an inferred or assumed relation, a relation that seems to imply an opposition between an active user and an inert material more or less available for use, arrangement or derangement. If the very relation between matter – nature reduced, as it were, to physics – and human life is seen as a relation of potential antagonism, it may be because the complement to an ergological view of matter is an ergological ego-of-work, or what Gaston Bachelard, following Maine de Biran, described as a 'cogito of striving'.[10] The self-sensing of such an ego, the way in which its being seems to be for itself, is as something that surges up spontaneously out of inertness, but is able thereby to stand up against it, in both a visual and an energetic sense, yet at the same time only seems to be able to come into being in reaction to the pressing in of inertness upon it. Inert is from Latin *iners*, *in-ars*, without art or work, either in the sense of being unworked or being itself incapable of working. But the interior reference to work means that inertness, like hardness, is never entirely inert, since it can impart or permit the demand that work be done. Alternatively, in Jean-Paul Sartre's category of the 'practico-inert', matter can appear as the sedimentation of human efforts of adaptation or transformation, making matter what Sartre calls 'worked inertia', or the artefact of past action.[11]

It is hard to be sure whether the seriousness of the idea of work derives from striving and struggle, or striving and struggle become serious by being reimagined as a kind of work. Perhaps in both cases the trick is turned by the imaginary transvaluation of suffering into willed purpose, subjection thereby being subjectified. In both cases, the phantasmagoria of seriousness depends upon the conversion of everything that is indifferently or inertially other than the self into its invigorating negative. Negativity works neutral adjacencies up into forms of work relation.

For there are two kinds of negative, that which is indifferently *un-* or *not-*, and that which says *no*, or to which we ourselves say *no*. The first is tolerative, the second privative. The first is part of an infinite, non-aggregating, non-interfering sum of adjacencies, the deific prospect of things *sub specie aeternitatis*, or under what William Empson calls 'the big top of the historical approach'.[12] If I contemplate my coffee cup, I can easily denominate hosts of things which it is not and which I am therefore unlikely to mistake for it: my cat, the carpet, the Berlin Wall and the doctrine of transubstantiation – there is, in fact, no limit to all the things that the coffee cup is trivially not, as an obvious but uninteresting condition of its being a coffee cup. The second kind of negative forms a zero-sum game, and is the kind of thing that quarrelsome primates, subsisting in a world of scarce resources, and the assault and battery of nothing-buttery, one thing or the other, and either-with-us-or-against-us, tend to get very het up about, existing, in fact, in a permanent state of pre-excitement about the prospect of such excitement. Empson suggested something like this difference in observations regarding the practice of literary criticism in 1950:

> There is a tendency to feel that, if the critic is offering a really efficient machine, it ought to be able to say whether marmalade is better than sausages; but even the most expert cook cannot say that; sometimes you want one, sometimes the other ... this kind of absolutism seems to be comical.[13]

The marmalade reappears in a different guise in Empson's comparison a few years later of the theory of the all-including collective unconscious to the 'Jam theory', that 'we have all human experience inside us, simply as the jam in our tin.'[14]

The problem, or very likely just one of them, is that any kind of (in)comparability, however delightfully and peaceably disparate it may appear, can serve to put the desperate competitive machine in gear. The disputational objection that one is illegitimately comparing apples and pears has always struck me as feebly self-defeating, precisely because apples and pears are so self-evidently comparable and in fact readily confusable, just like chalk and cheese and even, in their assonantal way, hawks and handsaws. But skipping is not pollen, to name, as much at random as I can manage, just one of the infinite numbers of things that skipping, or pollen, can turn out not to be, forever and ever, once you come to think about it, if you can be bothered. I think it would take a diabolically versatile kind of logico-poetic wangling to make skipping a jaw-thrusting naysaying of pollen, since it does not in any obvious way take pollen's place, or gainsay its existence. ('Come on! What is it to be? Skipping? Or pollen?') My readers will already have started imagining for themselves an exotic conceptual scheme in which pollen might indeed be construed as the opposite or antagonist of skipping (for example, it inanely occurs to me, as the indicative instances of an imaginary language built around the metaphysical duality of things spelled with a double l, like spelling, and things spelled with a double p). But this is evidence not of any pre-existing pattern of antagonisms, but only of how expert we are at finding ways to turn indifferent unrelatedness into adversary non-relation. That is what I am endeavouring to make my point.

Hegel's relation of negation usually does seem to involve this act of negativing, and therefore seems to prompt a self-defensive negation of its negation, making the negative the 'to-be-overcome', either through annihilation or the preservative annihilation of assimilation. Perhaps these two modes of the negative themselves exist in a privative relation, so that one might construe Hegel's famous 'labour of the negative' as a labour not just against whatever is constituted as or seems to present itself as negative, but, more importantly ('importantly'), a labour against the indifference that is the negation of the negative relation between spirit and whatever it supposes to be its opposite, and by supposing ends it.[15] Thought of in this way, the labour of the negative could be understood not as a labour bearing up against something experienced as a negation (distance, want, restriction, interdiction and so on), but as a labour on behalf of the relation of negativity. This is one of the many reasons that argumentative persons (and, given the affinity commonly assumed between impersonality and indifference, it is admittedly difficult to imagine any other kind) find equanimity in those they would have be their opponents so enraging, and, alas, also agonistically invigorating. Hence the charge of 'passive aggression', which is what passive persons are often accused of by aggressive ones. The labour of the negative is to keep negativity in being.

This is because negativity is an essential feature of the being of human beings, probably as a combined by-product of raw primate aggressiveness and the capacity, hugely amplified by language, to remember or project other states of things, in a way that seems to keep continuously actual and at-hand states which are no longer or are not yet, thus thronging actual existence with ad-hoc inactualities. If seriousness usually concerns the effort to keep things continuously in being, the seriousness of work maintains the importance of keeping effort in being, where effort is linked to the transformation that may be effected by work. Work, definable as 'the deliberate production by man of changes in matter for the purposes of man', is always a work of transformation, arising from more or less violent repugnance to the given, or to things as they are.[16] To work is to strive against givenness, even though work has by now been immutably bricked into the given for human beings. Working is therefore the overcoming of what impedes, or the negation of a negation, for work is also, and much more importantly, the production, preservation and, as we say, elaboration of the very relation of negativity that gives it its stimulus and 'reason'. The English word *strive*, of uncertain origin, embodies this ambivalence, for it may derive either from Old French *estriver*, to contend or quarrel, or from Germanic **strīban*, which has the meaning of endeavour; whatever the origin, striving for or towards has long been indistinguishable from striving with or against.

Work, then, is war – or, more strictly, the waging of war, where *waging* implies manner, method, strategy, some way of putting it into operation. To wage war is in fact to work on war, to transform the raw hurly-burly of the *bellum omnium contra omnes* by the scansion of rules of engagement (to wage and to engage are both variations of French *gager* and English *gage*). To wage, in the sense of performing, carrying on or carrying out, derives from the sense of giving a wager in pledging, the bargain struck by the first strike, and the effort to win. Work, like sport, according to George Orwell, is 'war minus the shooting'.[17]

One might take the will to strive to be explicable simply because it is one of the things about which human beings are so immensely serious, meaning that we commit ourselves to it with the same kind of commitment that work requires. But the kind of striving that is made universal in organized labour is not just the object of a particular kind of seriousness, but one of the cardinal modes by which seriousness exists and is made to subsist. That is, work is taken seriously because it is a prime means of producing seriousness. If this is circular, its circularity is not entirely inert. For one does not merely stumble on seriousness, that being precisely the opposite of what it means to be serious about something: one must win through, or beat a path to it. Work is a serious matter, because work is the proof of seriousness, and because the production of seriousness is itself always such a labour of striving, the striving that labour strives to make of itself, in its travail against the trivial.

War is the horizon and apotheosis of work, since the work of war requires a supreme effort of concentration and coordination of forces and resources: war requires that work itself be worked up into totality, so that there is no residue of any activity or purpose other than that of the struggle to win the war. Such total mobilization happens rarely in fact, partly because it is so hugely expensive, but its ideal form haunts ordinary understandings of work. And, since the mass mobilizations of the First World War, the ongoing convergence has become ever more complete. Once an entire economy and system of production has been focused on the waging of war, that economic system will always be part of long-term preparation for hostilities.

But total mobilizations, which put entire societies on a war footing, are, in fact, a sort of model for other kinds of militant project, religious, economic and political, of which they are the miraculous apparitions and actualizations. It may be the project of redemption for original sin, itself a generative model for many kinds of project. Or it may be the struggle for emancipation, from slavery or dominion. Or it may be the more general struggle for some unspecified fulfilment, against anything that seems in its mere being to negate that fulfilment. All these irritable or angry reactions require to be embodied in *projects*, in which one simultaneously launches oneself towards some future condition and takes on a kind of subordination to it. The slave who plans an uprising, the worker who pledges themselves to the revolution, the prisoner who digs a tunnel with a spoon, all, in their projects of freedom, actually choose one servitude, the unswervingly obedient service of their freedom, over another. Projection makes the strangely absurd affair of self-aware living in time a serious matter, a matter to which one must make oneself over.

And yet, if work is war and war is the essential form of work, there is at least one rather telling anomaly. 1 Maccabees 2 records that, in the second century BC, during the Maccabean uprising against the attempts of Antiochus IV to suppress Jewish religious practices, a thousand Jews were slaughtered when they refused to join battle with the forces of Antiochus on the sabbath. The followers of the resistance leader immediately determined that, like refusing to care for the sick, this was a suicidally self-contradictory principle that must be abandoned: 'At that time therefore they decreed, saying, Whosoever shall come to make battle with us on the sabbath day, we will fight against him; neither will we die all, as our brethren that were murdered in the secret places' (1 Maccabees 2:41). One might have thought this a pretty straightforward clarification, but debate about whether the waging of war is permitted on a sabbath has lingered, perhaps as a special instance of the continuing attempts to make the warlike lawlike.[18] If it seems obvious that work is always imagined as a warlike kind of struggle, and the conduct of war always requires many different kinds of war work and military operation, there is also something in war which seems opposed to work. For war may be regarded as the most intensely purposive action in which humans engage, especially for those who are defending their lives. Under these circumstances, war is an absolute necessity for survival, as are many other kinds of life-and-death struggle, against fire, flood, famine and other kinds of natural ills. As such, war must be won, once and for all, in a way that seems completely contrary to the practice of work, which is intended never to be finishable, or not in the absolute way at which war is aimed. To be sure, many human beings have, as we say, made their living as professional soldiers, but the turning of war into work that this practice involves seems to amount to a strange kind of deterrence. All work is a variety of war, even as work is a taming or sedation of the atemporal paroxysms of war into routine.

One works, as we say, for a living. Work has the importance it does because it makes merely being into a specific way of being. Work gives meaning because it finitizes what would otherwise be the horror of unstyled, unpurposed existence. Work fulfils but only by reducing living to the instrumentality of *living for*. Work embodies the projective nature of existence in joining the openness of living for or towards to the inevitable closure of having lived as and for that living-for. Work thereby opens up a free future that it is its purpose to foreclose. One works to have been. Work must always therefore be formative, dedicated to the formation of a work, even and especially the work that the worker must make of himself. To say that my work is fulfilling is to say that it has reduced me to an object without excess, in just the same way as alienating labour is supposed to. One need not mean one's work to function in this way, since it is the function of work to come to be the meaning that one's life has had. There is no escape from this process of working one's life up into some definite form or other, even if one forswears every conceivable kind of ambition or project for existence, for that forswearing will have in the course of time to harden into something that one swears by, as a sacred project of temper or torpor of which our lives cannot fail to have been the working through.

The need for work is implied in the condition of a being whose being is a question for itself. Answering the question of being, the question 'what am I to be, or to have been?', means understanding one's being as adversity or ordeal. This makes being a task, or the task of answering to the question of being. To be is to be challenged to be. One may fail in that task of answering, but one cannot avoid answering to that task as a task, since declining the challenge, like Melville's Bartleby, is nonetheless an answer to its demand. This necessity of response to the question of being is what makes work intrinsic to the kind of being characterized as human. To be a human is to live one's being as an affair – an *à faire*, something to be done.

It is Hegel who formalizes the principle that *Arbeit macht frei*. In labour, which is to say in the assertion of one's will over objective matter, one partially objectifies oneself, voluntarily limiting one's freedom for the period of one's labour. But the products of one's labour serve to enlarge one's freedom from necessity. The solemn exchanges of freedom and limit, life and matter, form a sort of animistic puppet play. Unlike Pinocchio, the woodentop imitation of life who strives to become a real boy, his father, the craftsman Geppetto (literally little log, or block), subdues himself through his labour in order to infuse his life into a lump of wood. Jean-Paul Sartre follows Hegel and the tradition of thinking about labour, which he inaugurates in his account of the mysterious dialectic involved in all labour, or the kind of purposive action for which Sartre uses the magic word *praxis*:

> One can say that *human labour*, the original *praxis* by which man produces and reproduces his life, is entirely dialectical: its possibility and permanent necessity rest upon the relation of interiority which unites the organism with the

> environment and upon the deep contradiction between the inorganic and organic orders, both of which are present in everyone. Its primary movement and its essential character are defined by a twofold contradictory transformation: the unity of the project endows the practical field with a quasi-synthetic unity, and the crucial moment of labour is that in which the organism makes itself inert (the man applies his weight to the lever, etc.) in order to transform the surrounding inertia.[19]

That this deadly earnest set of magical interchanges is essentially comic is suggested by the screw-turning Bergsonism of Sartre's formula for the subordination of workers to their work: 'Man becomes the machine's machine.'[20]

Militant seriousness is present even in the philosophical understanding of the human body, and specifically in the cathexis of the uprightness that characterizes humans, and the serious business it implies of standing one's ground, or standing up to or for things. In its effort to 'Contemplate all this work of Time', Tennyson's *In Memoriam* articulates the poetics of history turned from vertigo into groaning verticality:

> Till at the last arose the man;
>
> Who throve and branch'd from clime to clime,
> The herald of a higher race,
> And of himself in higher place,
> If so he type this work of time
>
> Within himself, from more to more;
> Or, crown'd with attributes of woe
> Like glories, move his course, and show
> That life is not as idle ore,

But iron dug from central gloom,
    And heated hot with burning fears,
    And dipt in baths of hissing tears,
And batter'd with the shocks of doom

To shape and use. Arise and fly
    The reeling Faun, the sensual feast;
    Move upward, working out the beast,
And let the ape and tiger die.[21]

To be upright is to assert one's will to negate the ground, and to display the continuing exertion of that wilfulness, in the doing of one's being. Hegel writes that the upright posture in man 'continues to be an affair of his persistent will; for the man stands only because and in so far as he wills to stand, and only so long as he wills it without consciousness'.[22] No wonder that so many cultures have striven to make such hard work of walking itself, or trained the human body to an uprightness that is a symbol of the spurning of earth, of a stasis ribbed and quivering with flexed will. No wonder, too, that the idea of having to strain every sinew simply to continue in being should so quake with ludicrousness, and that falling over should be the epitome of comedy. What keeps seriousness upright is not its indwelling virtue, but the precipice of absurdity on the brink of which it trembles, at once sternly refused and made momently imminent by its efforts of retraction.

There is an ambivalence in hardness that has substantial effects on the way in which we think about work. On the one hand, the hard represents the idea of a kind of ultimate and absolute limit, as embodied most powerfully in the absolute antagonism between subject and object, the subject being that which is overthrown by the object, that which it is thrown up against. On the other hand, since, as we have seen, hardness is not in fact an absolute and isolate condition but rather a relation between cohesion and susceptibility, it is also characterized by infinite degrees. The striving to overcome resistance can become the striving to overcome the inert, stony flavour of victory over the inert. In this, work is the striving to make striving absolute, as though it were striving to make itself autonomous of the alien and obdurate exteriority on which it depends for its excitement. Striving makes itself hard in bending the hard to its will, just as work is hard when it struggles to overcome the impediments of hardness. Work is only real work when it is hard work, even though it is always possible to set oneself in opposition to that hardness by working harder. Indeed, to work hard means to try to work even harder than one has hitherto, a built-in escalation that implies the risk that the reality of work may recede infinitely. In order to be work, then, work must be hard, and in order to be hard, work must always strive to work harder, in order to exceed itself, meaning that the limits of hard work are always, like the retreating horizon, soft.

Work turns the objects on which it works into what are called 'works', which seem at once finished and yet to possess the quality of unbroached potential that is characteristic of the artist-craftsman who has made them. Gaston Bachelard was always poised to recognize the ways in which the hard may be worked into softness, worked, as it were, into a working condition, for example in the iron works of the sculptor Eduardo Chillida, in which he discovers 'the *dream of hardness* . . . a muscular space, stripped of all fat and heaviness', in which, in other words, the iron has become a kind of self-fashioning body, imitating the shape of the body that has shaped it.[23] If the iron enters of the soul of the blacksmith, then his works may be said to have worked themselves out of purely spatial being and into temporal being. In Chillida's airborne works, which are 'somewhere between cages and birds, as if cages were on the point of taking wing', Bachelard finds at once a compounding of iron and air, and a 'synthesis of substance and movement, powerful movement finding in iron its proper substance'.[24] Work takes time, and in the process forges it, which is why, as will later be seen, the time of work must always look forward to a time of redemption and the perfection of time and work together.

Do As I Say

As Marx observes, work must always involve some kind of project. It is just this feature that, for Marx as for many others, distinguishes human work from the operations which seem to resemble it in the natural world, and which indeed human beings may often imitate. One works towards some end, which must always imply a gap between a current state and the end projected.

> We presuppose labour in a form that stamps it as exclusively human. A spider conducts operations that resemble those of a weaver, and a bee puts to shame many an architect in the construction of her cells. But what distinguishes the worst architect from the best of bees is this, that the architect raises his structure in imagination before he erects it in reality. At the end of every labour process, we get a result that already existed in the imagination of the labourer at its commencement.[25]

There are two aspects to Marx's definition of work. The first is that there must be some kind of reflexive relation between the one who projects an end and the one who effectuates it. The one who works

> effects a change of form in the material on which he works, but he also realises a purpose of his own that gives the law to his *modus operandi*, and to which he must subordinate his will . . . This means close attention. The less he is attracted by the nature of the work, and the mode in which it is carried

> on, and the less, therefore, he enjoys it as something which gives play to his bodily and mental powers, the more close his attention is forced to be.[26]

This reflexivity can take shared or collective forms, in which the worker subordinates himself or herself to the realization of an end shared with others, who therefore give themselves a law in common. But the outrage of slavery, or the alienated conditions of labour that approximate it, lies in the fact that it destroys any possibility of that self-relation, since the end towards which the slave works can never be their own end, even in part.

The second aspect of work is that it should involve both a gap and the closing of a gap between conception and execution – that is, it should take time: 'this subordination is no mere momentary act. Besides the exertion of the bodily organs, the process demands that, during the whole operation, the workman's will be steadily in consonance with his purpose.'[27] However, if the gap between conception and execution is at its maximum for the slave, or other exploited worker, it seems inconceivable that that gap could ever be reduced to nothing, precisely because the projective nature of work involves a conception that includes the requirement of having to be worked towards, or worked through. A projected end – whether a sonnet, a set of shelves or a three-course meal – must always include some implicit postponement, some prospect of the work necessary to achieve the projected end that will make it, as we say, worthwhile.

Reflexivity and postponement are related aspects of the same condition, for self-relation requires self-division. The attention required can only be maintained by a kind of tensioning of time, in which workers both maintain themselves in their work and yet effect a transformation, too, as they accompany the process whereby the work works towards the intended and finally completed 'work'.

The necessarily cooperative nature of many human undertakings, necessary because of the unignorable gains in efficiency that cooperation brings, means that the self-division between the worker and the self-monitoring attention that must be paid to himself or herself in the work process is often distributed between those performing the two kinds of work drily distinguished by Bertrand Russell, in arguing that work consists either of 'altering the position of matter at or near the earth's surface relatively to other such matter' or, alternatively, 'telling other people to do so'.[28] The question of whether the one who issues the instructions to others to do the work is or is not working has traditionally been a matter of some dispute. When Cleopatra says of Caesar's efforts to persuade her of his magnanimity in victory, 'he words me girls, he words me,' her words hurdy-gurdy the word 'word' into a kind of work, the work of words that was her author's own.[29] The question of the nature of the work done by the one who directs the work often dramatizes the contrast between the corporeal and conceptual understandings of work, or work's hardware and software. The beginning of Genesis, 'And God said, Let there be light: and there was light,' simply and powerfully enacts this magical sense of *fiat*, the abracadabra *be-it-so* of saying things into being. It is more snappily effective in the 'Fiat lux. Et facta est lux' of the Latin Vulgate than in the awkwardly strung-out English, which seems to have about it something of the potentate clapping his hands for retainers to scurry about performing the necessary operations. The invocation of the power of poetry in closing the gap between utterance and action is apparent in the slogan introduced to encourage the vigilance of travellers on British railways: *See it. Say it. Sorted.* The idea of the capacity of words to perform a kind of immediate work is at once mystical and one of the most common signs of the onset of serious mental illness.

The apparatus of mediated authority is one of the most powerfully cohering and yet also dynamic aspects of the work relation.

The names given to those who tell others what to do, in a work that they perform on those doing the work, seem to indicate that their role is perceptual rather than effectual. Their role is that of horseman to horse, or, in other words, a matter more of seeing than doing ('God saw the light, that it was good'): hence terms such as overseer, inspector, supervisor, superintendent or director. The worker performs the work, the manager has a responsibility to ensure that the work takes the form necessary to its completion. The worker supplies undirected effort, the manager gives it its shape, purpose, intelligibility or orientation.

Work relations thereby provide a physical approximation of the metaphysical relations between force and form. The ambivalence is neatly but amply implied in the word *order*, which means both to classify and to command, both a desired arrangement and the coercive force required to bring it about. In this case, the primary relation between a willing subject and an inert object is reproduced between different kinds of worker. The idiomatic expression 'to order about' shows their convergence, since to direct workers to move from place to place is a kind of mimicry of the work of purposively altering the state of matter that is the essential function of any act of work, and the force it is necessary to apply in order to give anything form, or to put it in order. The bawling of the sergeant-major on the parade ground represents an abstract diagram of these relations, with the forceful physicalization of the instruction (atte-e-n-*shun*!) seeming to act out that fantasy that the force of the order has literally shoved the soldiers into position, a position that mimics the reduction of a living body into a statue. The sergeant-major makes himself over into the image of pure, imperative force which, acting directly and immediately on the obedient bodies of the soldiers, makes them into pure, inert form. The OED suggests that the Latin *ordo* is 'perhaps cognate with *ōrdīrī*, to lay the warp before weaving, to initiate (an enterprise), on the assumption that the weaving sense was primary, and that *ōrdō* originally denoted "a thread on the loom"'. This might indicate that ordering, like working itself, is an action spread over time, between the openness of initiation, in which an order is given, and the closure of completion, in which some ordering has been achieved.

The principles of force and form have sometimes been invoked to distinguish living beings and processes from inanimate ones, or at least to characterize their relation. Thomas Khurana proposes that

> the processes that we – following the philosophical discourses around 1800 – call 'living' are processes inherently marked by a polarity of *force* and *form*. Living is what takes place within this polarity: a dialectics of force and form. It is neither the sheer productive force nor the mere resulting form but a certain interrelation, to be more precise, a *tension* of force and form.[30]

It will usually be possible, in any given circumstance, to distinguish the operations of force and form: the forms of the wheel and piston through which the expansive force of the engine is conveyed, the lozenge of willow that will allow a cricket ball to be propelled rapidly to the boundary. By operations, however, we must mean something that seems to perform the work of force, or something that will appear as a form. The drill sergeant can only act out his pantomime because he is enacting the form of the force he represents, recalling the fantasy of auditory execution that is satisfyingly laid out in the story of Joshua bringing down the walls of Jericho through the synchronization of trumpets and shouting, and ontogenetically confirmed in the power of the cry to procure comfort and relief that is rediscovered by every baby. The compliant company, on the other hand, can only assume its required form because it is obedient – that is, makes itself an object of hearing – and is capable of internalizing the external force in their movements. The form of force therefore requires the force of form. The fact that forces and forms are in fact both operations rather than objects means that force can never be permanently and definitively distinguished from form. As Khurana continues:

> It is of the utmost importance that . . . the form is the form of forces (produced by forces and organizing forces) and that the force cannot be thought of independently from form, but rather is a force of forms (producing forms and being itself formed).[31]

One may say that this dialectic of force and form characterizes not only the realm of the living in general but the realm of the kind of living that self-conscious life makes for itself, and so makes of itself, through work, understood as directed or formative force, or will-to-form. The form of force and the force of form play across the two meanings, verbal and substantive, of work, as well as the two equivalent meanings of order: the way in which one works to produce a work, and orders a particular ordering of things ('Clean up this mess': 'I will have the mushroom risotto').

Work relations are actually an allegory of the larger dialectic of force and form that gives work its character. These relations are a styling or staging of work, the form through which (the mediating-through-which signalled in the word *per-form*) the force of work is channelled. If work is an ungraspable necessity for humans, it is because it is a will to the forcing of form that cannot itself be conclusively precipitated into form. This is why the only real work must be hard work, a force seeking to bear up against something hard that seems to resist it. Work must be hard because it must strive to realize itself in such a way as always to exceed, or be able to exceed, its own realization.

The huge overestimation of mental functions among human beings, and the symbolic forms, like written or spoken 'orders', which those mental functions can so readily take, means that the relations between mental and physical ordering can often assume a magical character. Human beings have never accomplished any feat of invention, construction and organization to match the vast and millennia-long engineering of social life through the practice of work. The strike, which can never be general or anything other than an orgiastic episode, is the sabbatical proof that human life is essentially dedicated to work. The assignment of this present work is to demonstrate that the epic enterprise of human work – by which I mean, not what human work has accomplished but the accomplishment of the idea of work itself – is an expression and achievement of magical thinking.

The very concept of magical thinking revolves round the idea of work. As the doctrine of the omnipotence of thoughts, the functional principle of magical thinking is that thinking does not merely mirror the world, or foreshadow some future condition of it, but performs actual work on it. Magical thinking is the thought that thinking works on the world, along with the work that that thought does. But the work performed by magical thinking is a cause for concern as well as triumph. The point of magic is that it is undirected power that is capable of working on its own. The patient of Freud who suggested to him the term 'omnipotence of thoughts' was unnerved rather than overjoyed (or said he was) by the power that he believed his thoughts had to cause harm in the world.[32] The thought that thoughts perform work implies both a joyful and exalted sense of power and the austere sense of the necessity of channelling and tempering that power, so the thought of the thought-work of magical thinking gives rise simultaneously to the thought of the work that must be done to master it. Work is too powerful, magical thinking tells itself, to be allowed to work by itself: so it must be put to work. In the horse, sail or millwheel it is work itself that is worked on. This accounts for the strange ambivalence of magic, which at once allows the thought of things to be had for nothing – or nothing but the thinking, or the magical speaking that makes them so – and yet always also seems to require the literal 'elaboration', or working out, of logical systems, theories, techniques and technologies. The very word 'elaborate' seems to imply not just something worked out but a work that threatens to spiral out of control, or into a condition of deceitful vacuity.

In most ordinary circumstances, work is a sovereign defence against the temptation of magical thinking, the apparent proof on the muscles and through the sinews that mere thinking or saying will never simply be enough to make it so. At the very same time, the relation between the boss and the worker is a confirmation of the elation of the idea of work, as expressed in the fantasy of a command, the fantasy that the real work lies in the imaginary work of conception, government and man-management, without which the 'real' work of striving and straining becomes a vapidly time-serving charade.

The distributions of work functions between the master and the slave, the overseer and the operative, the conductor and the performer and the director and the actor can become a vast distraction, as the dynamics of esteem multiply in the space between conception and effectuation that should in principle be as reduced and efficient as possible. At every stage, force and form are driven to change places with each other. The ideal force of work makes what would otherwise be the empty form of the work-directive real, putting it into force, but in the process necessarily imparting to that force a kind of form. But the form given to the force of the work always threatens to diffuse that force into the impostures and wasteful distractions of work relations, which must always themselves be managed if they are not to drift into empty formality. The dramaturgy of work relations is the machinery required to make work real, making good the ontological deficit at its heart with stage business even as it derealizes the work by deflecting its focus away from its purported outcome. The form that channels a force, enabling it to exert its force, is also what impedes it and diffuses it in friction. At every point, the purpose of the work is on the point of turning into mere purport.

It is usually thought that this kind of dissipation is a problem to be solved. The problem solved by work may seem from close up to be how to bring work to an end. However, as the discussion of the history of efforts to imagine and effect redemptions of work in Chapter Five will conclude, the point of work is not to reduce work but to keep it going, which entails maintaining or if necessary manufacturing its necessity, and making sure it is of a kind that will allow it to be experienced as hard, in all the unexpectedly complex ways that have emerged in this chapter's discussion. For the time being, that process seems to involve a general move from apparently hard forms of work to soft forms. This is clear not just in the move away from manual labour and industrial processes to more abstract kinds of occupation, or from heavy lifting to bureaucratic sifting. It also involves new, ever more reflexive and densely recursive forms of relation between force and form, in which the mythical distribution of force and form between the master and the slave is internalized in forms of work ethic and work discipline.

Honest Toil

Work appears to be a primary and elemental conception, if etymology is a guide. The idea of work, like the word itself, does not seem to appear to be a development of some other, more primary conception, as is the case with many other words. We can assume the existence in Proto-Indo-European of a root **k^w^er*, meaning to do, make, shape or build, meaning that to work is to act or do. But work, for all its extraordinary range of applications in English and Germanic languages, is not the only word at work in English for the act of work. As usual, there is a Latinate alternative in the form of 'labour', along with words like 'toil' and 'craft'. It is in fact a complex task to discriminate the ways in which action can come to be regarded as work.

In pastoral writing, Arcadia was often characterized by honest toil, and the absence of any kind of guile:

> to buy reall goods with honest toil
> Amongst the woods and flocks, to use no guile,
> Was honour to those sober souls that knew
> No happinesse but what from vertue grew.[33]

Indeed, the idea that work began honest and was later on corrupted by forms of cheating and dissimulation is a powerful ingredient in ergogony, or the phantasmatics of work's origin. The myth of the Fall of work itself, from honesty into deception, alienation and other kinds of corruption, forms, as it were, a countermyth to the belief that work arises as a remedy for the Fall from felicity, as fallen humans work out their salvation. In fact, it seems likely that, as soon as work became a concept as well as a practice, as soon as it began to be distinguishable from the actions of which it consists (which may be as soon as there are the words like *make* and *do*, which appear to be primary in all languages), work entered into a symbolic mesh of meanings – things that work means and things that people mean to do through those meanings. It thus becomes possible for the idea of work to become entangled with the doing of it, meaning that work must from the beginning always be able to be something other than honest toil, pure and simple. Indeed, as with most theories of radical beginnings, the idea of the radical beginning of honest toil has required a great deal of working out and philosophical heavy lifting to be arrived at. This means that the honesty of work really lies in its future, as an unfulfilled dream of self-coincidence, even as the conceptions of what would count as honesty in work irresistibly become more elaborate. Following the historical rule that seems to apply to all radical imaginaries, the ideal of honest work is simultaneously deferred ever further into the future and recedes ever further into an imaginary past of simple and self-evident beginnings.

The principle of the economy of effort that applies to all entities and organisms means that work always aims to move away from inefficiency and towards greater efficiency, even if this is only on the whole, and in the long run (and it is often a very long run indeed). Nobody will persist for long in carrying books from one room to another one-handed when it is possible to carry twice as many using two – unless, of course, one is deliberately increasing the amount of work one wishes to do with one hand, as part of a programme of training or physiotherapy, in which case a different framework and programme of efficiency will have come into play, which will however maintain the principle of economy of effort in a different way. Work aims to effect desirable improvements in the world, and must always aim reflexively to improve itself into the bargain.

Work must be honest; work is perhaps honesty itself, or compulsion itself, ghosting the otherwise absent gerund of *musting*. You must work, but the *must* of things is the work you are compelled to do. Our speaking of honest toil, of the labourer who is worthy of his hire, makes of the idea of work an ideal of truth, even as it makes for the idea that truth must depend on striving or ordeal. Why? Why the will to truth or the war against error or ignorance? Can work that is not 'hard' really be work? Our language does not seem to make that very easy, even though it is usually indeed much easier to speak of hard work than to do it. The idea of work formally excludes pretence, since simulated work is not supposed to be work at all. And yet that definitional exclusion must always ensure that the question of pretence will be at work, or involve the purposive temporary suspension of purpose we like to call play, when it is a question of work. We might think, for example, of the paradoxical action of refraining from action, known as begging, which institutes a substitutive economy in which idleness becomes an active, even strenuous, form of performance. The animal that begs (begging being almost as widespread in animals as in humans) must always set the energy costs of their petition, which can be sizeable, against the likely gain on their investment in gifts of alimentation or copulative opportunity.

Michel Serres's suggestion that 'history passes from reality to language, from things to signs and from energy to information: from hard solutions to so-called soft ones' has been formalized in a model suggested by Stevan Harnad, who suggests that language may be understood as a form of symbolic currency that allows us to store up and transmit experience.[34] Just as I can earn money through a lifetime of labouring and then bequeath it to my daughter so that she herself never has to go to work, so language stores up and makes available for time-shifting and transmission the knowledge that would otherwise have to be gained repeatedly from the arduous and often costly rough and tumble of experience, or 'school of hard knocks'. Harnad describes this process as symbolic theft, because it allows us 'to steal categories through hearsay instead of having to earn them through the honest toil of learning them from direct exposure and trial and error feedback from the consequences of miscategorization'.[35] Harnad maintains that symbols must always be grounded in the sensorimotor interaction with the things that symbols refer to, which in turn enables the primary development of the capacity to categorize, or 'to do the right thing with the right kind of thing'.[36] Even though the intervention of the soft into the world of the hard produces very sudden and far-reaching transformations, it is nevertheless highly predictable as an outcome of the work that work performs on itself in the interests of efficiency (or, as it might alternatively be understood, work-reduction, or idleness).

One might extend Serres's principle that the hard moves to the soft to a brand name like Honest Toil olive oil. The oil is made by, or 'in the framework of', an English-Greek-Hungarian family from small-scale producers near Kyparissia in Messinia, on the west coast of the Peloponnese. The company is at some pains to emphasize that the oil is not blended or filtered as other oils commonly are, 'meaning it really is as unadulterated as possible . . . simply squashed olives'.[37] I have no reason to doubt these claims, which are made against, and perhaps in response to, a background of suspicion that so-called pure olive oils are in fact subject to various kinds of ancillary process. Olive-pressing has had a reputation for a long time as an epitome of laborious work designed to produce the reward of pleasure. Sometimes, as in the Jewish proverb that the olive must be squeezed to produce sweetness, it figures forth the lesson that suffering brings forth beauty or goodness. The pressing of olives provides an apt image for activities of destruction – digging, grinding, mixing, mashing – that themselves are transformed in work processes into a work of transformation. The long historical phenomenology of oil, imagined from the hygienic practices of the Greeks, as that which cleans or purifies, especially if it is in the form of the fantasy of what are called 'essential oils' (and is therefore accompanied by the counter-image of corruptive oil, in the form of animal fats and greases), assists materially in the making of oil's symbolic reputation.[38]

But the name 'Honest Toil' performs a different kind of work, a work on the idea of work itself, substituting the soft play of sounds for the hard work of treading and squeezing. Instead of the palpable work of pulping some physical mass, there is a minor work of modification that marks all the difference, and seems to make it too: the simple doubling of the dental that divides 'honest' from 'oil' with the little stutter, or geminate 't', of 'honest toil'. What the phrase also allows us to utter, in a pleasurable sort of reverberation, is the question of whether the act of transforming 'honest oil' into 'honest toil' is itself honest or not. The little jolt of pleasure at the joke is a sort of magical *honi soit qui mal y pense* inhibiting anyone who might suspect trickery. However, oil, which not only binds and preserves but slips and slides, is associated with guile as well as toil, the greasing of palms and the buttering up of superiors, as indicated by Cordelia's revulsion from the work of flattery indulged in by her two sisters to gain the favour of their father Lear, in affirming 'I want that glib and oily art/ To speak and purpose not'.[39]

In the last two centuries or more, a definitional perturbation has arisen in relation to the idea of work. From the beginning of the nineteenth century, it has begun to be suspected, suggested and then finally openly proclaimed that there is a special kind of work that represents the transcendence of work in two contrary senses: that is, it is both a transcendent form of work and a disturbing transcendence of it. This special, magic kind of work is known as art. During the course of the nineteenth century, it became common to contrast art to what is called craft, where art signifies a sort of ennobled or transfigured form of craft. *Craft* is a derivative from the German *Kraft*, work, force. Its physical sense survives in the word 'graft', to dig and, by transference we must assume, to labour or toil. But craft has become crafty, just as, in American slang, the drift of *graft* through ablaut modification into *grift* implies the work of theft or trickery. The meaning of work for human beings, and the question of its authenticity, or seriousness, is poised between engineering and ingenuity, doing things and '*not exactly doing things*', to evoke the field of enquiry that J. L. Austin mock-seriously marked out for future assay at the end of his essay 'Pretending'.[40] Indeed, the Proto-Indo-European root **k^wer*, to make or do, shows a tendency to generate words that are both an intensification and an inversion of the idea of work, implying a kind of trickery. Examples include the Lithuanian *keréti*, bewitch, enchant, and Russian *cary*, magic and *carovati*, enchant or charm.[41]

This drift (unless perhaps it is a drive) from honesty to deception is at work in other words, for example in the word *design*, which names the special kind of work involved in planning or preparing a work. In his essay 'About the Word Design', Vilém Flusser points out that, in English, design has connotations of cunning and deceit: to design is to have designs or be designing, just as to be an artist is to be artful, and there is artifice in every artefact. The suspicion attaching to artifice seems to have been slow to develop. Charles II praised Christopher Wren's design for St Paul's Cathedral when he saw it 1675: 'among divers Designs which have been presented to Us, We have particularly pitched upon one, as well because We found it very artificial, proper, and useful.'[42] As its pairing with propriety and utility makes clear, Charles II's praise of Wren's artifice does not yet imply artfulness.

Flusser's Aristotelian example of design trickery is the lever by means of which we might be able to lift ourselves to the stars: 'This is the design that is the basis of all culture: to deceive nature by means of technology, to replace what is natural with what is artificial and build a machine out of which there comes a god who is ourselves.' But Flusser ends his essay on the word *design* with an abrupt swivel, which, though disconcerting, is highly characteristic of his writing. In his final paragraph, he acknowledges that he might have taken a completely different track than 'to expose the cunning and deceptive aspects of the word *design*'.[43] He might, he assures us, have 'pursued another design', by explicating the word in terms of its relation to signs, omens and tokens – 'a sign of the times, a sign of things to come, a sign of membership'. Flusser's conclusion that 'Everything depends on Design' therefore leaves us uncertain which aspect of designing – deception or designation – is to the fore, and what kind of designs he might turn out to have on us, and to have as his object, in the essays that follow.[44] Flusser may mean simply that everything depends on design, or that everything depends on what kind of thing design is taken to be – on the design, so to speak, of design. Flusser's essays on technology will also be repeatedly pricked by the suspicion that it may be the things we design, or even the act of designing itself, that have designs, or are designing. The philosophy of design is to be given from 'Vom Stand der Dinge', the state, condition or standpoint of things, or, even, recruiting the German expression *Stand vom*, dating from, or as of this date, moving forward from, and through, things.[45] One of the most conspicuous of the disjunctures in Flusser's *The Shape of Things* is that between the deceptiveness of design and the question of the ethics of design: but this recurring question also acts as the generative principle of Flusser's philosophy-in-process of the process of design.

The association between deceit and designation in design points us to what is often regarded as a stark and absolute contrast between the physical order, of masses, forces and motions, and the symbolic order, of words, ideas and images. The simple word *form* slips with, or like, a *passe-partout* between these two realms, between the world of physical form and the mental world in which the abstract form of those forms is articulated. Form belongs both to the world of matter, the world in which everything must take physical form, and the mental world of abstract categories, which interpret the form of forms. But 'physical form' is itself a formal and not a physical category. The nowadays-ubiquitous word *information* begins by meaning not knowledge, or the transmission of what has previously been given a form, but the very act of shaping or forming itself. That of which you are informed – very often in early usages, the gospel, or revelation of divine truth – has the effect of reforming you, or imparting to you a new form. When, in his 1387 rendering of Ranulph Higden's *Polychronicon*, John Trevisa writes that 'Fyve bookes com doun from heven for informacioun of mankynde,' the informing effect of the information imparted is surely understood as a transformation.[46] In John Lydgate's affirmation of 1484 that 'crist was al by reson as I preue/ Fyrst prophete by Informacion', the two meanings, of imparting information and taking on physical form, or incarnation, are similarly held in exquisite balance.[47]

That Christ's incarnation has often been understood as an enactment of his role in the Trinity, as the executive force of doing or implementation, is indicated by the fact that he is referred to as 'the Word', translating Greek λόγος, *logos*, word, reason, logic. It is tempting to believe that a word like *logos*, which means both an order and the ordering that it effects, derives from a time in which doing things was not so clearly distinguished from saying them, or saying that you are going to do them. Such a time would be characterized by the magical thinking in which saying and making so are the same. But, while magical thinking has proved to be impossible to eradicate completely from human thought, it is hard to conceive of any human beings who could ever have been both possessed of language and unaware of the defining difference between a word and a work. The long centuries of doctrinal agonizing over how Christ could be both consubstantial with God and yet also represent him as his earthly lieutenant, or agent of his agency, may be seen as wrangles over the nature of the work done by God.

Indeed, they might even suggest that the idea of God, or of divinity, may be understood as a sacralization or apotheosis of work itself. This might go some way to explaining the rather strange fact that religious belief should itself be characterized by so many duties, constituting a veritable service-industry of observance. If the idea of God is an idealization of the idea of work, then it would seem appropriate, though in no sense literally required, that the worship of that principle should be an *opus dei*, a project of exacting, if also joyous, work. As we have seen, it is Thomas Carlyle who articulates most clearly and emphatically the principle of the Gospel of Work: 'properly speaking, all true work is Religion . . . Older than all preached Gospels was this unpreached, inarticulate, but ineradicable, forever-enduring Gospel: Work, and therein have wellbeing.'[48] In one sense, this gets things precisely topsy-turvy, since it is work that is the object of worship, rather than its means. But in another sense it intimates the centrality of a work-transcendental to every religious conception and practice, making them all religions of work.

For much of human history, it is the physical world that has been understood as the domain of work. Work, Michel Serres has suggested, is identical with the realm of space, which takes its form from being conceived and lived as a workplace:

> Euclidian space was chosen in our work-oriented cultures because it is the space of work – of the mason, the surveyor, or the architect. Hence the cultural idea of the practical origins of geometry that is a tautology, since the only recognized space is precisely that of work, of transport.[49]

We will leave aside for a moment, but a short moment only, the strangeness of the fact that such a space of pure work, of weight moved through a distance in the classical definition, must, in order to be workable, tractable, operable, be governed by an abstract, weightless space of shapes, lines, weights and measures.

The practice of art is still routinely represented, and surely by many experienced, as the opposite of earning an honest living. This practice is vitiated however by the fact that we seem to be running out of examples of classical delving/spinning, sweat-of-your-brow honest toil. In 2019, David Graeber published an influential lamentation on the vacuity of the occupations he calls 'bullshit jobs', which suggested that ever more employees in different areas of capitalist economies thought they were employed in a 'bullshit job', defined as 'a form of employment that is so completely pointless, unnecessary or pernicious that even the employee cannot justify its existence, even though the employee feels obliged to pretend that this is not the case'.[50]

Just as one might expect, the phantasmatics of work include literary and artistic representations of the act and fact of working, in which some of the peculiarities of the relation between work and art come into view. Literary works in particular have been drawn on heavily to assist and particularize the sociological imagination. But although there are certainly kinds of illumination to be gained about the lives of weavers, peasants, tinkers, clerks, washerwomen, merchants and even writers from works of art, we should be struck nevertheless by how allergic works of art tend to be to the representation of the work that these kinds of workers actually do. Work is strangely invisible in literary work. The strangeness of its invisibility derives from the fact the proofs and manifests of work are everywhere, but the work of work withdraws itself as work comes into the foreground.

This means in particular that work processes tend to be represented in symbolic or abbreviated ways. The factory scene in a film always begins shortly before the siren goes for a lunchbreak, therefore defining work by the transition to non-work. Despite efforts to increase viewer absorption by seeming to obey the classical unities, the deliberations in a courtroom drama are constantly being broken into by cries of 'Court Adjourned'. When Dickens attempts to characterize the work of the blacksmith's forge in *Great Expectations*, it is through transposition into the rhythmic motif of the work song 'Beat it out – old Clem!'[51] We may say that despite being drawn to the idea of work, the formal phantasmatics of art and literature are unable to keep work practices steadily in view. Despite being constantly adjured, or summoned to appear, the actuality of work is constantly being adjourned, literally put off to another day. When work is put on the stage, as at the end of George Bernard Shaw's *Mrs Warren's Profession*, it marks a transition away from any kind of dramatic 'action'. Throwing away a letter that might represent a change to her life, Vivie 'goes to her work with a plunge, and soon becomes absorbed in her figures'.[52] Showing somebody really working, as opposed to 'working', is equivalent to the act of turning on the light in dreams, an action that is always prevented or displaced in some way by the dreamwork whose job it is to keep the sleeper asleep, since turning on the light betokens awakening.[53] Artists have often been accused of indolence, but it seems to be art itself that is constitutionally workshy.

The reason may be simple: works of art may be about work but are in some dimly intuitive way expected to be means of distraction and recuperation from it. Works of art are not supposed themselves to be work at the consumption end. At the same time, though, works of art have found it impossible not to image themselves in the practices of work they depict, even though this may seem always to hint at the troubling suspicion that artistic work may not really be work at all.

As a professor of English, I used often, in high-level academic management meetings, to find myself putting up with withering accusations from my opposite numbers in the sciences that they were subsidizing our theological tomfooleries with their laborious laboratory work. (One might distinguish the hard sciences from the soft humanities with the single letter 'e', which appears to have been added during the seventeenth century to *laboratory* to form the word *elaboratory*, and then trimmed off again: those who work in what are now more sleekly called 'laboratories' labour, the word seems to teach us to think, while others merely 'elaborate'.) On one notable occasion though, the commercializing pressure of student recruitment gave me the opportunity for spiteful revenge, when the accounts we were reviewing seemed to suggest that in fact the Department of English, teeming with students and making the tills ring, was extending a very considerable cross-subsidy to the Department of Botany, in which the staff–student ratio was approaching a transcendental 1:1. Seizing my opportunity to turn the tables, I majestically enquired why the college should continue to maintain in existence a department that was so clearly incapable of paying its way. 'Because, Professor Connor,' replied the Master of the College quietly, 'we have mouths to feed in the Department of Botany.' I cannot recall or relate the story, though I often do relate it, without a frisson of shame, and ever since have felt I had something to expiate. There are indeed mouths to feed, but they are fed by processes that ultimately are symbolic rather than in any obvious or straightforward way laborious. David Graeber offers as an epigraph to one of the chapters in *Bullshit Jobs* the following quotation: 'In the Scilly Islands . . . the natives of that group are popularly said to have eked out a precarious livelihood by taking in each other's washing.'[54] He offers as a reference only 'obscure nineteenth-century joke', though there seems no particular reason why he might not have given its 1876 source in a report of a lecture, 'On the Uses of a Landed Gentry', given in Edinburgh by J. A. Froude, though the phrase does not in fact occur in the text of Froude's actual lecture.[55] Graeber's book is devoted to convincing us that such circumstances are so absurd that the requirement to work should be swept away by means such as a Guaranteed Universal Income, an idea that is increasingly being seriously discussed in a number of different countries. It seems much more likely that the point of work may be precisely to disguise this absurdity. The fact that the pretence of working is itself a kind of ordeal, privation or exploitation may be proof of the importance of ensuring that work is indeed hard, even – and in fact especially – when it is not particularly so.

This is perhaps part of the reason why the peculiar practice, or rather, perhaps, the peculiar category of practice, known as 'art' has got mixed up with the question of difficulty. Just at the point, from the late nineteenth century onwards, at which artists started to react testily against the expectation that their work required special kinds of skill or laboriously acquired technique, and began to insist that art in fact embodied the ideal of transcending vulgarly laborious craft, and just as the suspicion began to grow that the forms of modern art they produced did not really make many demands at all on their time or technique, so a set of occult beliefs began to be brewed about the special kinds of spiritual vocation and striving that were needed to be a modern artist. In fact, a special charisma had begun to be accorded to the figure of the artist from the Renaissance onwards, but from the late nineteenth century onwards the visionary power thought to be possessed by the artist began to be transferred to his or her products, which acquired their value not from the qualities of verisimilitude, beauty, absorptiveness and so on that had previously been readily recognizable by their audiences, but from the evidence they supplied of being the outcome of particular kinds of work that no longer seemed to be governed by accepted aims or techniques. In lockstep with this, the audiences for modern art were persuaded that their own responses needed ever more elaborate training, not least in the huge expansion of courses of academic study devoted to the understanding and interpretation of the different kinds of art that multiplied during the twentieth century. Increasingly, the point of a work of art was not to supply pleasure but rather to furnish difficulty, even if that difficulty was grimly expected to constitute a new kind of pleasure. Up until the end of the eighteenth century, making art had been thought to be hard, in order that its reception should furnish a kind of ease; by the end of the following century, it was the reception of art that was turned into hard work. The work that goes into the fantasy of difficulty in modern art is acidly mocked by John Carey in the course of his remarks on the case made by John Tusa for increased government funding of opera:

> 'The fact is', he explains, 'that opera is not like dipping into a box of chocolates. It is demanding, difficult.' Despite this assurance, the association of opera with difficulty seems questionable. What sort of difficulty, it might be asked, do those attending operas encounter? What is difficult about sitting on plush seats and listening to music and singing? Getting served at the bar in the interval often requires some effort, it is true, but even that could hardly qualify as

> difficult compared with most people's day's work. The well-fed, well-swaddled beneficiaries of corporate entertainment leaving Covent Garden after a performance and hailing their chauffeurs do not look as if they have been subjected to arduous exercise, mental or physical.[56]

Much twentieth-century art devoted itself to the paradoxical project of unworking, or working art free from the structures and expectations of work, in particular through a refusal to produce what are known or recognized as works of art. One form of this refusal is the idea of the readymade, as inaugurated in Marcel Duchamp's *Fountain*, a urinal signed 'R. Mutt' submitted in 1917 to an exhibition of the Society of Independent Artists in New York. Thereafter, it was open to artists to claim that their acts of choice, as dramatized by the displacement of objects from their familiar contexts into the context of the gallery, were enough on their own to make objects into works of art; or, what increasingly would come to the same thing, objects of speculation as to whether they were in fact works of art or not. This is really a replay of J. C. Maxwell's conundrum of the working-from-home demon who might be able to perform work merely through the action of selection or sorting. It was only a matter of time before artists would realize that there was no need for any kind of work-like object to act as a bait or decoy, since the very act of conceiving or projecting various sorts of actions or procedures might itself be regarded as art-work. The surprise is that it did in fact take almost half a century for what is called 'Conceptual art' to emerge, first of all in the USA and then in Europe. As Sol LeWitt explained in 1967, 'When an artist uses a conceptual form of art, it means that all of the planning and decisions are made beforehand and the execution is a perfunctory affair.'[57] As often as not the execution is so perfunctory that it can safely and perhaps even preferably be left to others to carry out, making the artist a kind of designer or commissioner, and the artist's idea 'a machine that makes the art'.[58] LeWitt does not go out of his way to suggest that the work of producing concepts is itself particularly hard work, and his statement concludes with the observation in a footnote that 'I dislike the term "work of art" because I am not in favor of work and the term sounds pretentious.'[59]

None of this could possibly have gone anywhere were it not for a peculiar kind of paradox that came to constitute the whole realm of art practice, or, since the point is that the practice is arbitrary and incidental, what we must call the mythos of art. On the one hand, the purposes, process and effects of art became increasingly self-determining, that is, meant to demonstrate the capacity of art to make of itself what it liked. Seen somewhat more expansively, one might also say that the point of a work of art seemed increasingly to be to dramatize the question of what kind of work it actually was, often by teasingly hinting that no work of any recognizable kind ('brush-work', say) might have been involved at all. One might expect such a project quickly to have diminished into nothingness, with the institutions and audiences of art drifting away to busy themselves with the many other modes of leisure and distraction that began to be provided by new media and technologies. In fact, however, the dissolution of the traditional understanding of the kind of work that might go into making a work of art went along with a dramatic consolidation of the power, fascination and prestige of the idea of art, as embodied especially in the theory that the sphere of art involved access to a special kind of experience, or world within a world, called the 'aesthetic'. Nothing proved the distinctness of the idea of the aesthetic, a term that in much common usage seems to mean simply 'being-art-ness', more than the apparent ordinariness of the kinds of thing presented as art – supermarket items, bricks, blocks of wood, light bulbs, empty rooms, unmade beds and so on, limitlessly, for what possible limit could there be to the capacity of art to turn non-art things into art things? The galleries, museums and concert halls that had previously existed to contain or make available the specific and distinctive kind of art-work that were the precipitates of the work putatively done by artists now became arenas for the performance of a special kind of work of vague musing on, or, as it was sometimes sternly called, 'interrogation' of, the nature of the work involved in art.

It has been drearily clear for at least a century that art can be anything – any kind of object, any kind of action whatsoever. But this does not in the least imply that anything can be art, since in order to be art (remembering of course, that being art is identical with being taken to be art, or being taken to be the kind of thing that other people would be likely to take to be art, and so on) some kind of claim, assumption or assertion needs to be made regarding the artistic status of the object or action in question. Being art depends on the magical operation of framing or put-up job that is necessary to turn an unartistic object into art.

And it is hard to deny that some kind of work, or at least some sort of operation, must have occurred, or be able to be assumed to have occurred in this process. *Work* and *operation* overlap almost completely in the range of their usages in English. It is hard to avoid the fancy that this operation is to be located somewhere between the heaving and straining of *work*, and the fancier kind of thing, both more elaborate and also more rarefied, that the Latinate *operation* might more often seem to mean, as for example in a military operation or a surgical procedure. For more than half the time that art has been assumed to be able to be anything, that operation has been able to be discursive, or institutional-discursive, as well as physical – that is, the soft kind of transformation effected by Maxwell's neat-fingered entity, of designating something as art, or declaring it to be so, or perhaps even just floating the possibility that it might be ('Art or not? You decide'). This process is at once wholly imaginary and completely real. What is more, it is wholly imaginary and completely real in just the same way as work is. By seeming to be the opposite of work, the work of art succeeds in being functionally identical with it. Art is whatever succeeds in being imagined to be art, in just the same hey-presto way as work is whatever succeeds in being imagined to be work.

3

At Work

The space of work is often necessarily itself the product of work, a worked place as well as a workplace. Designers like to urge the creation of a 'total workplace' that will deploy the principles of 'organisational ecology' to optimize the effectiveness of a particular enterprise.[1]

The intriguing intangibility of the work process makes the transition from not working to working a significant one, and one to which careful attention must be paid. Indeed, one of the most important ways of securing the definition of work is through the ceremony of the transition to what is recognized as a place of work. It does not seem to matter how abstract or conceptual one's work processes may be once one arrives at one's workplace, as long as some physical work, as defined in the classical sense, of moving a mass (one's physical person) through a distance, can be shown and known to have taken place. By being physical, one's journey to work enacts a rite of transition that is also symbolic. Working is, to a surprising degree, a matter of being in the right place at the right time – or, in order to be able to be there, getting to that place.

The history of the word *commute* retains the suggestion of transformation that is involved in travelling back and forth from one's home or residence to one's workplace. To *commute* had from the early seventeenth century the sense of exchanging one thing for another, from *com*, together + *mutare*, to change. This is the sense in which a judicial sentence of execution might be commuted to one of life imprisonment: the French *commutateur* still signifies a switch. The establishment of systems of public transport during the nineteenth century brought with it a provision whereby payment for a number of journeys over a particular period could be commuted into the single payment of a commutation ticket or season ticket. Commuting has now been transferred to the physical process of transfer from one place to the other, but the idea of the conversion of one condition into another seems vaguely to survive in the word. The commuter is the one who subjects themselves to a process of commutation, being transformed into a worker in a workplace.

Most literary representations of the act of travelling or being transported to work conform with the convention that it is a functional intermission in the day, something that simply must be got over in order to arrive at the place where one's occupation is. It is Dickens who, in *Great Expectations*, provides the most memorable representation of the journey between work and home as a translation as well as a noiseless transmission. As the law clerk Wemmick informs Pip, on the occasion of his first visit to his idyllically idiosyncratic cottage in Walworth he calls the Castle, because of its mock fortifications: 'the office is one thing, and private life is another. When I go into the office, I leave the Castle behind me, and when I come into the Castle, I leave the office behind me.'[2] As they return to the law office, Wemmick gradually reacquires the drily mechanical demeanour required of a law-clerk:

> at half-past eight precisely we started for Little Britain. By degrees, Wemmick got dryer and harder as we went along, and his mouth tightened into a post-office again. At last, when we got to his place of business and he pulled out his key from his coat-collar, he looked as unconscious of his

> Walworth property as if the Castle and the drawbridge and the arbour and the lake and the fountain and the Aged, had all been blown into space together by the last discharge of the Stinger.[3]

Wemmick consumes his habitual dry, hard biscuits in the office as though he were posting letters into the horizontal slit of his mouth. The synecdoche of the alternately loosening and tightening post-office mouth allows us to imagine Wemmick as himself a kind of package being posted to and from his office. One is posted to a position in order to fulfil the duties of what is known as a post.

During the worldwide restrictions on movement imposed in response to the COVID-19 epidemic that began in 2020, the shift in work practices, from working in offices to working from home (or living at work, as it came irritatedly to be known), intensified rather than eroded the symbolic importance of the transition from open or unmarked space into work-space. In part, this involved a shift from space to time, of course, as one 'set aside' periods in the day, rather than setting oneself aside from one's ordinary activities to perform one's work activities. But even the newly employed office menial renting a single room would sculpt a little enclosure in their living space to function as a workspace. The point was not just that the space was provided with working materials, most particularly, of course, the computer that allowed for the conjuring up of a virtual desk-top on top of the actual desk-top, or counterpane, as it might be, but rather that it allowed for a detectible movement between working and living, a movement without which the reality of work was deeply compromised. Even in houses without the luxury of a separate study or office, there would be a particular space that performed the office of an office-space. The fact that much of the work done at, or in the preferred preposition (presumably as sounding more dynamic), 'from', home, consisted of appearing on other people's computer screens, meant that a lot of work had to be invested in curating the décor of these spaces of work.

The inconsiderability, and even the invisibility, of the workplace as a specific kind of place is itself considerable. Places of work tend to be homogenized as 'the workplace' or a metonymy for the institution of work. To object that a study of workplace satisfaction or humiliation took too little account of the particularity of the actual places involved would seem like an embarrassing kind of triviality or literalism. But the generality attaching to the idea of the workplace, allowing indifferently for references to factories, farms, supermarkets, slaughterhouses, schools, offices, banks and hospitals, is itself telling. It is obvious that, although it is part of the purpose of an office to make available and keep on display certain kinds of adaptation to the process of working, there is no specific kind of place that a workplace must be, for what matters in a workplace is not the kind of place it is, but rather that it is a place of work, meaning the kind of place, which bizarrely enough can be any *kind* of place, in which work takes place, or is meant to. Workplaces can be steamy, sober, raucous, reeking, hygienic, orderly, chaotic, hushed, rushed or snug, but what they have in common is the fact of being marked as different from spaces of leisure, or whatever not-working is taken to be – simply living, perhaps, as though one knew what that was.

The spectral nature of workspace is suggested by the striking ambivalence of the apparently simple preposition 'at', in the phrase 'at work'. One can declare oneself – answering a phone call from one's daughter, let's say – to be 'at work', even though the very attestation is probably the indication that one has suspended the work that one might have been 'at' in order to make it. One need not and in fact cannot literally be at work, that is, performing actions that soothingly and in very sooth qualify as working, all the time that one is at work, that is, in one's workplace. And yet, at the same time, many find it surprisingly difficult to get to work properly, or at least to persuade themselves fully that they are at work, unless they are physically located in some kind of workplace.

The lexicon of labour in general is markedly locative. One has an occupation, and occupies a post or position. A job in a domestic household or a complex organization used to be known as a 'place' and is still known as a 'placement' in the case of temporary roles. Even when one is at work, one may be working to improve one's station by advancing through different kinds of grade. Of course, these places and progressions are part of the imaginary architectures of social standing. Nevertheless, these abstract relations derive from and are drawn back into the experience of physical space and place.

Workplaces do not merely provide spatial warrant for the division and possibility of passage between working and the condition of not-working that the invention of working allows to be retroactively invented. They also furnish outward and visible signs of the more abstract social divisions of labour and the distance to be travelled in what has become known as social mobility. Writing of the close physical proximity of manager and clerk in a nineteenth-century counting-house, Nikil Saval points out that

> From the shop floor the top of the Pittsburgh steel mill looked far off indeed. But in the six-person office, it was right next to you, in the demystified person of the fat and mutton-chopped figure asleep at the rolltop desk, ringed with faint wisps of cigar smoke.[4]

Nowhere were proximity and distance so ticklishly proximate as in the house co-occupied by the owners for whom it was a residence and the servants for whom it was a workplace, an arrangement common from the time of the Roman Empire all the way through to the early twentieth century. The derivation of the word 'economics' from οἶκος, *oikos*, the hearth, as a metonym for the family, is a clear indication of how the household provided a focus for work practices just as much as the street or field. As Alison Light observes of the Edwardian house with servants, 'The house on five floors worked hard to maintain the polar distances between its two tribes of women, but such boundaries were always clearer in the imagination than in daily life, where they were always being broached [*sic*]'.[5] The notorious 'servant problem' that preoccupied many in the late nineteenth century was focused principally on the difficulty of recruiting enough women to the rather menial functions that every respectable middle-class family required to be performed by servants. (*Menial* in fact derives from the Old French *maigné*, a household, itself derived from the Latin *mansio*, a place of remaining.) But the servant problem had much larger dimensions, of tension, resentment, embarrassment and other kinds of emotional complexity, that arose from the shared occupation of spaces that were both domestic and professional, with the scope in particular for the kind of bitter anxieties and rivalries between women that are the regular accompaniment of strongly patriarchal social systems. The mythical figure of the housekeeper, the servant appointed to, or, in many stories, aspiring or rising to, the position of exercising authority over the other servants, embodies many of these tensions.

In her essay 'Mr. Bennett and Mrs. Brown' (1924), Virginia Woolf used the breaching of these spatial boundaries as a shorthand for broader forms of social space-agitation:

> The Victorian cook lived like a leviathan in the lower depths, formidable, silent, obscure, inscrutable; the Georgian cook is a creature of sunshine and fresh air; in and out of the drawing-room, now to borrow the *Daily Herald*, now to ask advice about a hat. Do you ask for more solemn instances of the power of the human race to change?[6]

The rationalization of work practices, both physical and bureaucratic, and applied both to factory and office (the latter now the name not of a function or duty but of a physical space in which different kinds of function were executed), meant that a workspace was not only worked in, but increasingly worked on. What this process of working was increasingly aimed at, with the result that it increasingly became the identifying 'look' of work, became known as *efficiency*. Until the nineteenth century this word was part of a philosophical or theological lexicon, and signified the fact or action of being an operative agent. An *efficient* might be the name for any kind of effector of an effect: so when Richard Hooker referred in 1604 to the 'diuine efficiencie' which must lie behind and determine all of the workings of nature, he was pointing to the existence and application of a power rather than to any markedly neat and tidy way in which it might be exercised.[7] The development of thermodynamic principles in the work of Clausius, Kelvin and others during the nineteenth century introduced the idea of comparative measure into the idea of efficiency, making it not just the process of doing work but a measure of the effectiveness with which the work was done and its effects achieved. In essence, this amounted to a secondary work exercised upon work, or effort expended on the aim of reducing effort. The focus on outputs gave way to a focus on the relation between output and effort. The product of this work on work was an improved form of work, in which doing less work could be made equivalent to doing more work with one's work. Space, as a source of waste or delay, was contracted to its minimum. The workplace became a space in which space, in the sense of free, waste or empty space, was abolished. The workplace became a machine for the contraction or evacuation of space, a test-bed of proximities supposed to allow of asymptotic approaches to ideal states of immediacy (ideal because immediacy would not allow for any of the movement through distance of which work must always be constituted). Communication and information technology had a central role in this process, with telephones transmitting messages and instructions faster than could be done by the physical movement of persons.

The inaugurator and principal representative of this way of thinking Frederick Winslow Taylor made the shift of focus clear early in his book *Principles of Scientific Management*, in glossing the phrase 'maximum prosperity', which he argued must be the aim both of owner and worker:

> The words 'maximum prosperity' are used, in their broad sense, to mean not only large dividends for the company or owner, but the development of every branch of the business to its highest state of excellence, so that the prosperity may be permanent.[8]

Taylorism or Taylorization is popularly supposed to be part of a move towards ever more ruthless rationalization of the workplace, reducing workers to the status of machines, or, even worse, machinery, that is, subsidiary parts of larger machines. It is less often noticed that there is paradox built into the principles articulated by Taylor. The paradox lies in the fact that efficient work is focused on the maximization of outputs, through what Peter Sloterdijk calls the extension of *Explizierung*, explicitation.[9] Instead of a focus on the aim or outcome of work, said focus shifts inexorably and irreversibly to the forms and methods of work. Initially, it is easy to see how this kind of reflection must lead to improvements. By rearranging my desk, I can reduce the time I spend repeatedly groping about for my reading glasses. In the long run, however, the process of efficiency-management builds in a range of functions of systematic self-maintenance that will eventually begin to bring the enterprise to a standstill. These arise from the paradox that it is not enough for a process to be efficient: in order to confirm its efficiency, it must countersign the fact with the look of efficiency, not least because the fact of efficiency will always need to be checked. The question of whether the idea of the look of efficiency – which must always represent, at least logically, a kind of surplus or excess over simple being – aids or impedes efficiency is a harder conundrum to unravel that is supposed. Efficiency, which comes into being as the conscious effort to resist or reverse the Second Law of thermodynamics, inevitably tends to confirm it. Nor is this an accident: entropy depends upon the struggle against entropy to achieve its ends, if ends they may be imagined to be.

A modern university can be taken as a paradigm case here. Universities are in essence rather elementary enterprises. They exist to teach students and engage in exploratory research. That is it. However, this gradually comes to require a vast and proliferating apparatus of accessory functions, many of them originally having to do with the maintenance of the physical fabric of the university – cleaners, painters, technicians, porters, drivers, gardeners – and then, increasingly, and invariably in the interests of greater efficiency, the maintenance and improvement of the medical and moral condition of its employees, or human resources. The pursuit of efficiency, as a doubling of one's work with a continuous care for avoiding any superfluity in it, and therefore arduously and elaborately maintaining the look, feel or ideal of efficiency, is an epistemic tax that all institutions impose on themselves, insofar as all systems will tend over time towards introversion, quietly forgetting their alleged objects in favour of the goal of optimized self-maintenance. Only very wealthy universities have sufficient resources to be able to bear up against the tide of slack, processual mud that they themselves increasingly exist oozingly and usuriously to exude.

Efficiency of this kind is usually thought of as reducing time, but space and place are really at the heart of the work upon work that efficiency enjoins. The saving of time requires the materialization of duration in visible, countable and therefore comparable forms. Space is the accountancy and accountability of time.

The factory has the reputation of being a space maximally rationalized for production. Almost from the first, however, the factory was also a symbolic shrine dedicated to demonstrating the glory as well as the power of industrialized work. The skyscraper office blocks which became the signature of mid-century American bureaucratized capitalism soared like cathedrals in Chicago and New York, the concrete and glass forms effecting a symbolic merger of extravagant display and the display of sober functionality. Sometimes they borrowed the look of an older kind of factory or industrialized product, like William Van Alen's 1930 Chrysler Building in New York; more often they mimicked the kind of office furniture which they typically contained, especially the filing cabinet or screen. For W. H. Auden, writing in and of New York in 1939, 'blind skyscrapers use/ Their full height to proclaim/ The strength of Collective Man'.[10] The abstract look of work which these buildings possessed singly was multiplied in the downtown areas of cities 'whose silhouettes looked a lot like the wild spikes and dives of a GDP chart', as Nikil Saval suggests.[11] The downtown skyscraper not only exteriorized the look of the workplace, concentrating attention on its external forms rather than its internal workings (the look of the skyscraper becoming therefore something like its 'external workings'), but spread the look of work to many other kinds of building, including hotels and residential blocks.

Workplaces can be regarded as formalized versions of what Tim Ingold has described as 'taskscapes':

> tasks are the constitutive acts of dwelling. No more than features of the landscape, however, are tasks suspended in a vacuum. Every task takes its meaning from its position within an ensemble of tasks, performed in series or in parallel,

> and usually by many people working together . . . It is to the entire ensemble of tasks, in their mutual interlocking, that I refer by the concept of *taskscape*.[12]

But Ingold's concern is with the temporality of the landscape, or more generally with the temporalizing of one's natural environment, a process that always makes it more than a backdrop, or a mere inert space-within-which. This is the precise reason why a workplace is not a taskscape. A taskscape is a practical co-constituent in the performing of tasks, as the field of operations within which every task must be performed. As Ingold says, we perceive the temporality of the taskscape 'not as spectators but as participants, in the very performance of our task'.[13] A workplace may be a field of operations too, but it does something further: it crystallizes an image of the work-function to be performed in it. A taskscape is a setting; a workplace is a mise-en-scène or projective *setting out* of the work that will take place in it. The taskscape is a space of work, the workplace is a space for work. A taskscape temporalizes space, a workplace spatializes the time of working. Where a taskscape comes into being through the work that may be performed in it, a workplace makes it possible and necessary for what takes place in it to be work.

The idea of a taskscape aims to despecialize space: a workplace is by contrast the specialization of space for the purposes of work. Ingold's aim is to resist or reverse the abstraction of humans from their environments. In his conception, a taskscape is all quality without quantity, or any possibility of abstract division or limit. This is why 'you can ask of a landscape what it is like, but not how much of it there is.'[14] By contrast, workplaces are characterized by the principle of abstraction, in their separation out of special places dedicated to the act of work. Surprisingly, however, the cleavage of space effected by the mine, factory, nursery or kitchen borrows from a logic of spatial consecration that is more familiar in the church, museum, academy or other sacred space. This is because the sacralization of space is in fact dependent on the spatiality of sacralization, since all making sacred is the creation of apartness, the magical overestimation of the cognitive capacity of humans to effect abstract divisions in space.

Where religious or other kinds of sacred space abstract the sacred from the merely actual – the workaday – the workplace effects a sacralizing abstraction of the actual. The workplace borrows the logic of the sacred space but inverts it through its devotion to the fact of work imagined as a kind of pure actuality. This may be why monasteries provide so readily adaptable a ground plan for the modern factory, college campus or labour camp. And yet this is also the very reason that workplaces can never embody pure actuality, even though it is their apparent purpose so to do, since the very idea of its purity contaminates its actuality with abstraction.

Although human beings have long clustered together to perform different kinds of productive process, in order to achieve efficiencies of scale and to exploit the power of massed labour, the factory, as the emblematically specialized workplace focused typically on the mass production of a single type of product, is a relatively recent development in human history. One of the most conspicuous early examples of factory production was the Venice Arsenal, founded in 1104, which systematized the building of ships to a considerable degree. Factories were and are means by which space and time can be concentrated together to maximize productivity, and for this reason depend upon an ever-greater distinction of productive work from unproductive non-work activities. Space is required for this concentration, and must always in fact be one of its products. That is, a space designed for the maximization of production is itself one of the products of this maximization. This reflexivity is particularly characteristic of the factory, and is what makes it the essential form of the workplace, as the place of production that depends on and reproduces the production of place.

There is a tendency in factory production not just towards concentration, but also, to maximize the benefits of that concentration, of centrifugal dispersa to the periphery of towns, partly to offset the polluting effects of the by-products of production. The traditional placing of tanneries away from the centres of towns, to protect their inhabitants from the noisome stink of their emissions, is representative of this tendency. Factories always produce waste by-products, and can themselves be thought of as waste products in which, as in the alchemist's kitchen, purification is inseparable from the pollution that is a kind of spatial unconscious of every productive activity. This purity–pollution dynamic is a constant of the factory, of whatever kind it might be, be it a sawmill or data centre.

This dynamic, in which the concentration of space in places of work coexists with the separation and dispersal of those spaces of concentration away from spaces of inhabitation, is typified in a development like the iron-forging works advanced in Coalbrookdale during the eighteenth century. However, the development of factories during the Industrial Revolution in Britain produced a remarkable reflux, as designers of factories began to try to imagine different dispositions of space. The most distinctive feature of the factory was its contagious capacity. As a place of work that was itself a working on and of place, the factory began to extend its reach far beyond the factory gates, and, throughout the nineteenth century, gave rise to visionary projects for the reconceiving of the relations between work and life. The factory expanded to become a whole town, reworked in the accents of work. It aspired to be factory of place, as a spatial exemplification of the morality of work. Robert Owen's production of a whole mill village in New Lanark, incorporating housing, educational and leisure facilities, is an early example of this strange new mixture of diffusion and concentration. It was followed by developments such as William Hesketh Lever's Port Sunlight on Merseyside.[15] The idea of what would come to be the 'model village', built to provide accommodation for industrial workers and to demonstrate the improving power of industry and commerce, was well enough established by 1844 for Benjamin Disraeli to be able to rely on readerly recognition of the phenomenon when the hero of his novel *Coningsby* approaches the village built by the mill-owner Millbank:

> About a quarter of a mile further on, appeared a village of not inconsiderable size, and remarkable from the neatness and even picturesque character of its architecture, and the gay gardens that surrounded it. On a sunny knoll in the background rose a church in the best style of Christian architecture, and near it was a clerical residence and a school-house of similar design. The village too could boast of another public building; an institute where there were a library and a lecture-room; and a reading hall, which any one might frequent at certain hours, and under reasonable regulations.[16]

Set a little apart from the village is the mansion of Mr Millbank, which provides Disraeli with an apt formula for the particular kind of self-consuming theatrics constituted by the model village:

> The atmosphere of this somewhat striking settlement was not disturbed and polluted by the dark vapour, which to the shame of Manchester still infests that great town, for Mr. Millbank who liked nothing so much as an invention, unless it were an experiment, took care to consume his own smoke.[17]

In one sense, this is an image of continence, for the emissions, metonymic of the spreading contagion of riot and disease, which would otherwise invade the space around the factory, are kept in their place. At the same time, it is an image of the consumption of place, as the work of the factory effects the work of its own self-effacement in the landscape.

The space of the office generates functions that internally mimic its ways of concentrating space. This is typified by the institution known as the meeting. Efficiency tends toward entropy through its optimization of time, which means the suppression of wasteful variations in levels of productivity. As in dense traffic, the time taken to stop and start exacts a frictional cost that means that traffic moves more slowly than it would if optimized to travel at what might seem like an inefficiently low speed. Offices are designed to maintain a steady metre rather than an unsteady rhythm. But optimization also exacts a cost, in boredom and lassitude and the diminishing productivity they can produce. Some means must accordingly be found – or, more likely and more precisely, will tend spontaneously to be produced – to introduce a locally irregular but globally regulating variation into the entropically over-optimized beat of work. The solution depends on the gas law decreeing that temperature, which here may be glossed as emotional intensity, covaries with density. Reduce the volume in which a given quantity of a gas is contained, thereby increasing its pressure, and the temperature will rise. The resulting exchangeability of heat and motion gives rise to what is known very exactly as thermodynamics. The meeting is the social-symbolic equivalent to the simultaneous decrease of volume and increase of pressure. The rhythm of contraction and release effected by the alternate convergence and diffusions of groups of workers makes for a chronotopically pulsional piston effect – chronotopically because meeting at the same time and place brings about a meeting of time and space. Such possibilities of compression may be much more important in nonmanual work environments that are otherwise deprived of the rhythms which allow for corporeal forms of entraining and recharging.

This language is metaphorical, of course, for what is being described here, somewhat fancifully, is social-symbolic rather than material physics. And yet we should acknowledge the force of the analogy between these different modalities of force: by definition, magic is imaginary action that does not in fact work as it is supposed to, and yet magical ideas have measurable efficacy. Phantasmal physics are still physics.

But the invigorating syncopation of work-time introduced by the institution of meeting can itself all too easily be subject to entropic quasi-optimization. Anybody who has spent any time in a large, information-based organization will know that huge amounts of institutional time and effort can come to be devoted to the preparation for, conduct of and, of course, reporting of meetings. The meeting is understood and experienced as a joining of forces. But most meetings do not in fact have an external object on which that force may be exerted. Indeed, the conduct of meetings is determined largely by their function of reasserting the continuity through self-consulting of the organization. Meetings are intended to be, or are at least meant to mime, the act of collective deliberation: the forming of forms of collective intent that will create difference and distinction. But collective will tends always to be bent backwards and sideways into the will to collectivity, a will to the kind of willing that collectivity allows. Meetings act out processes for the forming of purposes, but their real function is to transmit the fact of those purposes having been formed; thus the purpose of most meetings and committees is to generate reports which are transmitted to other committees. This is a familiar complaint, but the blunting of function and effect effected by meetings is in fact one of its most important functions, for it prevents the meeting from breaking out of the web of interdependence within which it is organizationally suspended. Meetings are potentially very potent devices indeed, capable of producing rapid and unpredictable intensifications. It is important for this reason that these intensifications are ritualized, in order to maximize their eruptive force, while also maintaining their function of monitoring and maintenance. One of the most important functions of workplaces is to act as a frame or container for these minor, internal contractions and relaxations.

This transformation is performed most impressively by the device known as the 'chair', the person who metaphorically enacts the process whereby the meeting operates on itself. The chair is nominally in charge of the meeting, because at some imaginary centre. But the real responsibility of the chair is not to govern proceedings but to enable and enact the 'sense of the meeting', or the meeting's sense of itself. This reflexive self-awareness must be externalized, in a process which transforms a diffuse and ambivalent event into an artefact: the record of the meeting, be it a report or minutes. The work performed by a meeting is to make the meeting work, to form it into a work, even if it appears to be fulfilling a regulative or governing function in relation to the work of the organization more broadly.

Electronic communications have recently proved able to simulate this effect of tuning space and time. Where the meeting draws together those sharing a space into a shared duration, the online meeting uses the experience of that synchronized duration to create a virtual workplace, which serves now not as the conditioning setting of the meeting but the outcome and effect of the time spent in the meeting. Rather than the workplace making it possible to hold meetings, meetings precipitate a temporalized workplace.

It might seem self-evident that a workplace is a place for work or a place in which work takes place. There is however a subtle but telling distinction between a place of work and a place for work, a distinction that in modern workplaces seems increasingly to make all the difference. A place of work is conceived of as coextensive with the work done in it. A place for work is less tightly twinned with the work it locates and allows. Like the office of a groovy accountant

I once visited, a place for work might seem to resemble a sitting room, with its cushions, cocktail cabinet and record player. Such hybrid places are often a marker of professional status. Where a place of work provides a defining here-and-now for work, the place for work provides a kind of alibi, a place in which work might take place but need not, depending on the disposition of the worker. A place of work provides a habitat; a place for work provides a habitation or place of residence. The place for work advertises the fact that its occupant is free in principle to turn it to other uses. In their resemblance to the kind of studies that might be styled a 'den' or a 'snug', there may be the suggestion in such spaces of the burrow, formed centripetally by the turnings of the occupant's body, rather than held in readiness to receive its occupant.

Such places have become characteristic of workplaces designed to pay their employees the compliment of pretending that the work they perform in them is voluntary, and subjective rather than subjecting. They are common among advertising agencies, tech companies, consultancies and other undertakings keen to salute the 'creativity' of their workforces by seeming to want to foster it. Workplaces of this kind may appear to offer themselves as spaces of play rather than places of work, though they are subtly styled to make it clear that they are really playing at being playspaces.

Laboratories

Many of the spaces designated for different kinds of work have themselves become mythical, chief among them, perhaps, being the studio and the laboratory. The earliest and classical form of laboratory was the chemistry laboratory, described by Peter J. T. Morris as a 'matter factory'.[18] Its origins lie in the alchemist's workplace, which had already by the sixteenth century become established as a topos, with characterizing forms of equipment.

And yet one of the singular things about alchemy is that, though alchemical workplaces are readily visualized, there is no settled name for them. Alchemists sometimes have 'dens', and even, perhaps because of the wizardly associations, 'lairs'. Sometimes they are accorded the dignity of a 'studio', or a 'workroom' and, from the seventeenth century, a 'laboratory' or 'elaboratory'. Tellingly, alchemists are also sometimes sited in what are called 'kitchens'. These last named seem particularly appropriate, since a furnace or kiln features in many images of alchemical workshops. Examples include Thomas Wijck's *The Alchemist in His Studio*, Cornelis Bega's *The Alchemist*, David Ryckaert III's *The Alchemist and His Wife*, Domenico Maggiotto's *The Alchemist*, François-Marius Granet's *The Alchemist* and David Teniers the Younger's *The Alchemist*, and *The Bald-Headed Alchemist*. Often, as in Peter Breughel's *The Alchemist*, the furnace is simply a grate with a chimney.

At the centre of alchemical practice is the skilled application of heat, inherited from the crafts from which alchemy derived its practice and much of its knowledge. These were pottery, metallurgy – in its familiar form of the blacksmith, in which melting, alloying and annealing through the action of heat were central – and no less significant, and even more pervasive, the crafts of cooking. The culinary arts in particular made for a network of links between the practice of transmutation in nature and the operations of the human body, the latter of which were thought of primarily as the action of internal 'concoctions' or cookings. Tellingly, concoction was the process that produced animal spirits through a series of imaginary 'digestions', and thus formed the passage between the body and the soul. There was even a special kind of alchemical furnace, the Athanor, the name deriving from *al-tannoor*, an oven, normally used for baking bread, and designed to provide a steady heat for the process known as 'digestion' (a sort of dissolution). The furnace, at once familiar and exotic, was central to the process whereby ordinary arts and handicrafts were transmuted into the quasi-imaginary art of transmutation that alchemy is.

As simultaneously the process and the place of heating – literally, the forge or 'fireplace' – the furnace partakes in the strange duality of heat that was, until the nineteenth century, understood as at once an action and an imaginary substance. Indeed, the oven is perhaps a mise-en-abîme of the alchemist's den, lair or laboratory itself, the place in which place is transformed. In alchemy, as in the writing about it, matter is meta: it is always in close commerce with metaphor and metaphysics.

The furnace has a double operation in magico-imaginary conception. First of all, of course, it transforms, through destruction or dissolution, and therefore enacts the mutability that is the essential characteristic of matter. But it also confirms and perfects, through processes such as forging and annealing. These two operations are acted out in the biblical story of the preservation of Shadrach, Meshach and Abednego, to give them their Babylonian names, in the 'burning fiery furnace' (Daniel 3:6). I always somehow assumed when I heard the story told in school assembly that the fourth figure who is seen walking about in the flames, sometimes identified with the protective angel Michael, was in some sense a kind of by-product of the flames, as though heat could not only destroy but proliferate (as indeed, in some senses, it can). It seems right that the best circus trick in the whole Bible should have given rise to an early nineteenth-century reworking in Sadler's Wells, in which a magician would crawl into a hot oven with a raw steak on a plate: some time later, the oven door would be opened, and the magician would be revealed unsinged, but with the steak in his hand odorously well done.

The furnace has a particular centrality in Ben Jonson's 1610 play of simulation and trickery, *The Alchemist*. The furnace is one of the pieces of equipment named at the beginning of the play, in the course of the row between the confidence tricksters that forms its opening scene. Face reproaches Subtle with all the work he has done to set him up as an alchemist:

FACE: I ga' you count'nance, credit for your coales,
Your stills, your glasses, your *materialls*;
Built you a fornace, drew you customers,
Aduanc'd all your black arts.[19]

The furnace requires attentive and judicious application of the bellows, personified by Face, as evoked in the words of Sir Epicure Mammon:

MAMMON: That's his fire-drake,
His Lungs, his *Zephyrus*, he that puffes his coales,
Till he firke nature vp, in her own center. (*Alchemist*, 315)

Jonson means us to see Mammon himself being kept alight by Face's vaporous words, which maintain his glow with the oxygen of cupidity. Mammon's servant Surly makes the sneering connection between inflammatory talk and rekindled libido: 'The decay'd *Vestall's* of *Pickt-hatch* would thanke you,/ That keep the fire a-liue, there' (*Alchemist*, 316).

The furnace is also at the centre of what Surly calls 'the whole work' of alchemical imposture, the incubation of idiocy:

SUBTLE: Why, what have you obseru'd, sir, in our art,
Seemes so impossible?
SURLY: But your whole worke, no more.
That you should hatch gold in a fornace, sir,
As they doe egges in *Egypt*! (*Alchemist*, 325)

Subtle gives the furnace the name that was frequently applied to it in alchemical and esoteric literature: Athanor. Athanor is sometimes taken to be the name of a mystical hill, enclosing volcanic combustions, though, as mentioned above, it was in fact a special piece of apparatus, the digesting furnace, which maintained a constant heat and therefore mimicked the action of fermentation and incubation, alchemy here borrowing from the arts of baking and brewing. George Ripley evokes the Athanor in his *Compound of Alchymy*:

> by little and little increase
> Their paines, by heat, aye more and more,
> The fire from them let neuer cease.
> And so that thy furnace be surely apt therefore,
> Which wise men call an Athenore,
> Conseruing heat required most temperatelie,
> By which thy matter doth kindly putrifie.[20]

The Athanor is an apt image for *The Alchemist* itself, a play in which the aim of the devious Face, Subtle and Doll is just to keep the fires of foolish desire alive in their bubbled clients for as long as possible. The furnace is never seen on stage, nor are any of the alchemical stage properties, perhaps because the whole rolling boil of the play's frenetic business is an image of the furnace in operation, an imaginary thermodynamics and a thermodynamics of imagination. *The Alchemist* brings together in its space of performance three separate but imbricated kinds of work. There is first of all the ongoing 'Great Work' that the tricksters continually evoke in order to lead their victims on, extracting money from them for investment in various kinds of equipment and laboratory supplies. For the Anabaptists, this work is allied with the great work of Christian redemption. Tribulation Wholesome urges Ananias:

> When as the *worke* is done, the *stone* is made,
> This heate of his may turne into a zeale,

And stand vp for the *beauteous discipline*,
Against the menstruous cloth, and ragg of *Rome*.
(*Alchemist*, 341)

Second, there is the plot itself, and the various ways in which Face and Subtle 'work' on their victims, or delightedly observe its workings. Dol remarks coyly to Sir Epicure Mammon 'You are pleas'd, sir,/ To worke on the ambition of our sexe' (*Alchemist*, 363). Jonson here is allowing a collusion between the two senses in which 'work' could be understood: to work in the sense of to strive concertedly and purposively towards a goal, or 'exert oneself for a definite purpose', in the OED's crisp formulation, and to work in the sense in which a process or mechanism works, and in the more specific sense of a churning or chaotic movement, as of boiling, fermentation or germination, in which something apparently works spontaneously, of and on itself.

Third, there is the work constituted by the play itself, which knits together the two other senses of work, drawing them together in the space of simultaneous work and work-simulation, known as the play-house.

The twin jeopardies of the furnace are that it will go out and that it will overheat and spontaneously combust, an ever-present danger with the application of heat in a confined space. When, around 1630, Jan Baptist van Helmont produced carbon monoxide through heating charcoal, the first gaseous compound to be distinguished from air, he decided to call the substance 'gas' because of its resemblance to the Greek χάος, *chaos*. In a sense, the furnace is not so much an object as the objectification of the dissolution that does away with objects: as such it is a kind of anti-object, or *objet-décomposé*. The furnace is a type of thermodynamic accelerator: it has the transformative powers of heat, but also its destructive powers.

From the very beginning in *The Alchemist*, there is the foreboding of a thunder that will eventually discharge itself flatulently when the plot, along with the imaginary or purely 'projected' laboratory, off-stage, and yet encompassing all of the visible action elaborated onstage, is blown up:

> FACE: O sir, we are defeated! all the *workes*
> Are flowne *in fumo*: euery glasse is burst.
> Fornace, and all rent downe! as if a bolt
> Of thunder had beene driuen through the house.
> *Retorts, Receiuers, Pellicanes, Bolt-heads*,
> All strooke in shiuers! (*Alchemist*, 378)

Most words over time move from concrete to metaphorical. 'Explosion' seems to be an exception, for most of the seventeenth-century usages of the word relate not to substances or physical processes but to the explosion of ideas, beliefs or conceptions. In fact, to 'explode' often meant to jeer or laugh off stage.

The word that Jonson uses to embody the double direction of his play's process, compounding itself and violent decomposition, is 'projection'. Projection is an alchemical term which refers to the final consummating transformation that produces gold. But the word also alludes to the work of speculation, both poetic and pecuniary. And projection also anticipates the final explosion, of expulsive laughter, that will be the vaporizing outcome of all the farcical plottings and frenetic dissimulations. Explosion holds together Jonson's brilliantly prescient understanding of the close imbrication of capitalism with fantasy, magic, libido and the spectacular dreams of the playhouse, the double of the dream-theatre that is alchemy itself.

One may take 'the lab' to be the most developed form of imaginary workplace. In academic settings, a lab can nowadays just as easily be a place (or just the idea of a place) where those in the humanities would work together, as well as scientists. Imaginary workplaces are necessary to provide grounding for the many kinds of imaginary work in which human beings engage. One of the most important forms of idleness is the idleness of imaginary work – the fiddle-faddle as it has seemed to many of philology and other modes of self-elaborating technicity, for example. The strangeness of this is that such forms of imaginary work can do real work in forming the imaginary of work: the idle can become the ideal. Among other things, it is of course possible for idle spaces to be laboratories for the elaboration of new kinds of work to do.

If one can be 'exploded' off the stage, the experimental theatre of the laboratory has similarly always been at risk from the materials on which it worked. The development of pneumatic chemistry during the eighteenth century heightened the dangers both of poisoning and of injury from explosion: Michael Faraday, who had developed a fascination with experimental science from reading the books on which he was employed to work as a bookbinder, got his first opportunity to work at the Royal Institution after Humphry Davy injured his eyes in a laboratory explosion and employed Faraday as an amanuensis.[21] The arrangement that had been used to draw off the heat and smoke from the alchemical furnace was adapted to form the apparatus that came to be known as the 'fume-hood'. When the space below the hood was closed off, it began to be known as a 'fume-chamber' or 'fume-cupboard'. The glass doors or the fume-cupboard made it a kind of interior doubling of the space of the laboratory, much as the visible space inside Robert Boyle's air pump had been. The laboratory was theatrical in that it involved the production of the space in which to observe the effects of the operations performed by the experimental scientist.

And indeed, observation, display and the display of observation have come more and more to constitute the work of the laboratory. Alchemists' lairs or dens tended to be secret places, hidden away both physically and in the elaborate allegory that conceals the physical operations undertaken. The sustained joke of *The Alchemist* is that the actual scene of the Great Work is never seen, and never could be. But the development of the demonstrative ethics of experimental science, which required that scientific claims be proved, and be able to be reproduced, in practice, made for a new, ever more theatrical visibility in experimental science. The word laboratory is in fact older than 'elaboratory', which arose precisely in ironic reference to the pseudo-work performed in the earlier kind of workshop. Robert Neville described heresies as 'nothing else but the inventions of worldlyminded men, working out of the Elaboratory of their Fancy, some new Doctrine'.[22] But the laboratory moved from being an elaboratory, a place of complex obfuscations, to being a place where things were made plain, such that Walter Charleton was able to look forward to the time which 'shall have brought up some more worthy Explorator, who shall wholly withdrawe that thick Curtain of obscurity, which yet hangs betwixt Natures Laboratory and Us'.[23] During the eighteenth century, the laboratory became ever more a place of ostension and sometimes spectacular display, as experiment passed across into experience, and the work of science passed over into spectacle.

There were two distinct audiences for the work of scientific demonstration. The first was a non-scientific public, who were treated throughout the eighteenth century to different kinds of scientific entertainment, designed to show both the wonders of nature and the powers of science to be able to put them on show. The many kinds of electrical demonstration were a leading form of scientific display during the eighteenth century. But the second audience was made up of the scientific investigators themselves. Theatricality has always been at hand in the spatial dispositions of work. The use of the term 'shop floor' presumably derives from the practice, already common in the eighteenth century, of setting aside the ground floor of a residence to act as a shop or place of sale, the proprietors using the upstairs as living quarters. By the end of the nineteenth century, the shop floor was the name of a large space in which productive manual or mechanical operations were carried out, so named because it was often at the floor level of buildings in which superiors worked in upstairs offices. The theatrical nature of this arrangement, as well as its use for supervision of workers by managers, is suggested by the explanation given in the *Engineering Magazine* in 1898 that 'the "shop floor" means the area of effort, the theatre of those operations which distinguish a factory from a vacancy.'[24] A workplace is both actual and symbolic, because its function is to symbolize the actuality of the work that is supposed to take place in it: position underwriting supposition.

Playhouses

Far from being reduced by the moves to diversify and deformalize office design, with the softening of the hard lines of spatial division that characterized the office of the mid- to late twentieth century, office work has become ever more saturated by theatricality. Clive Wilkinson, the head of an architecture firm, who described himself not only as an architect and designer but as a 'workplace strategist', is unusual in turning the condition of theatricality which has implicitly attended the workplace, and sometimes erupted into uncanny visibility, into a self-conscious design principle, suffusing the whole set-up of setting to work:

> The reality is that work in its most engaging form has the potential to become theatre – which is a total experience, immersing and engrossing at its best . . . the workplace itself can and should function as theatre, where workers are alternatively the players and the audience. And through this drama, and the unveiling of a corporate culture of permissiveness to engage fully, the work community may constantly invigorate itself.[25]

Needless to say, the understanding of theatre offered here is a positive one, evoking thoughts of community and creativity and quietly passing over all of the many ways in which theatre is also implicated in obsession, coercion and vicious fixation. Wilkinson subscribes to the view that, even though designers can only 'set the stage' for these processes to come into being, they nevertheless create the conditions in which, 'freed from excessive management and control, work can become serious play and the associated activity become a state of flow.'[26] The tendency for work to crystallize into spectacle is quite consciously intensified to the point of inversion, in which work itself becomes pure theatre. This might offer a condition in which the alienation of labour is either entirely overcome, in which case one wonders whether those involved can be said to be working at all, or in which, as Terry Eagleton once wrote, we might be alienated even from our own alienation.[27] Alienation is a terrible thing, but the apprehension or awareness of alienation is probably not altogether so. Indeed, the powerful tug of Hegelian thought within Marxist conceptions of alienation not only allows for the dream of a work before or beyond alienation but insists on the necessity of the encounter with otherness in all forms of work capable of offering any kind of enlargement or fulfilment.

Contemporary work processes in technologically developed countries take ever more dissipated or decompressed forms, allowing for the conception of a life streaked and marbled with episodes of work. In such circumstances, the epic scenography represented by the mill, mine, factory or other romantic pandemonium seems to dematerialize, making of what had been the demarcated space of work a minimally everywhere. The iconography of hell is never far away from the theatrics of work. The Yorkshire song collected by F. W. Moorman, professor of English Language at the University of Leeds, or perhaps himself elaborated from what he records as a Yorkshire proverb, 'From Hull and Halifax and Hell, good Lord deliver us,' concludes with the sedate triumph of the old countryman who has returned to his cottage after a life of industrial toil:

> But now, when all wer childer's fligged,
>   To t' coontry we've coom back.
> There's fotty mile o' heathery moor
>   Twix' us an' t' coal-pit slack.
> And when I sit ower t' fire at neet,
>   I laugh an' shout wi' glee:
> Frae Bradforth, Leeds, an Huthersfel',
> Frae Hull, an' Halifax, an' Hell,
>   T' gooid Lord's delivered me![28]

But the kind of historical landscape that in allowing for spatial division also allows for the return or retirement from the place of work has been worked over into an indifference in which space offers no visible warrant either of work's existence or its remission. The words of Marlowe's Mephistopheles anticipate the aspatial or hyperspatial condition of damnation in which work can be everywhere at work, even where our occupation is gone:

> FAUSTUS: Where are you damn'd?
> MEPHASTOPHILIS: In hell.
> FAUSTUS: How comes it then that thou art out of hel?
> MEPHASTOPHILIS: Why this is hel, nor am I out of it.[29]

The dominant emotional tonality attaching to work is perhaps no longer terror or rage but a tender kind of melancholy at the fact that, while work itself continues, the place of work seems to have evaporated into ubiquity. Nowhere is this more intensely embodied than in the phenomenon of the museum of work, or its near relative the 'working museum'. Such museums tend to occupy the actual locations and buildings where the work being memorialized was practised, so mills, breweries and other kinds of industrial plant. The Magna Science Adventure Centre near Rotherham, for example, recreates in a dramatic sound and light show called 'The Big Melt' the operations of one of six electric arc furnaces in the Templeborough steel works. The British BBC TV series *The Repair Shop*, screened from 2017, which was itself filmed in such a museum of work, is a demonstration of the force of the mediatized theatricalization of work. Strikingly, one of the oldest forms of the museum of work is the most reflexive of all, namely the museum of museum practice, in which a museum will put on penitent display its own superseded working practices and discredited modes of exhibition.

For the last fifty years or so, it seems to have become compulsory for the country houses and stately homes of Britain, which would previously have invited visitors to muse admiringly or yearningly at the adornments of the leisured classes, to develop displays of servant quarters, centring in particular on reconstructed kitchens, with accompanying activities like cheese-making or pastry-rolling on offer for the visitors to try out.

The purpose and promise of such displays is that the country house or castle is revealed to have been a kind of factory, in which all the constituent parts are compacted together in an activity of cooperative work. There are no outcomes for this work, other than the workings of the house itself, but there scarcely needs to be, since keeping up a large enterprise like a stately home is an exacting enough aim in itself. All houses are subject to the work required to keep the house going, and stately homes and what in Ireland used to be called Big Houses exist through and for this complex, coordinated project of housework, which obviously extends far beyond the work of dusting, darning and digging, since such houses exist largely to perform the work of display, through entertainment and such like. Whole houses were sometimes acquired and fitted out for the purpose of entertaining a monarch, whose own purpose was largely to furnish a rationale for the building of such houses, through the possibility of their ruinous arrival along with their voracious retinues. Indeed, the visitors to National Trust and English Heritage properties and their equivalents in other countries are active inheritors of this work of predatory upkeep. Typically, it is the expense of keeping such houses going which makes it necessary for the owners to make their properties over to the nation, who may allow the 14th Viscount to linger on in a fourth-floor apartment like an official ghost, at the price of allowing gawpers to trample up and down their erstwhile property at the appointed hours. The put-up job of simulating the work of a country house – cleaning the portraits, pruning the parterre, maintaining the fetish-wardrobe of stable-hand and servant-girl costumes for the staff of the house whose job it is to pretend to be the staff of the house – is in fact sturdily continuous with the work of performance that it was the job of the house to perform in life.

The country house as factory of appearance rhymes oddly with the function of advertisement that actual factories have often performed. As Gillian Darley has commented, 'The imaginative application of exuberant ornament to factories led to a kind of commercial *architecture parlante*, arousing interest in the product and acting as a permanent free billboard.'[30]

Homework

The work of maintaining a country house is perhaps to be thought of as a sublimated form of the thing known as housework, which has come to absorb so much in the way of dream-energy and the energy of dreaming. The irritation and agony that are bound up with the politics of housework largely derive from the bitter oxymoron that the house should be the location of so much work while also being allegedly the place of work's remission. If the role of the traditional housewife is to keep the house for the one who must be supported in doing the real work in a household, namely the kind of work that involves, as we say 'going out to work', this is a demeaningly auxiliary role. It is not at first sight clear why this should be so, since the male breadwinner in a traditional household arrangement might very well in fact go out to fulfil an occupation that is itself auxiliary in the same way. What, aside from the absence of wages, of course, makes the wife who gets on a step-ladder to clean her windows less rewarded or recognized than her husband who goes out to clean others' windows as a professional window-cleaner?

The problem of housework is very likely that it is a certain kind of work that does not count as work – payment being an important way of making something count as work. It is sometimes suggested that housework is the particular kind of anguish it is, for those for whom it is, because it is non-productive. Unlike the coalminer, farmer or watchmaker, the housewife is engaged in work that keeps things as they are rather than subjecting them to the processes of transformation that are said to be characteristic of human labour. It is the fact that housework is housekeeping which means that a woman's work is never done. Simone de Beauvoir articulates this view eloquently in *The Second Sex*. As opposed to man, who 'can find expression in projects', woman is permitted only the project of turning the prison in which she is confined into a 'realm':

> The housewife wears herself out marking time: she makes nothing, simply perpetuates the present. She never senses conquest of a positive Good, but rather indefinite struggle against negative Evil . . . The battle against dust and dirt is never won.[31]

If this is true, it is only true of the reputations of male and female work, since, as women have quickly found, there is just as much sterile circularity in the world of work outside the home. If there is an enraging difference between housework and going out to work, it cannot be quite the difference between immanence and transcendence that Beauvoir here makes out. As Hannah Arendt observes, almost all labour in fact consists of this immanence, and the generalized emancipation of labour that occurred through the twentieth century threatens also to generalize what Arendt sees as the futility of labour that never produces anything durable: 'The danger is that such a society, dazzled by the abundance of its growing fertility and caught in the smooth functionality of a never-ending process, would no longer be able to recognize its own futility.'[32]

As usual, the focus on the physical aspects of housework – whether it is boring, time-consuming, unproductive, never-ending and so on – is not really relevant to the ceaseless state of unhappiness and aggression that is focused on the question of housework. If it were the physics and not the phantasmatics of housework that mattered, one might have expected the host of allegedly labour-saving devices that appeared from the end of the nineteenth century onwards to have made a difference. But, if anything, the reduction of the laboriousness of domestic labour exacerbates rather than relieves the tensions associated with it. As Susan Strasser observes, consumer convenience may reduce labour, but it increases isolation and reduces the rewards of satisfaction that might have belonged to household skills and crafts.[33] Laura Humphreys agrees, seeing domestic technologies as part of an intensified industrialization of the home rather than a reduction of housework. Even a simple device like the carpet sweeper

> speaks to a worsening of conditions for women in the home, whether paid or unpaid. New technologies bring new modes of cleaning, new patterns of consumption, and new standards of cleanliness. They are sold as labour savers, saving time, money, and energy in the home; the spotless maid smiles

> as she pushes the carpet sweeper over a pristine carpet. However, labour-saving devices are a marketing trope, not a product of progress. With new technologies in the home come new standards that demand more work, as well as a loss of control and self-reliance through dependency on bought equipment and supplies.[34]

One of the surprising problems with housework is that it can so easily be mistaken for what is thought of as unalienated labour. William R. Beer reports that some men making the transition from employment outside the home to a partial or complete role of maintenance within it saw housework as a kind of 'antidote to alienation', and characteristic of the traditional workplace:

> In housework, one carries out all phases of work. Work and home are integrated; one is not working for the abstract value of wages, but for loved ones. In no other realm of work, save, perhaps, that of the artist or craftsman, are people surrounded by the products of their labor. The tools of their labor belong to them. The fruits of their toil belong to them.[35]

At the same time, the real horror of housework is that nobody really has to do it, in any kind of contractual sense. If one does feel impelled to mop the kitchen floor, or dust the bookshelves, it seems clear that whatever reward might accrue from it is not really for anyone's benefit but one's own. At least part of the agony of housework must surely be the feeling that one has somehow been tricked into a kind of addiction to it. The Wages for Housework movements of the 1970s aimed at a radical demystification of the role of the housewife, in their demand that women's domestic labour no longer be regarded as a free or natural resource. As Silvia Federici affirms in her essay 'Wages Against Housework' of 1975, '*It is the demand by which our nature ends and our struggle begins because just to want wages for housework means to refuse that work as an expression of our nature.*'[36] Writing in 1903, at a point when the economy of the household was moving from a servant model towards the unstable model of the traditional nuclear home, Charlotte Perkins Gilman offered a no-nonsense analysis of what she called the 'home as workshop', which concludes that it is the most wasteful way imaginable to ensure the reproduction of the labour force: what ship's company provides a personal cook for every sailor on board?[37] Such an analysis predicts that, were people really paid to perform housework, market forces would rapidly ensure that the vast majority of sole providers of domestic services ('housewives') would be made redundant. Gilman and Federici in fact converge on this point, since Federici makes it clear that 'to demand wages for housework does not mean to say that if we are paid we will continue to do this work. It means precisely the opposite. To say that we want wages for housework is the first step toward refusing to do it.'[38]

The literally fantastic non-necessity of most forms of domestic labour makes the phantasmatic demands placed on those performing it intense to the point of intolerability. That housework on the traditional model should be so palpably residual yet so stubbornly ubiquitous means that it must be viewed as a neurotic-devotional activity as well as, sometimes still, a straightforwardly coercive one. The condition of house-rage consists of a revulsion against the absence of alienation, a condition of having been made to perform all the parts in the play of employment, master and slave, mistress and slavey, locked together in vicious embrace. Perhaps the most important feature of housework is that, in the absence of the distance that would allow the workplace to provide a stabilizing scenography, a scenography which allows and requires one to move between the conditions of audience and spectacle, thereby ensuring that one does one's work rather than undifferentiatedly having to be it, the house becomes a nightmarishly compressed space which allows for no relations of distance, projection or objectification. So the worst thing about being a housewife is also what is sometimes supposed to be the best, or at least a compensatory, thing about it, namely that it is an arena of female self-ownership, allowing a woman 'confined within the conjugal sphere . . . to change that prison into a realm', for this means that in it, narcissism curdles into claustral rancour.[39] Because it is not an accredited theatre of work, the house becomes a dream theatre pulsating with tension, aggression and misery. Instead of the house being set up for a particular kind of work, housework becomes the transferential setting for every imaginable and imaginary kind of resentment, deceit and suspicion.

Unlike carpentry or schoolteaching, housework encompasses many different kinds of work. It is remarkable, though, how the development of the modern home has concentrated all the multifarious domestic demands – which might at one point have included cooking, childcare and the care of the elderly, a great deal of fetching and carrying of wood, water and different kinds of animal husbandry – into one essential and unifying function. Over the period from the late nineteenth century in which nuclear housework acquired its essential form, housework has become almost completely identified with various kinds of cleaning. The humiliation of housework, religiously cathected in the washing of the disciples' feet in John 13 and given sexual orientation in the career of Hannah Cullwick along with male practitioners of voluptuous drudgery, is centred on acts of purification, rather than the acts of making, mending, production or cultivation that would have been to the fore in most household economies up to the late nineteenth century.

And because housework is no longer about anything other than cleaning, it is no longer about cleaning at all. The purgative process makes housework the vehicle of especially powerful libidinal drives and demands, which reach far into myth, ritual and the most desperate passions of obsessional practice. Insofar as females are identified with the house that they are charged with cleaning, they may be possessed by a fury of purification that can easily shift from the dirt that invades the house to the house itself. The rage for cleanness smears across into a rage against the house that incessantly demands to be cleaned, both of them, of course, powerfully identified in the person of the housewife, who, as herself both wife and hearth, must toil to sluice away the corruption that she herself embodies. Care, rage and revenge are laminated in the music-hall song-recitation 'A Mother's Lament', of uncertain authorship, which brings together in comic-grisly Gothic the themes of maternity, pollution, purgation and abortion:

> A mother was washing her baby one night;
> The youngest of ten and a delicate mite.
> The mother was poor and the baby was thin;
> 'Twas naught but a skeleton covered with skin.
> The mother turned 'round for the soap off the rack.
> She was only a moment but when she turned back
> Her baby had gone, and in anguish she cried,
> 'Oh, where is my baby?' The angels replied:
> *'Oh, your baby has gone down the plug hole.*
> *Your baby has gone down the plug.*
> *The poor little thing was so skinny and thin,*
> *He should have been bathed in a jug (in a jug).*
> *Your baby is perfectly happy;*
> *He won't need a bath anymore.*
> *He's a-muckin' about with the angels above,*
> *Not lost but gone before.'*

Freud makes an influential passing remark about the obsession with house-cleaning in his *Fragment of an Analysis of a Case of Hysteria*, usually known as the 'Dora' case, in his brief, disdainful sketch of Dora's mother, from whom he suggests Dora may have inherited her predisposition to mental illness:

> I never made her mother's acquaintance. From the accounts given me by the girl and her father I was led to imagine her as an uncultivated woman and above all as a foolish one, who had concentrated all her interests upon domestic affairs, especially since her husband's illness and the estrangement to which it led. She presented the picture, in fact, of what might be called the 'housewife's psychosis'. She had no understanding of her children's more active interests, and was occupied all day long in cleaning the house with its furniture and utensils and in keeping them clean – to such an extent as to make it almost impossible to use or enjoy them. This condition, traces of which are to be found often enough in normal housewives, inevitably reminds one of forms of obsessional washing and other kinds of obsessional cleanliness.[40]

We can put aside without casualty the suggestion that there is an obsessional form of cleaning that can be easily distinguished from the ordinary, as it were rational or merely instrumental kind. Even in animals, cleaning and grooming is a task that tends to be autonomous, becoming implanted in the animal's behaviour as the kind of need beyond external necessity which I am trying to maintain is centrally implicated in the phantasmatics of work. We must doubt that there is any kind of cleaning work that is entirely free of an obsessional component, especially when it is redoubled by the devotional-obsessional forces at work in the idea of work.

The housewife's psychosis is a kind of revenge by the woman wived to the house that imprisons her. But, since she is herself identified with the house, and her revenge a kind of sealing of that identification, the revenge on the house is also a revenge on herself, and for that matter a weird revenge on her vengeance. In one sense, the act of cleaning is a radical, symbolic expulsion of all the other residents in the house for whom the housewife is supposed to provide, as indicated in the small detail which, whether or not it really was true of Dora's mother's house, is certainly familiar enough from the whited sepulchres to which houses maintained in extreme states of cleanliness can be reduced. In the quotation just given, Freud observes that the furniture and utensils of Käthe Bauer's house are cleaned 'to such an extent as to make it almost impossible to use or enjoy them'. In such a practice, the house, which is intended to be made available to its inhabitants, is sequestered from them, and the one supposed to make the house the giver of commodity and convenience becomes the hoarder of them. The appropriative nature of such obsessive cleaning is strangely of a piece with the process described by Michel Serres, in which '*appropriation takes place through dirt*' – the animal who urinates at passing points to mark its territory, the diner who spits in their soup to ensure it remains untouched when they leave the table. The work of the housewife mediates between the two meanings of propriety distinguished and associated by Serres: 'either proper means appropriated and consequently dirty or proper implies really neat and therefore without an owner'.[41]

The classical association in psychoanalysis between hygiene and what might appear to be its opposite, anal eroticism and the fascination with faeces, manifested in hoarding and retention, is assumed by Sándor Ferenczi in his casual observation in 1917 that

> Sufferers from 'housewife-psychosis' [*Hausfrauenpsychose*] employ their insatiable passion for cleaning by preference on lavatories [*Aborten*, in Ferenczi's original German, a word that can mean both lavatories and miscarriages].

> A combination of cleanliness (anal character) and coprophilia (anal erotism).[42]

Ferenczi goes on to assert an association between excremental and economic functions, in his claim to have observed

> marked avarice, concerned, however, only with quite special expenses; such as paying for the laundry or toilet paper. Very many people who in other respects live well economize noticeably in changing their linen, and can only with difficulty decide on the purchase of fresh toilet paper for their households (avarice – anal character + filth – anal erotism).[43]

Ferenczi summarizes the magical economy of dirt and purgation in a marvellous story he claims he was told by a patient:

> A patient could not recall any kind of coprophilic manipulations, but soon after related without being asked that he took a special pleasure in brightly shining copper coins, and had invented an original procedure for making them shine; he swallowed the piece of money, and then searched his faeces until he found the piece of money, which during its passage through the alimentary canal had become beautifully shining. Here the pleasure in the clean object became a cover for satisfaction of the most primitive anal-erotism. The curious thing is that the patient was able to deceive himself as to the real significance of his transparent behaviour.[44]

Just as the reader, or this one certainly, is beginning to wonder about the satisfactions that such interpretations might offer to the analyst, flushing out secrets and picking over the overlooked dross of everyday actions for the glister of significance, Ferenczi – unawares or not, it is hard to tell – adds a footnote that implicates the physician in the alchemical operations of telling and weighing: 'The case reminds one of the coprophilic joke in which the doctor who had succeeded in expelling by means of a purge a piece of money that a child had swallowed was told he could keep the money as his fee.'[45] After a reference to the magic money-pooping donkey in the Grimm fairy story 'The Wishing-Table, the Gold-Ass, and the Cudgel in the Sack', Ferenczi observes 'The word "Losung" (= deliverance) means proceeds of a sale (in business), but in hunting speech it means the faeces of wild animals.'[46] He perhaps regards it as unnecessary to point out that *Losung* also means solution, as of a puzzle or riddle, or is perhaps tricking the reader into thinking they have seized on this unconsidered trifle for themselves.

If one allows for a modulation from the spatial concern with the maintenance of the household to the endless and inconclusive temporality of housework, one might also see in the pruritic satisfactions of the urge to clean the operations of something like Freud's death drive, in which one secures life by driving out the dirt that both assails and asserts liveliness. The drive to cancel out excitation can itself become venomously eroticized, as encapsulated tidily in Samuel Beckett's rendering of a maxim by Sébastien-Roch Nicolas de Chamfort:

> Live and clean forget from day to day,
> Mop life up as fast as it dribbles away.[47]

There are those for whom the problem and offence of housework is principally that it is of such low status. Anyone and everyone ought to be capable of housework, which is perhaps part of why it is so galling for women that men seem to feel so little impulsion to do it. Though it certainly seems possible to perform domestic tasks poorly, it seems oddly difficult to perform them well, or in a manner that might be deserving of praise without it sounding patronizing. The universality of housework is just what makes it so degrading to be defined, as women seem to be, as uniquely qualified to do what could be done by anyone.

Attempts are sometimes made to relieve the burden of domestic drudgery through efforts at revaluation, as though women are not oppressed by having to do housework but rather housework is devalued because of being the sort of thing that women do, not being thought capable of much else. For Mary Townsend, housework holds out the rosy prospect of grasping the Heideggerian condition of being-in-the-world, or being-as-a-dwelling:

> When I recover my respect not only for domestic work but also for the task of keeping a home, I have taken a step toward ending my homelessness, not as modern, as thinker, or as woman, but as mortal.[48]

As such, housework is not just a degraded, bestial kind of occupation that is inimical to intelligent existence, for it can also become 'the very ground of thought'.[49] This view is perhaps in accordance with the claims of Kathryn Allen Rabuzzi, who suggests that the access women may have to an apprehension of the sacred in the work that they perform in the home, in which they double as the embodiment of the mystery of embodiment itself, may form the basis for a veritable 'theology of housework'.[50]

It is not surprising that the spiritual travails of housework should have become apparent and articulate less in periods in which women were assigned to menial or domestic occupations than in periods in which they began routinely to have access to other kinds of opportunity and occupation. Domestic labour thereby becomes more than laborious, or menial, in being a reversive denial of the powers of thought and self-conceiving. This may be why D. H. Lawrence can so readily invert the traditional dispositions of women as nature and man as culture at the beginning of his 1913 novel *The Rainbow*, in which it is the working men whose 'brains were inert, as their blood flowed heavy with the accumulation from the living day', and women, or rather 'the woman', who

> strained her eyes to see what man had done in fighting outwards to knowledge, she strained to hear how he uttered himself in his conquest, her deepest desire hung on the battle that she heard, far off, being waged on the edge of the unknown. She also wanted to know, and to be of the fighting host.[51]

Freud makes a less exalted kind of connection between housework and epistemopathic longing in the example he added in 1920 to the section of *The Psychopathology of Everyday Life* in which he deals with the forgetting of names. Pausing to note that such phenomena can be a symptom of hysteria as well as simple parapraxis, Freud quotes a passage from Ferenczi to demonstrate the distinction:

> 'At the moment I am treating a patient, a spinster getting on in years, in whose mind the most familiar and best-known proper names fail to appear, although her memory is otherwise good. In the course of the analysis it has become clear that this symptom is intended by her as a documentation of her ignorance. This demonstrative parade of her ignorance is, however, really a reproach against her parents, who did not let her have any higher education. Her tormenting obsession to clean things ("housewife's psychosis") also comes in part from the same source. What she means by this is something like: "You have turned me into a housemaid."'[52]

I cannot pretend not to have felt something of the same vengeful stirrings in my own mute but high-minded meditations on the metaphysics of housework amid the thought-annulling boom of the hoover I steer during our own Saturday cleaning observances. But the problem with such attempts at transvaluation may be that, for persons who might actually be capable of the philosophical or spiritual somersaults effected by Rabuzzi, Townsend and myself, there would no longer be any problem to solve. For most people, however – and assuredly, it seems, for most modern women – the rage and resentment focused on housework do not arise from the low or lowered self-esteem it engenders, or not just from that. The frustration and despair come not from the negligible value of housework, but rather from its imperious overestimation, along with its inevitable, absurd, ghastly failure to fulfil the ideal demands made of it, or to repay the huge cathexis it apparently cannot help but demand. So it is not the vacuous and ignominious mundanity of housework that matters, it is the fact of its seeming to matter so much, when it is, as we say, so close to home, when it is the work not just of keeping house but of making a place to be at home, a place for others to come back to after work.

It certainly does seem that the close relationship of the sacred and the profane, the *sain* and the *sale*, in the very idea of the house, a Möbius strip knotted into a clove hitch, is powerfully at work in the misery as well as the missing glory of home life. In such a structure there is no distance or distinction possible, for the breathing possibility of space has been slurped back, solemn-sinisterly, into the solipsism of place. It is not surprising that housewives caught up in the clammy 'shades of immanence' insistently evoked by Simone de Beauvoir should so often seek to create carceral apartness through appropriative and colonizing routines like that of Käthe Bauer, at least according to Freud.[53] These routines both vengefully put the house beyond use and give the housewife the commanding distance from the house of the housekeeper, as the one who no longer keeps house for its occupants, but keeps them from it. In efforts like this to make the house work as a way out of the work it demands through housework, housework seems to play house for much of the enigmatic pain and longing that attaches to work as such, which seems to be, among all the other things it is, an indwelling urge for exertion, literally, from *ex-* + *serere*, an unbinding, and a demand to build a mode of being – and make oneself at home – in a way that depends on the capacity to put distance between you and it.

4

Off Work

Phantasmatics, like fantasy more broadly, often implies the work of wish-fulfilment, subserving the pleasure principle. In this kind of projection, wish comes to the aid of need. But, if there is always some pleasure associated with the work of fantasy, that pleasure is rarely straightforward or unmixed.

Perhaps the most ambivalent form of the phantasmatics of work attaches to its absence or negative, in voluntary leisure or the enforced idleness of unemployment. At various points in the history of mechanized substitutes for work, the prospect has arisen of the dissolution of the need for work, a prospect which is viewed both with excited longing and with dread. Christophe Dejours et al. begin their introduction to *The Return of Work in Critical Theory* by dismissing what they describe as 'the myth of the end of work', arguing that, as jobs in certain areas decline, 'there has been a continually growing number of tasks done by humans worth paying for – the exact opposite of the end of work scenario.'[1] The question here is whether 'worth paying for' is entirely the same as 'necessary'. This compensatory ratio seems in fact to indicate that work has less to do with needs extrinsic to the work, things that the work is necessary *for*, than might appear – otherwise why might those new forms of occupation arise that have not seemed necessary or worth paying for before? The truth would seem to be, by contrast, that as the external need for work recedes, only the internal need remains, radioactive in its intensity. In fact that need for work in general is not merely residual but amplified by the need to justify work, a need which becomes sharper and more bewildered than when it seemed more obvious what secondary products work was needed for – chopping wood, building houses, growing plants, making clothes, cooking food, teaching children, treating illness. Our focus might therefore be less on work and more on the need for it, and possibly even the need for that need. Under such circumstances it might very well be the case that work may be more worth paying for the more unnecessary it becomes. We might regard work as worth paying for not because its outcomes are desirable, but because of an apprehension that, unless it is paid for, it might vanish. This puts us not in the world of objective necessity but just where we, or at least I, need to be for my present purposes: in the sphere of phantasmatics, or psychological necessity. What, if anything, can account for the continuing need for work in the absence of any necessity for it? And even if it should prove to be beyond us to account for this sense of the need for work, what is it like to live with this need, and how do we live it out, or indeed put it to work?

One answer to these questions is simply that work is an unhelpful habit or addiction which we should just roll up our sleeves and learn to live without again, eschewing the ersatz gratifications of work, as we tell ourselves in different kinds of Edenic fable, whether of the nursery or the south seas. We do, after all, sometimes say that we 'give up' work, as though it were more of a reprehensible indulgence than a compulsion. The austerity of this renunciatory prospect, made palatable only by the absurd consolation that the project of learning to do without work may turn out to be as laborious as the work with which it dispenses, suggests that the project of letting go of work may often be regarded in part as a way of clinging to it, insofar as it represents a kind of compulsory programme of disciplinary self-renewal. Many of the urgings and exhortations to projects of self-enrichment that are supposed to sweeten the post-employment years seem designed to fill with factitious purpose what would otherwise be a painful void.

Tellingly, there is no single, obvious or neutral name for the opposite or absence of work. 'Sabbath' and 'holiday' both suggest a formal framework of restriction and requirement, while 'idling' and 'unemployment' carry a strongly negative charge of disapproval. 'Leisure' seems to be reasonably neutral, though its origin in the Latin *licere* – to be allowed, have licence or be available for sale – suggests that freedom from work is conceived as special remission from a work-demand and 'availability for work', as it used to be called in the UK, that is general and perpetual.

Hobby

A word used in English for the kind of thing at which we work for fun or relaxation aside from our work is 'hobby'. Indeed, there is a tendency to think of the pursuit of hobbies as itself definingly English, so much so that many languages, including French, German, Italian, Russian and Indonesian, have taken over the English word. Hobby, in use from the fifteenth century onwards, was the name for a small, ambling horse, originally typically of Irish breed – probably as a derivation from Robin, from which the dumpier Dobbin may also derive. An allegorical tale of 1581 suggests that the hobby was regarded as rather an inferior kind of mount:

> I then being weary was willing to see the warrens & other pleasures, which when my gouernesse *Folly* vnderstood, she told the tale to Lady *Voluptuousnesse*, and the [she] consented to hunt or hawke with me, whereof I was right glad. Then I apparailed my selfe in hunters guise, taking in steede of my helmet, a hat ful of fethers, for mine armour,

> a horne: & I lept vpon *Temeritie* my horse. *Voluptuousnes* had a hobbie, *Folly* a Ienet, & the other Ladies euery one of them a Palfray.[2]

Towards the end of the sixteenth century, references began to appear to toy horses, consisting usually of a stick with a horse's head, that were known as cockhorses or hobby-horses. They became a metaphor for foolish or childish distraction, as in the advice given in Thomas Lodge's *An Alarum Against Usurers* of 1584 that 'Spangled Hobbie horses are for children, but men must respecte things which be of value indeede.'[3] A rather more elaborate version consisted of a wickerwork frame which was fastened around the waist of a morris dancer or performer in pantomime, like an exoskeletal bustle, the performer capering skittishly to suggest the movements of a spirited horse. This is the sense in which the anonymous author of the anti-Anglican Marprelate pamphlets uses the term 'hobby-horse', in reference to the poem 'Mar-Martine' which had been written against him:

> Then among all the rimers and stage plaiers, which my Ll [Lords] of the cleargy had suborned against me. I remember Mar-Martin, John a Cant. his hobbie-horse, was to his reproche, newly put out of the Morris, take it how he will; with a flat discharge for euer shaking his shins about a May-pole againe while he liued.[4]

The association between the cock and the hobby seemed to depend on, or at least certainly to allow for variations on, the ancient and surely inextirpable association between idiocy and tumescence, fallacy and the phallus. The hobby-horse was often associated both with the pagan priapism of the maypole and the jutting absurdity of the one scandalized by it – the one who is, as we say, stiff-necked. The figure of the hobby-horse animates this association throughout Ben Jonson's *Bartholomew Fair*, which comes to a climax with the scene of the mock-disputation between the toy-maker Lanthorn Leatherhead and the ferociously anti-idolatrous puritan Zeal-of-the-Land Busy, who denounces him as representative of the idolatry of the fair in general: 'Thy Hobby-horse is an Idoll, a very Idoll, a feirce and rancke Idoll: And thou, the *Nabuchadnezzar*, the proud *Nabuchadnezzar* of the *Faire*, that set'st it vp, for children to fall downe to, and worship.'[5] The idolatry of the hobby-horse is a matter of a toy that is taken to be something real or serious. The pleasure of *Bartholomew Fair*, as of many other Jonson plays, lies in the play's own self-mocking participation in this play of seriousness and idiocy. The play is itself a thing of simulation, made of air and pasteboard, a 'sport' or 'Fayring', even if it is able to represent itself officially as a simulation of serious matters, as Jonson's prologue, addressed to King James, attempts to:

> Your Maiesty *is welcome to a* Fayre;
> *Such place, such men, such language & such ware,*
> *You must expect: with these, the zealous noyse*
> *Of your lands* Faction, *scandaliz'd at toyes,*
> *As Babies, Hobby-horses, Puppet-playes,*
> *And such like rage, whereof the petulant wayes*
> *Your selfe haue knowne, and haue bin vext with long.*[6]

The ancestor of the pedalled bicycle in the early nineteenth century was the velocipede, or speed-walker, also known as a 'hobby-horse' or 'dandy-horse', a set of wheels with a saddle which one propelled with one's feet, as Fred Flintstone was required to propel his stone car. The name 'dandy-horse' may have been suggested by the fact that these contrivances became so fashionable among the Regency beaux, but perhaps also, if contemporary illustrations provide any clue, because of the prancing posture required by the apparatus, in which one built up speed by the dainty, skimming employment of the toe rather than the flat of the foot, allowing one to foot it as featly as Camilla over the tips of the standing corn.

The essential comedy of the hobby-horse is Bergsonian, in that it involves the interplay between a freely choosing subject and their own self-objectification. The one who rides their hobby-horse sits astride a cock-horse that is sustained by nothing but the tumescence of their own fantasy, and so is in a sense ridden by what they affect to ride and guide. In Laurence Sterne's *Tristram Shandy*, reason itself seems to have become idolatrous, or hobby-horsical. Sterne plays with the notion of an interchange between a subject and the objects of his obsession:

> A man and his Hobby-Horse, tho' I cannot say that they act and re-act exactly after the same manner in which the soul and body do upon each other: Yet doubtless there is a communication between them of some kind, and my opinion rather is, that there is something in it more of the manner of electrified bodies, – and that by means of the heated parts of the rider, which come immediately into contact with the back of the Hobby-Horse. – By long journies and much friction, it so happens that the body of the rider is at length fill'd as full of Hobby-Horsical matter as it can hold; – so that if you are able to give but a clear description of the nature of the one, you may form a pretty exact notion of the genius and character of the other.[7]

Flann O'Brien will offer variations on this idea in the centaurian exchange of vital essence he imagines between people and their bicycles in *The Third Policeman*, a book which pays elaborate homage to Sterne's philosophical hobby-horsery in the solemn footnotes devoted to the theories of the fictitious de Selby.[8] Sterne's characters, including his own narrating persona, suffer from the madness not of distraction but of contraction, which nevertheless itself paradoxically expands to take up all the ontological space, as the idea of the hobby-horse becomes the organizing, hobby-horsical preoccupation of Sterne's whole text. One may aptly wonder of its comic theatre of benignly relentless obsessions, as Samuel Beckett does in *Company*, 'What kind of imagination is this so reason-ridden?'[9] One cannot take seriously the one who concentrates all their will and possibility into a single obsession, even as seriousness depends upon just this kind of narrowing. To be a serious person means making oneself austerely less than the bundle of accidents, propensities and general openness to possibility that all beings must essentially be; but that very reduction deprives one of the possibility of being taken seriously as the kind of being we think of as human. The concentration of will and resolution is the determination to make something of oneself, as opposed to simply being made fluttering use of, be it by others or by time and circumstance. What one makes of oneself thereby is a kind of puppet; and, like the hobby-horse strapped around the waist of the rider, the puppet spreads its woodenness like rising hemlock back into the fairground rider. The hobby-horse, like the hobby, are different modulations of the caricature of seriousness, both of them toys that, like the Freudian fetish, insist on the desperate gravity of the work of covering over the absence of seriousness. 'Toy' is thought to be from the Latin *theca*, sheath, hull, vagina, casket, and the Greek θήκη, case, chest, tomb, whence also *apothecary*, *bibliotheque* and *boutique*: a toy covers over the fact that it is a covering for emptiness.

It is striking that the development of the work disciplines associated with industrial civilization brought with it a formalization of leisure activities, which became less an alternative to one's work, and more a kind of laxative accessory to it. This is certainly the argument of Theodor Adorno, who, with Max Horkheimer, in the chapter 'The Culture Industry' in their *Dialectic of Enlightenment*, sternly counselled that 'Amusement under late capitalism is the prolongation of work,' such that 'The liberation which amusement promises is freedom from thought and negation.'[10] It is indeed difficult to conceive the austere Adorno retiring to his shed after dinner for a spot of fretwork, so it is not surprising that, in his essay 'Free Time', he could not disguise his disgust at the idea that he might be suspected of indulging in a hobby:

> When the illustrated weeklies report on the life of one of those giants of the culture industry, they rarely forego the opportunity to report, with varying degrees of intimacy, on the hobbies of the person in question. I am shocked by the question when I come up against it. I have no hobby. Not that I am the kind of workaholic, who is incapable of doing anything with his time but applying himself industriously to the required task. But, as far as my activities beyond the bounds of my recognised profession are concerned, I take them all, without exception, very seriously. So much so, that I should be horrified by the very idea that they had anything to do with hobbies – preoccupations with which I had become mindlessly infatuated merely in order to kill the time – had I not become hardened by experience to such examples of this now widespread, barbarous mentality.[11]

Adorno directs at the hobby the solemn jeer elicited by the idea of amusement 25 years earlier in 'The Culture Industry':

> If we suppose with Marx that in bourgeois society labour power has become a commodity in which labour is consequently reified, then the expression 'hobby' amounts to a paradox: that human condition which sees itself as the opposite of reification, the oasis of unmediated life within a completely mediated total system, has itself been reified

> just like the rigid distinction between labour and free time. The latter is a continuation of the forms of profit-oriented social life.[12]

But Adorno makes himself ridiculous by not recognizing or taking seriously the paradox of the hobby, a strange lapse in a writer who tends to see paradox coiling in everything. For the absurdity of the hobbyist, who devotes himself to an occupation as seriously as he is supposed to devote himself to his official trade, thereby issues a reproach to the empty and adventitious coercion of the day-job. The hobbyist quietly affirms the truth that people do not want to be free of the need to work, but rather want to be free to assign themselves to their ownmost devotion.

By the end of the nineteenth century, the idea of the hobby was beginning to be recruited to the critique of organized labour relations. The *Hobby Horse*, the magazine of the early arts and crafts movement the Century Guild, proclaimed in 1889:

> To take delight in work, to lose all sense of toil in the effort to make beautifully, that is what an age of Art gives to her craftsmen; and how much of the work of this life is of the nature of a craft.[13]

The inaugural issue of the magazine evoked Don Quixote in launching the venture:

> In case our 'Hobby Horse' ride out, unknown to us, into circles beyond those compassing personal friends, we think it well, by way of introduction, to give to such new acquaintance some fair notion of the intention and character of our union; some unburdening of our hobbies; some reasons for riding them now and again through a public highway – a highway that is, too frequently, a veritable 'rotten row'.[14]

Since 1973, Robert A. Stebbins has lent himself to the investigation of what he has called 'serious leisure', as part of a larger sociology of the amateur. At the centre of his work is a conception of the seriousness with which his correspondents devoted themselves to their leisure pursuits. The 'Concepts' page of the Serious Leisure Perspective website explains that

> The adjective 'serious' (a word Stebbins' research respondents often used) embodies such qualities as earnestness, sincerity, importance, and carefulness. This adjective, basically a folk term, signals the importance of these three types of activity in the everyday lives of participants, in that pursuing the three eventually engenders deep self-fulfillment.[15]

In a recent synthesis of the project to which he has devoted himself over almost half a century, Stebbins emphasizes that serious leisure pursuits are taken seriously because they provide 'personal enrichment, self-actualization, self-expression, self-image, and self-gratification'.[16] The apparent unavailability of non-tautological accounts of what seriousness might consist of may suggest that serious pursuits provide these gratifications, or the prospect of them, precisely because they are taken seriously, where it is the taking that matters. So the seriousness of serious leisure may in fact consist precisely in the arbitrariness of that taking. The one who takes their leisure seriously is triumphantly demonstrating the emptiness of a choice of pursuit which, unlike ordinary forms of work, has no obvious or official necessity, and therefore could be anything. It is a poker-faced caricature or charivari, which is closely analogous to the child who earnestly devotes themselves to activities like pushing buggies or moving plates around in a dolls' tea-party, which demonstrate how well they have observed and internalized the human habit of taking work seriously. This does not in the least mean that such activities are not really taken seriously, though it might imply that it is the taking that makes them so.

Sabbatical

The history of sabbath prohibitions provides ample indication of the exacting and laborious nature of the terms and conditions attached to the formalized leaving off from work, reminding one of the comical parade-ground order 'Sta-a-and *Easy*,' with the stiffly alert posture of readiness it mandates. Not-working has to become a much more positive and elaborated thing than merely not working. At the same time, the prohibitions that secure the condition of ease readily and steadily exhibit the retroactive difficulty of defining what will actually count as work. The sabbath, or the day sanctified by the prohibition on doing work, is at the centre of Jewish faith. It is a leading example of the cohering force of collective refraining or non-action that I have designated cohibition.[17] The 39 categories of action forbidden as *melachot* amount to a definition of work, as *melacha*, the word used in Genesis to refer to the world-creating labour of God: 'And on the seventh day God ended his work which he had made; and he rested on the seventh day from all his work which he had made. And God blessed the seventh day, and sanctified it: because that in it he had rested from all his work which God created and made' (Genesis 2:2–3). The *melachot* include not only obviously laborious actions such as digging, gathering and bricklaying, but accessory or enabling actions for the performance of work, along with actions that may sometimes occur as part of work, but need not necessarily, one might have thought, constitute work in themselves. For example, the climbing of trees is supposed to be eschewed because of the danger of tearing off a branch in the process, which may be regarded as a form of the forbidden labour of reaping. A great deal of attention is paid to the indirect requisition of work, such as the use of tools and technologies, or the commanding or requesting that work be done by others. The preoccupation with this epiergonomic domain of the preparation for work, and the unintentional performance of it – by dragging a chair leg across loose soil in such a way as to seem to prepare it for sowing – makes work a source of mystical fascination in the rabbinical tradition.

Technology, especially in electronic forms that seem to effectuate automatic processes or action-at-a-distance, affords many interpretative challenges and opportunities. Making things work by flipping switches or pressing buttons is not permitted.[18] In 2001 the Israeli Knesset made it a legal requirement that any new multi-storey building equipped with more than one elevator must ensure that at least one of them is a 'shabbat elevator', which can travel to all the required floors without needing to be, as we so commonly now say, 'operated' by pressing buttons, an institution which serves Alan Dundes as the prompt for an anthropological investigation of the function of subterfuge in Jewish reasoning.[19] Work, it seems, lurks everywhere, like sin, not as Sisyphean labour always needing to be renewed, but as a distraction, temptation or impious compulsion sowing itself through everything. The work which the sabbath attempts to transcend or transfigure is, it increasingly seems, perversity itself. It is the delirious opposite of the burglars working at their work of pretence of window-cleaning, as though window-cleaning or burgling could spontaneously break out in the midst of our ordinary action. It is a work that will break free of intention and start to work itself, and so may turn out to be artificially and autonomously at work everywhere. The countervailing work of suppressing the possibility of these perverse insurgencies of work grows ever more demanding, absurd and solemn at once, especially with the expansion of the realm of seemingly authorless systems.

It is really not surprising that the elaborate work of finding ways to obey the probably impossible commandment to refrain from work on the sabbath, in what Pinchas H. Peli calls 'the painstakingly meticulous effort to define forbidden work', should have led to such deep, renewed and seemingly unconcludable meditations on what exactly one is to understand by work.[20] It is often suggested that what marks out such actions as work for the *melachot* is that they are creative or productive, though it is probably a more precise explanation that they tend to be productive of order or arrangement, which one might sometimes think of as the opposite of creativity. It is striking, in particular, how many of the proscribed actions involve sorting – for example the category gathered together under the Hebrew *borer*, winnowing, filtering, combing or otherwise unmixing – matched by actions of productive mingling or combining, as in the kneading of clay or mixing of cement. The action of writing – explicitly forbidden on *shabbat* – cannot but effect both kinds of articulation, joining and separating. Erich Fromm suggests that in the sabbath ritual, '*"Work" is any interference by man, be it constructive or destructive, with the physical world. "Rest" is a state of peace between man and nature.*'[21] Keeping the sabbath therefore involves a radical act of letting things be, of refraining from acts that aim to alter the state of nature or exercise any kind of transformative mastery over it. But nothing could be more radically against nature than striving to leave nothing unchanged in nature. Letting things be is as drastic an abracadabra as a *fiat lux*. In a natural condition of things, entities and organisms are constantly effecting change in their environments, consuming and discharging energy and information. Not even a deceased organism leaves its natural environment unchanged – indeed, the explosion of chemical and microbial activity in and around a recently expired body means that the condition of death constitutes a dramatic tampering with things as they are. Attempting or, more accurately, pretending to suspend this constant condition of metabolic exchange is a change in the order of things that is imitative of just the act of creative mastery effected by God on the seventh day by giving rise to the sabbath condition of suspension.

The point of these objections and reservations is not to suggest that sabbath prohibitions are difficult or impossible to fulfil, since the whole of the centuries-long wrangle about the nature and meaning of the sabbath is based on just this condition. One might even wonder if the difficulties of defining work are not so much the predicament of the sabbath as its organizing purpose. The commandment to remember or keep the sabbath is the injunction to slog without cease at the insoluble question of the nature of work and the hold it has over us. I am obviously at it myself at this moment. Like so much in Judaic doctrine, or, more especially, interpretative commentary on it, or doctrine about doctrine, these requirements build a sort of rational reverie, a comico-philosophical working through of the paradox of Maxwell's demon, which asks in a similarly fundamental way what work might essentially be, and in particular raises the question of whether the work of arrangement, or 'working things out' in one's head, as we say, performs work just like the more obviously corporeal work of moving matter through space, or weight through distance.

For, amid all of the arduous deliberation on what is and is not permitted, there is one glaring Ur-issue or meta-problem: namely, whether the kind of assiduous winnowing required to determine what is prohibited on the sabbath, and also to make sure that one is observing it, should itself fall under the sabbatical veto. Is working things out, like the demon who simply distinguishes fast-moving particles from slow-moving ones in Maxwell's thought-experiment, working? Does a thought-experiment like Maxwell's itself do any kind of work? It is not that there is any absolute difficulty in making an exception for this kind of activity, since thinking about the sabbath is almost as concerned with exceptions, suspensions and variations as it is with the making of rules. The institution of the eruv, the physical zone within which it is permissible for Jews wishing to observe the sabbath to carry or propel items, such as keys, medications, walking sticks or push-chairs, without violating the rule forbidding such carriage outside the home, is the most outward and visible sign of such suspension. The eruv has the effect of deeming the outside space to be in fact part of an inside domain, though not every sabbath prohibition is suspended within it: one may still not touch a pen or open an umbrella (apparently because it resembles raising a tent, and, in all fairness, it can indeed often be a bit of a palaver). Orthodox Jews may feel they have to resort to practices that can be regarded as wearing rather than carrying (keys attached to a belt in such a way as to constitute adornment rather than a function). The eruv usually consists of a symbolic designation, typically through poles connecting lengths of almost invisible fishing wire. Though its function is symbolic, the equipment's physical integrity is so important that it is required to be checked every week for signs of damage.

The zone of exclusion constituted by the eruv – a zone in which the exclusion of certain activities is itself excluded – is of interest not because of the magical thinking of which it gives evidence, which is perfectly of a piece with other forms of obsessional self-restriction practised in Judaism as well as in most other religions and indeed forms of life – but because of the fact that non-Jews can so easily work themselves up into feeling invaded or constrained by it. This may well be because of the aptitude, both of humans and of many animals, to see mark-making as an assertion of ownership or, in Michel Serres's terms, to treat pollution as appropriation.[22] I really cannot, as we say, 'take exception' to such a set of signs without in the process indicating that I feel in some way included in them, despite the fact that I know, or ought to know, perfectly well that they can have no jurisdiction over me – that I am, in fact, excluded from the exclusion of sabbatical exclusion that they effect. Barry Smith concludes his philosophical exploration of what he calls 'the ontology of the eruv' with the suggestion that it is found provocative because it 'seems to interfere with our freedom to exercise exclusive jurisdiction over the region of space in which we live'.[23]

The projections and performativities of the eruv may seem to have taken us quite a long way from the question of what it means to suspend acts of labouring on the sabbath. But in fact the squabbles over magical power to which the epistemic erotics of the exception give rise return to the central problem, already met with several times in this book, and around which the act of sabbatical suspension turns, namely whether information (the order of signs) is continuous with energy (the order of physics, or what Serres calls 'the realm of ordinary work and the displacement of objects'), such that they can be thought of as forms of work capable of impacting on or being converted into each other.[24]

Still, the question must always remain, or importunately recur, of whether the act of exempting is itself to be regarded as exempt, and, if so, according to what principle. This might be regarded as a diabolically deconstructive predicament, or just a disrespectfully idle whimsy; but equally, suspending the force of a requirement can be regarded as wholly obedient to the principle of the sabbath itself, which is nothing other than suspensiveness sanctified. Joseph Livni and Lewi Stone suggest that the seven-day cycle represented by the sabbath may have had a very important function of social stabilization among the rankless or covenantal social groups of Israel, setting up an oscillatory dynamic of profane and holy, transgression and atonement, that resembles the stabilizing rhythms revealed in mathematical epidemiology. The 'weekly Sabbath pulse' may then be regarded as 'a vaccination process whereby the Sabbath immunizes individuals from transgression', an immunological stability-in-instability.[25] Although the Jewish sabbath is imagined and experienced as a day of universal rest and joy, and so not a device to ward off evil fortune, but a commandment of God, as opposed to the Babylonian *Shapatum*, which was a day on which it was regarded as unlucky to work, the fact that it is a commandment actually secretes compulsion within the release: 'whosoever doeth any work in the sabbath day, he shall surely be put to death' (Exodus 31:15).[26]

The idea that the sabbath is not in fact a remission from work, but rather an imperative to a different kind of working, is not at all new, or restricted to the perspective of the unreligious outsider. It is at the centre, for example, of Abraham Joshua Heschel's reflections on the nature of the sabbath:

> Labor is a craft, but perfect rest is an art. It is the result of an accord of body, mind and imagination. To attain a degree of excellence in art, one must accept its discipline, one must abjure slothfulness. The seventh day is a *palace in time* which we build.[27]

The remission from work effected by the institution of the sabbath is therefore part of the project of the redemption of work, in its offer of a higher form of work – not craft but art, not indolence but joyful employment. Giorgio Agamben has made the institution of the sabbath the embodiment of the principle he calls inoperativity, which is related to the capacity possessed by humans and any other animals possessed of a symbolic capacity that allows them to conceive of negation; it permits them to decline, refuse, set aside or leave off, as well as to do, opening up the vast domain of abstitution:

> What is at stake is the capture and inscription in a separate sphere of the inoperativity that is central to human life. The *oikonomia* of power places firmly at its heart, in the form of festival and glory, what appears to its eyes as the inoperativity of man and God, which cannot be looked at.[28]

God does not merely rest on the seventh day, but sets it apart from the other days for that reason, reversing the valence of merely not working to create the positive negation, reinforced by the commandment to remember and repeat his action, of the suspension of work. Plainly, since omnipotent creators cannot get tired, or be in need of any kind of rest and recreation, this must be regarded as not just the creation of a new kind of thing, namely rest or not-working, but also, in a gesture reiterated over and over again by every kind of performance artist, from Diogenes to Duchamp, the creation of an entirely new kind of work, in the office of abstaining from work. This primary act, the first time in history that God has left off working, is therefore, like all such inaugural acts, double as soon as it is singular: it is the first time and so thereafter able to be recalled and reiterated as the substitutive sign of primality. Setting a particular day apart, like any setting apart of person, place or utterance, both makes the day incomparable and asserts the suspensive power of setting apart as such. It is this power to celebrate – the suspensive power in general of exempting things from the general – which is itself implicitly celebrated in the many forms of Agamben's inoperativity.

Agamben elevates inoperativity into an absolute principle. His argument depends on the assumption that human beings have no essential purpose to fulfil, meaning that there is no necessary work they absolutely by their nature have to do. The weakness in the argument comes when this absence of essence is made itself into the kind of essential principle which it cannot ever be. For not having to work in no sense implies having not to work, just as not having to be polite to people does not imply the necessity of being rude to them, or not having to be alive implies the necessity of suicide, though there have been hard-liners who have been immovable on this last point. There are in fact occasions when Agamben recognizes that it is the very worklessness of the 'Sabbatical animal' that makes the devotion to projects of work irresistible:

> Human life is inoperative and without purpose, but precisely this *argia* and this absence of aim make the incomparable operativity [*operosità*] of the human species possible. Man has dedicated himself to production and labor [*lavoro*], because in his essence he is completely devoid of work, because he is the Sabbatical animal par excellence.[29]

A programmatic refrainer like Melville's Bartleby the Scrivener could easily be set to work by the expedient of earnestly enjoining him to refrain from working. Insofar as he is consistent in his refusal to work, or indeed to do anything he is required or requested to do, he will find himself having to cleave strenuously to his project of disinclination, like the alien computers routinely out-reasoned by Captain Kirk in *Star Trek*. The principle that humans often put more effort into avoiding work than they would have to expend in performing it points to a similar reversibility. From this paradox derives my characterization of work in this book as an unnecessary necessity, though this characterization does not imply that the necessity of this non-necessity is to be regarded as any redemptive principle, or one that is actually capable of redeeming anything.

The projection of the sabbatical principle may be called phantasmatic, not just because it is pretence but because it is projective – the embodiment of the wish to be able to conceive of such a paradoxical thing as non-laborious labour, or resting toil. Perhaps the most astonishing embodiment of this idea of the perfected form of unemployment is the 'rest' that epitaphs assure us is to be found in the ceasing of existence altogether, as though death were the absolutization of the sabbath. There is sometimes bliss in repose, or at least in the prospect of it; but those who remember the torture of being required, as young children sometimes still are, to sleep before night, may find horror rather than comfort in the long and chilly night shift of the wait for awakening. Still, as a kind of interlude made permanent, to be broken only by an awakening out of time altogether, death can seem like a blissfully ultimated form of sabbatical. Beckett allows Dan Rooney something like this perspective in *All That Fall*, with the realm of work as the proleptic peace of death. As compared with 'the horrors of home life, the dusting, sweeping, airing, scrubbing, waxing, waning, washing, mangling, drying, mowing, clipping, raking, rolling, scuffling, shovelling, grinding, tearing, pounding, banging and slamming', Dan finds solace in the thought of being in his 'silent, backstreet, basement office . . . buried alive, if only from ten to five, with convenient to the one hand a bottle of light pale ale and to the other a long ice-cold fillet of hake. Nothing, I said, not even fully certified death, can ever take the place of that.'[30]

Work is doing, a word that is so ordinary it is apt to be enigmatic: 'I have been doing some work on that.' When we say 'this arrangement simply will not do,' we mean that it will not work or serve its purpose. 'You do not do, you do not do,' the speaker lilts witchily at the beginning of Sylvia Plath's patricidal poem 'Daddy', magically unmagicking the patriarchal power.[31] We 'do' work in a way that we cannot be said to do idleness, unless, of course that idleness is construed as a service of time, or purposive occupation, such as a piece of performance art consisting of being idle, a wearisomely common convention. 'What do you do?', we say when enquiring of a person's identifying occupation: 'Hunter-gatherer' was the unsurprising reply of the bearded caveman in the 'Origin of Smalltalk' sketch in *The Armstrong and Miller Show*. But of course hunter-gathering is not something that a caveman can be said to do, or at least do 'for a living', even though his remaining alive may depend on it – and perhaps even because of this, because it is not something he might otherwise choose not to do. Hence the prolongation of the cavemen's polite exchange in the sketch, as though other career paths might have been open for them: "You?" "Hunter-gather too." "Oh."' Working is not just doing, it is *doing* that doing, where the most important feature of the doing is that it is thought to result in things getting or having been done, brought to some state of completedness. Idleness is not work, not because idling is entirely inactive – we should scarcely accuse a perching stylite or a prisoner in chains in an oubliette of idling – but because the idler does not get anything done, in the sense of bringing something about as a result of their purposive action. One can easily say 'my work here is done,' but English does not allow us to say 'my idling is done' or 'my unemployment is done' in the same sense – namely that of having accomplished something rather than it simply being over.

So one uses one's time productively when one works, and is unproductive when one idles. But perhaps we do more than use time or waste it. What one principally produces through working is time itself, as something other than pure persistence or dissociated succession. What appals in idleness may therefore be that it unstrings the tension of tense, thereby voiding time of sense. The tension between unemployment and occupation, occupied by the ambiguous action we call 'acting', fills out the sparse two hours' traffic of Beckett's *Waiting for Godot*, coming to a climax in Vladimir's exchange with the boy who comes to tell him that Mr Godot will not come that night:

> VLADIMIR: What does he do, Mr. Godot? (*Silence.*) Do you hear me?
> BOY: Yes, sir.
> VLADIMIR: Well?
> BOY: He does nothing, sir. (*Silence.*)[32]

It is often assumed that the ills of unemployment derive entirely from the economic deprivation with which it tends to be associated, and there is no doubt that the ills can be appalling. But the greater anguish of unemployment may be the paradox into which one is thrust by it, whereby one is simultaneously given time – indeed, one has what we call 'all the time in the world' – while also being deprived of timing, or temporality, that quality of scansion or regulated variation that seems to be as much a requirement of a life as of a sonnet or symphony. The many modes of scanning with which we have become familiar in modern life suggest an action of lateral ranging, as in 'horizon-scanning'. But the origin of the word in Latin, *scandere*, to climb, makes it clear that the action of scanning involves the intersection of the vertical with the horizontal, or what structural linguistics define as the paradigmatic axis of selection acting always perpendicular to the syntagmatic axis of combination: the either/or with the and/so. The tension or tuning of this relation, as frequently noted by Michel Serres, is visible in the fact that *time*, *tempus* and *temps* are derivable from both τείνω, to stretch out or lengthen, and τέμνω, to cut or divide.[33]

That impossibility of structure in idleness, or even of the sense of position, seems close to the condition of impersonal existence evoked by Emmanuel Levinas in his descriptions of the impersonal condition of the *there-is* commonly experienced in insomnia. Insomnia belongs to the night, in which, as the New Testament assures us (John 9:4), no man can work, and yet which is a refusal or sustained suspension of the sleep that should belong to the night: 'What we call the I is itself submerged by the night, invaded, depersonalized, stifled by it. The disappearance of all things and of the I leaves what cannot disappear, the sheer fact of being in which *one* participates.'[34] In a sense, insomnia is a kind of active idleness – from which one might seek relief and resetting of the alternating engine of work and rest by getting up to read or hoover – just as unemployment is a kind of insomnia.

It may seem at first that the tuning of temporality that is given by work is contradicted by the fact that it is work that is associated with the reduction of time to grey uniformity and neutralized routine. There seems little doubt that work routines have become more standardized over time, but it seems unlikely that there was ever a time in which work was entirely free of structured iteration, since even animals will rarely persist with an unproductive action once they have found a more efficient way of catching the bird, digging up the root, climbing the tree and so on. In fact, as the primal scene of my time as a teenager at the unbelievably boring deburring machine, as described in my *Living by Numbers*, seems to show, there are ways in which even actions reduced to purely quantitative repetitions can be subject to variation, such that the temporality of repetitive work may form something like a musical drone which is itself an element in variation.[35] As argued elsewhere in this book, the idea of work seems to be inseparable from some kind of redundancy, or the action of reducing variation to uniformity. Work without any kind of redundancy – that is, without any kind of recurring pattern which would become drudgery if repeated indefinitely – would in fact be indistinguishable from idling.

This is the sense in which work truly gives, not life, the zero-degree existence which is not so easily dispensed with as all that, but a living, in the sense of a way of life. Badgers, beavers and bacteria are life forms, but they do not produce forms of life, for the very life forms they are means that they cannot form their lives in any other ways than those which are currently available to them, or not, at least, by any kind of design of their own. Indeed, for this reason, they may, and even must, have life (*bios*), without it being possible for them to have lives (*biographies*), except through fictionalizing projection on the part of creatures like us, who do. Work is indeed the vehicle and effect of reflexivity in symbolic creatures, their condition as being for themselves, subjects in being subject to themselves.

This is the case most particularly at the ultimate point at which all possibility of working recedes, in extreme debility, fragility or other physical incapacity. Even at this point, there may be the pressure to work purposively at the action of seceding from life, through the various modalities of the *ars moriendi*, or art of dying, which retain their force, in a world in which more of us than ever are unconvinced of the existence of a deity or of any other mode of existence than the earthly. The *ars moriendi* treats the approach of unbeing as though it were something that can or must be brought into being – something to be done, even as it may be something to get over and done with.

The horror of this condition is expressed in the term *redundancy*. The word originally suggested abundance, both deriving from *unda*, a wave. Following a formal entertainment in the Hague in 1641, Queen Henrietta called her host Prince Frederick, 'in your eloquence[,] a younger *Iupiter*, out of whose redundant brain the *Minerva* of eloquence is extracted'.[36] 'Redundant' here has an interestingly dual force in information theory, in which it refers to extra or surplus elements in a system of communication that may not be strictly necessary for the conveyance of a single message, but the superfluity of which in the system is important, since high probability makes for predictability.[37] If you are working on a crossword clue, you are in a much stronger position if you have two consonants from a five-letter word than if you have two vowels, because vowels are much more common than consonants. Put differently, if you are trying to shout a message in high wind, or through a noisy phone line, the message is more likely to be guessed if the receiver can make out the consonants rather than the vowels, because vowels, being more redundant, that is, abounding, are more guessable. Redundancy therefore signifies a kind of necessary non-necessity, as in the redundant back-up system that an engineer may wish to include in a design. As such, there is an ironic sense in which the very definition of work to which I cleave in this book, as the unnecessary necessity, makes work itself an example of redundancy.

However, as applied to human beings, especially from the beginning of the twentieth century onwards, redundancy has become identifiable not with plenitude and copiousness, but with sterility, uselessness and vacuity. To be made redundant is to be turned from a resource to a cost: where redundancy could once refer to an unused potential, it now signifies that for which there is no further use. George Bernard Shaw articulates the self-aggrandizing desire to be put to aggrandizing use in his preface to *Man and Superman* in 1903:

> This is the true joy in life, the being used for a purpose recognized by yourself as a mighty one; the being thoroughly worn out before you are thrown on the scrap heap; the being a force of Nature instead of a feverish selfish little clod of ailments and grievances complaining that the world will not devote itself to making you happy.[38]

The desire to be, in that word that has become so staled by custom and casual employment, 'employed', at once subjected but thereby given a more swelling subjecthood than is available through any other means (Shaw's sense of himself offering a good example), is nowadays routed through the particular kinds of project represented by the idea of 'one's life's work', though it extends historically through many other modes of grandeur, thereby, as Shaw smartly points out, connecting Bunyan to Nietzsche.[39] To employ and to exploit have come to seem like opposed conceptions, though they are closely twinned variations on the same idea, expressed in Latin by *plicare*, to bend or fold: employing is folding in or implication in something, while exploitation is the explication or unfolding of possibility. This is why one bends to a task, or plies one's trade, though to ply, like to bend, is both active and passive. In employment, one exploits oneself, perhaps even in the process making one's life into what may be termed an exploit, or series of exploits, in the sense of adventures or grand or complex undertakings. Employment is a complex form of compliance.

Idling is characterized by the verbal oddity that it is expressed as a form of action as well as a state of inaction. An idle engine is not quite the same thing as an engine that idles, for the latter makes for a condition of readiness to act. In humans, to idle may attract disapproval where simply being idle may not. One may be called indolent if one is idle in a certain sense, but being idle in the sense of being unemployed or laid off may mean that one is yearning for work. Idleness has long been regarded as the opposite or refusal of occupation, in both spatial and temporal senses, with frequent bills and proclamations being devised to suppress this assertive or aggressive kind of idleness, like the Act Against Vagrants, and Wandring, Idle, Dissolute Persons of 1656. The fact that English has the verb *to idle*, which can be used to signify a strangely stubborn and paradoxically active devotion to doing nothing, or nothing to any purpose, suggests that attitudes towards idleness are centred not on the fact that it is a failure of or disinclination to action, but on the fact that it is a parody or simulation of action, a doing that does nothing, or a mere ado, or business.

In Christian tradition, the Devil is strongly implicated in idleness. Jerome wrote 'Fac et aliquid operis, ut semper te diabolus inveniat occupatum,' which Chaucer renders in 'The Tale of Melibee':

> And therfore seith Seint Jerome, 'Dooth somme goode dedes that the devel, who is oure enemy, ne fynde yow nat unocupied . . . For the devel ne taketh nat lightly unto his werkynge swiche as he fyndeth occupied in goode werkes.'[40]

Milton's industrious, not to say downright industrial, Satan might seem to be a conspicuous exception here, but in fact it is an important part of the mythology of the Devil that he is always busy. The idleness with which the Devil is associated is not that of sloth or lethargy, but that of noise or accident, which is to say, directionless or chaotic activity. The word 'mischief', as employed in Isaac Watts's jolly 'For *Satan* finds some Mischief still/ For idle Hands to do', has as its primary signification mishap, or ill-fortune, perhaps from *mis* + the Old French *chever*, from *chef*, head, meaning to miss one's end, or fail to *achieve*.[41] The word comes quickly to be moralized and personalized in signifying a deliberate wrong or harmful action performed by an agent ('You'll do yourself a mischief'). This seems to be a clear indication that the Devil may be the embodiment not of inertia but of noise, not of inaction but un- or ill-directed action. Idleness also came to be associated with the curiously busy corruption of fermentation, through the folklore belief that idle fingers would breed worms, referred to in Mercutio's speech in Shakespeare's *Romeo and Juliet* which imagines the chariot of Queen Mab drawn by 'a small grey-coated gnat,/ Not half so big as a round little worm/ Prick'd from the lazy finger of a maid'.[42] Robert Greene evokes the same idea in his retelling of the fable of the ant and the grasshopper, which ends with the ant transforming the grasshopper into a worm: 'Packe hence (quoth he) thou idle lazie worme . . . For toyling labour hates an idle guest.'[43]

The medieval devil Titivillus, whose job was to gather up in a sack 1,000 slips of the tongue for his master, Satan, every day (why? what was he going to do with them? Nothing, perhaps, which may be the most characteristically satanic thing) exemplifies the paradoxical industry of noise-harvesting that is regarded as the Devil's occupation. The modulation of Titivillus into the figure of the 'printer's devil' suggests the association of misspeaking with misprints.[44] So the work of the Devil is a diabolical double negative: not work, exactly, but a disconcerting kind of not not-work. The Devil is the vehicle for this convertibility of the interference with work into a work of interference.

One may sometimes even today hear some arrangement praised or recommended as being 'business-like'. But the word 'busy' has a divided profile. It can imply absorbed intentness, as it does in

Johnson's definition, 'employed with earnestness', in line with his definition of 'business' as 'Serious engagement: in opposition to trivial transactions'. The OED explains that it is cognate with West Frisian *beuzich*, working, diligent, industrious, and Middle Dutch *bēsech*, useful, occupied, Dutch *bezig*, and Middle Low German *bēsich*, diligently employed. All of these meanings imply what we rightly call 'occupation', being taken up with or taken over by some activity, or being *besetzt* in modern German.

But *busy* also probably has the same Germanic base as a number of words, like Middle Dutch *bisen*, Middle Low German *bisen*, *bissen*, *bēsen*, Old High German *bisōn* and regional German *bisnen*, all having the sense of 'to run around wildly, to bolt (especially of cattle)'. Johnson gives as his second definition of busy 'Bustling; active; meddling . . . Troublesome; vexatiously importunate or intensive'. When the dying Henry IV shrewdly advises his son 'Be it thy course to busy giddy minds/ With foreign quarrels', a quotation given by Johnson, the busying that is supposed to steady the giddiness is allowed to partake sonically and substantively of it.[45] This idea persists faintly in usages like 'none of your business' or the term 'busybody', defined by Johnson as 'A vain, meddling, fantastical person', and illustrated by Jeremy Taylor's reference to 'tatlers, and busie-bodies, which are the canker and rust of idlenesse, as idlenesse is the rust of time'.[46] Ben Jonson's Zeal-of-the-Land Busy from *Bartholomew Fair* similarly conjoins serious and frivolous kinds of work. So business means both earnest occupation and a kind of distracted idleness.

The division is dramatized by Shakespeare, for whom the word *business* usually refers to sober, serious or even solemn matters, in *King Lear* in particular, in which Cordelia says Christically 'O dear father,/ It is thy business that I go about,' and Albany concludes that 'Our present business/ Is to general woe.'[47] But if the noun *business* is serious business in Shakespeare, the adjective *busy* points to a rather more suspicious condition. There is in early modern usages the sense that business is a kind of facetious imitation of work, as one might see in an animal: dropping the juice of love-in-idleness on to the eyelids of Titania, Oberon looks forward to its workings: 'The next thing then she waking looks upon/ (Be it on lion, bear, or wolf, or bull,/ On meddling monkey, or on busy ape)/ She shall pursue it with the soul of love.'[48] The use of the word 'business' to mean the fussy, time-filling action on stage, which makes of doing a mere ado, seems to have been in use from the late seventeenth century. The association of apes with imitative or mischievous action crystallizes in the mid-nineteenth-century phrase 'monkey-business', after the Bengali *bădrāmi*, parallel to the modern Sanskrit *vānara-karman* (*vānara* monkey + *karman* action, work, employment).

There is one kind of pseudo-work in particular that one must imagine is supplied by the Devil for idle hands, on which many of the feelings provoked by the idea of idleness converge: that of masturbation. During the years when masturbation was written about the most, from the eighteenth century onwards, it tended to be seen as a sort of parody of the work process, especially as a sort of empty mechanism, as suggested by words like *fiddle* and *fidget*. *Fiddling* suggested both triviality and trickery, as did *wanking*, which rapidly migrated to a metaphor for wasteful or idle behaviour – 'wanking around'. Although a great deal of writing from the eighteenth century onwards was devoted to what were represented as the grave dangers, spiritual and physiological, attending the practice of masturbation, its characteristic tonality is a mixture of the furtive and the absurd. What is frightening about masturbation is the fear of being seen or caught doing it, so, in other words, its emptiness and inanity. What is feared in the threats and suspicions directed at masturbation is the revelation that one may in fact be nothing, and the absurdity of the fact that in the fear of exposure, the masturbator has nothing to fear, though that is exactly what they fear. In fearing being reduced to nothing, one fears also that one's fear is exposed as nothing. All of these ideas are in accordance with the long tradition that associates the Devil not so much with positive evil as with counterfeit and imposture. The original sense of Germanic words like the Old English *ídel* is empty, useless, void or vain. The fourteenth-century Wycliffite Bible renders 'the earth was without form and void' (Genesis 1:2 – *inanis et vacua* in the Vulgate) as 'The erthe was idel and voide.'[49]

The phantasmatic work that is directed at the various inflections of the idea of unemployment is a strong intimation that it may be as indeterminable as the work from which it provides blessed or accursed remission. In a world in which symbolic labour – that is, the engineering of symbolic forms and images, or the labour on appearance rather than the mere appearance of labour – is as salient as the corporeal labour of moving mass through distance, it may be a difficult matter to be sure that one is ever idle. The way in which digital technologies allow for the patterns of our attention to be spontaneously self-archived, in what has come to be known as 'data', allows us to be made unknowing employees of media companies who find ways of making profit from our attention, or, as it might better be understood, the dazed shapes of our semi-subliminal stimulus responses. This susceptibility can trigger a diffuse kind of outrage at the thought that our leisure might be turned without our knowing it into work, along with the bewildered sense that somehow we have been tricked into working for nothing when we did not even know we were working at all. Those who have toiled historically at the oar, the coalface or childbed might view labour of this variety, propt on beds of amaranth and moly, as a desirably slumbrous form of enslavement.

Perhaps the most obvious concentration of feelings and attitudes towards work is centred on the dream of its abolition. One of the liveliest and most systematic of these attempts is by Bob Black, in an essay of 1981 entitled roundly 'The Abolition of Work'. Black defines work as '*forced labor*, that is, compulsory production' and argues that it should be abolished in order to make possible not ease but play, defined as wholly voluntary action: 'Play is always voluntary. What might otherwise be play is work if it is forced.'[50] Black's principal argument against work is simply that it is not only unpleasant – boring, tiring and productive of a 'demeaning system of domination' – but unnecessary. For all the unconditionality of his views – 'No one should ever work' are the opening words of his essay – Black does not pretend that they come from nowhere, for there is a long tradition of puzzlement and dismay among those who have thought hard about the question of what work, considered not as an action but as an institution, might be for, and what it might be like to forswear it.[51] They include Bertrand Russell and Daniel Bell.

Russell's arguments are not as absolute as some others'. His 'In Praise of Idleness' of 1935 is really an argument not against work as such, but against the perpetuation of unnecessary work. Russell argues that the institution of work is a kind of superstitious residue of a system in which leisured classes benefited from the surplus labour of the majority of the population, beyond that required to keep them alive. 'The morality of work is the morality of slaves, and the modern world has no need of slavery,' writes Russell.[52] Russell's point is that, as proven by the ability of the economy to produce enough necessary goods during the First World War, even though half of the labour force were removed from productive labour for war work, this system of thought and practice is simply no longer required:

> Leisure is essential to civilization, and in former times leisure for the few was only rendered possible by the labours of the many. But their labours were valuable, not because work is good, but because leisure is good. And with modern technique it would be possible to distribute leisure justly without injury to civilization.[53]

Russell's argument really calls for a pragmatic readjustment of attitudes to what he takes to be the economic realities of modern life, in which machines seem likely to be able to do much of the work. He accepts that a certain amount of altering the position of matter will continue to be necessary, but not nearly as much as we pretend, meaning that the morality of work previously required to make people contented with their lot is really a fantasy that serves no purpose and should be dispensed with. Russell does not wonder why this slave morality has persisted so long, but probably should do. It seems at least possible that the work ethic is not just silly or residual but is doing some kind of work (whether or not that work is fatuous, or, come to think of it, in large measure because it is).

Most arguments against work in principle, as opposed to simpler arguments that aspects of work can be unpleasant, are built around the conviction that you can never have too much of a good thing, and that therefore the more of a good thing you have, the better. The *ne plus ultra* of this argument is the belief that eternal life would be better than mortality. But there are quite strong objections to be made to all such arguments. The strongest form of this objection is the view that the value of all good things is constituted through the abeyance of bad things that they represent. Without this abeyance, any good thing infinitely extended and prolonged must inevitably itself become a bad thing. Indeed an infinitely extended good thing would be bound to become, not just no longer as good as it at first promised to be, but an infinitely bad thing, the kind of thing for which we tend to reserve the term 'evil'. The assumption that more good is always better than less depends either upon an excess of imagination, the willingness to give credence to a wholly imaginary condition of unceasing or ceaselessly augmented bliss, or a deficit of imagination, in the failure to project concretely what the actuality of such a state would be bound in the end to be. Viewed in this way it is possible to consider every argument against the principle of work as in fact an argument against certain features of the institution of work. Any absolute argument against work is bound to preserve certain aspects of the way work is lived and imagined in its characterization of the desirability of a life lived without or beyond work.

This is because the idea of work is essentially ambivalent, even paradoxical. Most of the bad things about work are necessary to the good things about it. Indeed, one may press this point home in saying that the only good things about work are in fact identical with the bad things: take away all the toil and trouble and there is nothing left. To point out the many negative features of work without reference to this paradoxical economy is to resemble the Cambridge examinee who, in living memory (mine), solemnly advised his or her examiners that 'there can be a dark side to tragedy.' The phantasmatics of work, when they tend to either the glorification of work or the glorification of what might surpass it, are often the result of an effort to resolve this condition of paradox into the fairytale simplicity of good and bad.

At the end of his *Work and Its Discontents*, Daniel Bell suddenly turns away from the kind of socioeconomic functionalism that has dominated his analysis up to that point, centred on the organization of work and the possibilities that might flow from automation, to entertain, in a lurid, sputteringly inconclusive flare, the possibility that work may be 'a way of confronting the absurdity of existence and whatever lies beyond'.[54] He ends by wondering what will keep that sense of inanity at bay:

> Although religion declined, the significance of work was that it could still mobilize emotional energies into creative challenges ... One could eliminate death from consciousness by minimizing it through work. As *homo faber*, man could seek to master nature and discipline himself. Work, said Freud, was the chief means of binding an individual to

reality. What will happen, then, when not only the worker but work itself is displaced by the machine?[55]

The importance of work, therefore, is probably less that it conduces to happiness than that it can assuage the hunger for seriousness that we may continue to surprise in ourselves. That seriousness has always consisted to some degree in the fact that, to count as work at all, work must be difficult, even and especially as it becomes difficult to know quite what counts as work and why. Take away the fascination of that difficulty and we may expect other kinds of striving to take its place, perhaps in the examination room, or on track and field, but, as they cease to be able to be otherwise managed, more likely on new kinds of battlefield. It seems unlikely that the reduction of the requirement to work, or even the relinquishment of the institution of work altogether, along with whatever condition of rapturous or uplifting leisure is supposed to take its place, will suffice to keep at bay the sense of the absurdity and anguish of living towards death.

For intensely and incorrigibly associative creatures like human beings, the most powerful analgesic against the sense of absurdity and the dread of more-or-less impending annihilation is congregation and the huddling together in various kinds of collective endeavour, where it is the joining in that does the work rather than the utility of the endeavour. This accounts for much of the horror and disdain directed at idleness, which is supposed, by Russell and others, to belong to a work ethic and slave morality that has arisen specifically in a modern world of totalized and highly regulated work practices, but in fact is to be found in the language and popular representations of many cultures: the staple targets of the universal work of contumelics, or formalized mockery, are the lazybones and the fool, which are often regarded as equivalent. A sequence of Sumerian clay tablets dating from around 4,000 years ago contains the invective of a scribe father against his indolent and undisciplined son: 'why do you idle about? Go to school, stand before your "school-father," recite your assignment . . . Come now, be a man. Don't stand about in the public square, or wander about the boulevard.'[56] The father reminds his son that the work he requires him to attend to is not manual labour like digging, ploughing or building: it is the labour of inscription imparted at scribal school, the results of which we are currently reading, and the purpose of which is the enforcing of repetition and redundancy in the system of human relations:

> Among all mankind's craftsmen who dwell in the land, as many as Enki (the god of arts and crafts) called by name (brought into existence), no work as difficult as the scribal art did he call by name. For if not for song (poetry) – like the banks of the sea, the banks of the distant canals, is the heart of song distant – you wouldn't be listening to my counsel, and I wouldn't be repeating to you the wisdom of my father. It is in accordance with the fate decreed by Enlil for man that a son follows the work of his father.[57]

The purpose of school is to teach habits of attention by inscribing the disciplines of work in the otherwise fitfully wandering hands and eyes of the young. Steady attentiveness is both the message and the method of the work of inscription, with song and poetry the internal inditing of this injunction to inscription, its exhortations anticipating the iterations of work practices themselves. The essential instruction of all writing is therefore not only, as Michel Serres suggests, 'keep me warm', but 'join in'.[58] Work is itself the communication of this exhortation to keep working, or keep alive the faith in the operativity of work. It is not hard to imagine a reform of work according to the sabbatical principles that Giorgio Agamben summed up in the term 'inoperativity', but as soon as any kind of inoperativity became a collective work, it would revert to performing the work of collective formation.

The idler or lazybones who is so regularly mocked, reproved or disdained is not just a parasite, for parasitical relations make up the whole sphere of work relations: more injuriously, he is an infidel. Parasitism is in fact perfectly capable of preserving and propagating work relations; idleness, however, is apostasy, more loathed by far than simple disbelief, because it leeches away the belief in the power of believing in common, like the osmotic suction of the Haemorrhissa (Mark 5:30).

The abolition of work depends upon the principle that work is a bad thing and that it is self-evidently the case that bad things should be removed or diminished as much as possible. Most of us see no flaw with this kind of reasoning when applied to other bad things, for example poverty, hunger and disease. But work differs from these kind of ills in that, although work is for many an appallingly bad thing with little or nothing to redeem it, there seem to many people to be substantial values associated with work that hunger and disease do not have. This is why almost all of the arguments against work are not arguments for idleness but in favour of conditions that will make a kind of free or transfigured work possible. Imagination tends to stall very quickly when required to characterize this state, even though it is usually assumed that human beings freed from compulsory work will spontaneously devote themselves to improving and absorbing projects of craftwork and philosophical contemplation, like the friend described at the beginning of William Morris's *News from Nowhere* who is coming to take his turn at being a ferryman on the river:

> He is a weaver from Yorkshire, who has rather overdone himself between his weaving and his mathematics, both indoor work, you see; and being a great friend of mine, he naturally came to me to get him some outdoor work.[59]

Things get complicated as soon as one begins to conceive the panoptical kinds of measures that might be needed to produce and regulate this spontaneous condition of *ne quid nimis* moderation. For it would be necessary not just to make sure that no one was compelled to work, but that no one was permitted to work to excess, lest they thereby accumulate wealth, power and status. It may well be, as we tend to be assured, that the appetite of people to accumulate work and power through surplus-producing labour would spontaneously wither, but if it did not – and it is hard to know how one could be sure that it would not spontaneously arise and, like a new pathogen, spread quickly among a population with little or no resistance to it – it would have to be forcibly curbed. This suggests that, in a world without systematic and compulsory work, career opportunities in the secret police at least, even if necessarily on a part-time basis, would be assured.

None of this is meant to discourage projects for the abolition of work, that kind of thing being employment for others; rather, it is to make unmistakable the formative part that such projects themselves play in the phantasmatics of work. The dream of idleness is never idle, in its earliest sense of vain, empty or vacuous. The dreamwork of the dream of work's end is in fact the final instalment of the work of keeping inanity at bay.

So work is a chronotopic connivance, a matter of when as much as of where. Wemmick's repeated journey to and from work is the demonstration that a place of work is also a means of dividing up time and in the process existing it. It is not surprising that the most powerful and far-reaching philosophy of work, as found in Hegelian dialectic, should take the form of a struggle in and with time. Where philosophy had striven to establish universal and therefore atemporal truths, Hegel gave philosophy the task of showing the task-like nature of living in time, and subordinating time itself to the action of working. The dialectic is not just the abstract schema of a process of struggle, onward and ongoing;

it is itself the outcome and effect of a struggle against unworked time, or what Joseph Conrad describes in a letter of 1907 to John Galsworthy as the effect of overwork:

> You know that materials subject to breaking strain lose all elasticity in the end – part with all their 'virtue' on account of profound molecular changes. The molecular changes in my brain are very pronounced. It seems to me I have a lump of mud, of slack mud, in my head.[60]

Conrad's phrase is expressive because mud is usually thought of as too compacted to be regarded as slack, though slack, perhaps related to the German *Schlacke*, metallic dross, is a word for loose or unproductive coal, as well as a low-grade mixture of dust and small lumps of coal, as in 'nutty slack'. However, the idea of active slacking, in the sense of slackening, neglecting or, in school and service slang, idling or underperforming, has had a surprisingly busy history in English. Slaking, which is a version of the same word, survives nowadays only in the slaking of thirst, but has been employed to signify many different kinds of diminishment or relaxation.

Despite the disapproval apparent in the mistaken mishearing of lackadaisical, meaning affectedly or languidly melancholic, and so prone to uttering 'Alas and Alack' or 'Lackaday', as 'laxadaisical', languor and slacking have developed a positive force, in the form of a word that is etymologically related to both of them: *relaxation*. The thematics of relaxation are omnipresent in modern life, in which relaxation has become a complex mode of employment and injunction, in a systematic application of William Blake's 'Damn braces: Bless relaxes.'[61] As an ideal, relaxation is really the chiasmic mirror of idleness, since, where idleness is a suspiciously busy form of inaction, relaxation is an efficiently, less-is-more form of focused inaction. So contemporary humans apply themselves with oxymoronic industriousness to 'relaxation exercises', a phrase for which nobody seems to have had any use before 1900.

Relaxation has some sombre streaks in its history, however. It was an early medical term for paralysis, and, in the Spanish Inquisition, relaxing a heretic (Portugese *relaxar*) meant yielding them up to the secular authorities for execution, as in William Stirling-Maxwell's remark that 'fourteen heretics . . . were "relaxed", or, in secular speech, burnt in May 1559.'[62] Perhaps 'relaxing' might be revived as an alternative to the contemporary euphemism 'letting go'. Relaxation is a term in physics for reversion to a state of equilibrium. Thermodynamic theory, which began as an effort to produce a physics of work defined entirely in terms of measurable quotients, which was timeless in the sense that all the equations ought to be written forwards and backwards. However, it has ended up constituting the only reliable cosmic clock for measuring the cosmic elapse of time, in the entropic tick-tock of the conversion of energy available for work into energy put irretrievably beyond employment. The state of relaxation towards which we strive in working is in reality the coming night in which no man can work, the onset of which all work advances.

What might vanish with universal or near-universal unemployment? It is unarguable that this might include some very bad things, including exhaustion, work-related disease, ennui rising to a suicidal sense of futility, coercive social practices and the suppression of the opportunity to develop civilization in only the ways that enhanced leisure is supposed to be able to. What, however, should be considered as the goods, phantasmatic or projective though they may be, that might also be diminished in a world that has moved beyond work? These must include notably status, structure, subjecthood and sociality.

Working, in the systematic kind of way that is involved in having what is known as an occupation, fulfils a need that is hugely powerful among all social creatures, namely the need to have recognition and respect. Financial reward is much less important than the status conferred by one's mode of work – and, as the intense rivalries between peers and near-equivalents indicates, it matters more to have relative standing than absolute wealth. Absolute wealth very quickly reverts into quite localized tussles over standing among wealthy neighbours: media billionaires struggling to develop systems of space travel, footballers striving to prove their repute through ever-more-inflated transfer fees and salaries. Status is closely allied to the principle of recognition that, since Hegel and following the decay of traditional systems of rank and caste, or perhaps we had better say their transformation, has come to seem ever more important in modern societies.

Working also establishes an active relation to time. If it is true that organized working practices often bring about a calculative homogenization of time, work nevertheless brings time under tension. Work allows time to be saved, invested and harvested, and in the process brings about an economy of time. It is in fact only the principle of quantification that brings about the possibility of qualitative differentiation and equivalence that makes it possible serially and seriously to live one's life rather than simply to be alive.

It is in this way that work creates the sense of reflexive self-relation that is necessary to form a subject, namely a being capable of voluntarily subjecting itself. A subject has to be able to be subjected, and a protagonist requires an agon.

Finally, the for-itself relation in work internally duplicates the for-others relation that is essential for social living, which is in its turn essential to the status, structure and subjectivity just discussed.

All of these positives depend to some degree on a *quand-même* or *and-yet* principle in that they rely on the overcoming of the self-evidently bad things about work just itemized. Work is characterized not only by bad things but by things that are only prevented from being wholly or unambiguously bad by being work. This principle of active ambivalence may be the most important feature of work. And it is in the living out or active existing of this ambivalence that the phantasmatics of work are most potently in operation. It is certainly the case that humans do not have to live in this mode of striving and have indeed done much to immunize themselves from the instinct to strive that they have all inherited. Indeed work may be the most important way in which this immunization is achieved.

5

Working Out

During the last two centuries, work has become political, in the sense that it has become the subject of large-scale efforts at design and management and the functions of deliberation these efforts required. In previous eras, work had been the means whereby various projects had been accomplished. From the early nineteenth century onwards, work moved from being the method for fulfilling certain ambitions to being the object itself of methodical organization. This is not at all to say that work had never been organized before this time, but from now on it would be work-process as such and in the abstract that would need to be rationalized. More and more, the work of planning that had been directed separately at special areas of social concern, such as the armed services, agriculture, construction, transportation, religion and education, were brought to bear on the planning of work, conceived as what connected and was held in common across all parts of social life, a social life that itself came as a result to be thought of as a work in progress.

As a result, work moved into the centre of political life and theoretical reflection. This is how Hannah Arendt sees the rise of 'a society of laborers', based on the universally shared horizon of work:

> This society did not come about through the emancipation of the laboring classes but by the emancipation of the laboring

> activity itself, which preceded by centuries the political emancipation of laborers. The point is not that for the first time in history laborers were admitted and given equal rights in the public realm, but that we have almost succeeded in leveling all human activities to the common denominator of securing the necessities of life and providing for their abundance. Whatever we do, we are supposed to do for the sake of 'making a living'; such is the verdict of society.[1]

The most obvious sign of the production of work as the cohering centre of social life was the development of the various styles of abstract social knowledge that continue to exercise a considerable monopoly on our understanding of work today: political economics, the sociology of institutions, occupational and organizational psychology. The formation of work as a general object of analysis produced ever more concrete and specific ways of existing it, or living out one's relation to it. By becoming more abstract, work also became more versatile and adaptable, more apt to impose its logic at every stage and in every aspect of life. Following Michel Foucault, the governmentality of life in general has been called 'biopolitics', naming a form of power which is constantly

> working to incite, reinforce, control, monitor, optimize, and organize the forces under it: a power bent on generating forces, making them grow, and ordering them, rather than one dedicated to impeding them, making them submit, or destroying them.[2]

Most importantly, this was a productive rather than repressive power, a power that was put to work to produce social relations as a product of the work process. It is assumed that work was subjected increasingly to the calculative structures and processes of an economic logic that extended into more and more areas of human life, but this economic logic itself performs the subsidiary or instrumental function of allowing for the drawing together into commensurability of different kinds of activity as instances of work. Foucault begins his *History of Sexuality* by outlining the repressive hypothesis that sexuality is subject to systematic repression

> because it is incompatible with a general and intensive work imperative. At a time when labor capacity was being systematically exploited, how could this capacity be allowed to dissipate itself in pleasurable pursuits, except in those – reduced to a minimum – that enabled it to reproduce itself?[3]

But he proceeds from this to a 'general working hypothesis':

> The society that emerged in the nineteenth century – bourgeois, capitalist, or industrial society, call it what you will – did not confront sex with a fundamental refusal of recognition. On the contrary, it put into operation an entire machinery for producing true discourses concerning it.[4]

At the heart of this view of things is the metaphor of the 'network', a metaphor which the structures of electronic and then digital communication has made both more abstract and more literal, both in analysis and in experience, meaning that a large part of the work of many employees consists of the action known as 'networking'. The principal idea of the network is a set of relations that have been worked into the form of a net, which is normally thought of as constricting movement; but the network of which Foucault speaks is a set of abstract arrangements that allows everything to work on and through everything else, actively and multidirectionally.

Marxist analysis depends upon the idea that capitalism abstracts work into 'labour power'. The emancipation of labour means its return to experience. However, the centrality of work does not mean that work is evacuated of meaning, but rather that life is suffused by the meaning of work. Indeed, the very idea, and ideal, of 'living labour' is the proof of this universal identification of life and work.[5] So the abstraction through generalization evoked by Foucault does not lead in the direction of alienation, but rather into multiple forms of embodiment and empirical instantiation. Because work is everywhere, it is actively *existed* as every possible kind of thing. The politics of work is then increasingly a psychopolitics, at once more intense and more intensively distributed than any previous kind. As work has become the subject of ever more active and impassioned kinds of individual and collective cathexis, it has given rise to ever stronger and more perplexed currents of dream, dread, desire, demand and sometimes desperation. As we saw in Chapter Four, a leading emphasis of late twentieth-century feminism was the recognition and dignification of domestic work as labour, transforming the home, the phantasmal masculine refuge from work, back into an extension of the workshop or workplace, as it had in fact often been before the twentieth century, and so fully part of the ergic plenum of modern life. The work–life balance is something one has to plan, administer and 'work at', like so much else, which is why it is such a preoccupation of Human Resources departments. Far from being kept in balance, work weighs on both sides of the scale.

The scientific, economic and political energies brought to bear on work have made it the engine not only of a psychopolitics but of the phantasmatics that provide their source material. There had been many insurgencies, uprisings and revolutions in previous centuries, prompted by many kinds of ambition, deprivation, rivalry and resentment, many of which centred on different classes and conditions in society, but none of them before the revolutions of the early twentieth century was centred on anything like a theory of the value of labour or a labour theory of value. Only a phantasmatics of work could have brought about a revolution not to emancipate humans from labour, but to emancipate labour itself.

Because work has become identical with what is known as the 'social bond', it has become the target for every conceivable kind of social rage, aimed at the inequities of work, and social hope, aimed at the redemption of work.[6] Indeed, the latter form of political ideal has a claim to be the leading strain in the phantasmatics of work. If work fulfils the role of a global religion, then the redemptive transformation of work is its millennial horizon of salvation. This is the principal sense in which work constitutes a human project, of the most unified and general kind. Work is both the object and process of this project of renewal and transfiguration. The salvific horizon of work is nowhere attested to more emphatically than in the modern glorification of work insisted on by Hannah Arendt, a glorification which interprets every example of the misery and waste of work as arising from the perversion, forgetting or non-fulfilment of its true nature. Arendt herself constructs a three-stage process of widening human self-fulfilment, moving from labour through work to action. It has often been the role of art to embody the possibilities of work in its prelapsarian or reborn condition. In the title of his book *Making Work Human*, Glen U. Cleeton offers a hint of the chiasmic structure whereby humanity is thought to form itself fully only through work that has itself been humanized. Man can only redeem himself through a work he has made it his task to redeem.[7]

Work has had an important role to play in religious thinking, and especially in the kind of religions that centre on the principle of redemption. The need for redemption suggests that every incarnate soul is born with some kind of moral or spiritual arrears which it will be the work of their lives to pay off, in the process clearing the soul (both the individual soul and the soul of mankind) from its corruption and buying back its lost perfection. In Christianity in particular, work has a dual function. First of all, it signifies the fallen nature of humans, who are condemned to two kinds of work for their disobedience: the fact for the woman that 'in sorrow thou shalt bring forth children,' and for the man that 'in the sweat of thy face shalt thou eat bread' (Genesis 3:16, 19). But the work to which humans are condemned is also a transformative engine which grinds culpability into felicity. So the curse of work is also the machinery for the lifting of the curse, and the means of regaining blessedness is cancelling out time by offering your life-time to it in the form of labour. The economy or structure of administration (οικονομία means household management) through which the godhead produces its own division of labour through the three persons of the Trinity is mirrored in the structure of deferral in which humanity both sets itself aside from itself in its work and returns to itself in the redemption or return on expenditure that work is supposed to effect.

Not all religions are centred on quite such an explicit temporal contour of sin and salvation as Christianity, but the idea of redemption through work nevertheless operates within some that are not. The Islamic principle of *jihād*, for example, which has tended to be associated by recent commentators with fighting or military endeavour, is perhaps better understood as a derivative from the root *jhd*, which signifies striving, struggling or exertion more broadly.[8]

Religious perspectives on work can often be regarded as reflections of the sociologization of religion into expressions of ethnicity rather than as what might be thought of as specifically religious understandings of work. One way in which the redemption of work can be projected is through recourse to what are taken to be religious or scriptural understandings of the inherently redemptive nature of work against the corrupt or worldly forms into which work may decay through the operations of sin, often nowadays called capitalism for short. Such understandings of work can then be traded as a biblically sanctioned political economy:

> Economisation of the social life, when perceived as domination of economical calculations above culture and religion, creates the social gap of richness on the one hand and poverty on the other. Economy always needs cultural and religious corrective mechanisms to avoid marginalisation of those who are not able to face the challenge of social competition. The economic models contained in the Bible provide such methodological tools.[9]

Giorgio Agamben tracks the ways in which, through words like *ministry*, *service* and *office*, an idea evolves of priestly practice, the result of which is 'the transformation of being into having-to-be and the consequent introduction of duty into ethics as a fundamental concept'.[10] This idea of religious observance passes across into secular forms, so that ministry both expands and dissolves into the secular sphere of administration, and divine service transforms via the service offered by servants and retainers to abstract institutions like the Civil Service and the service industries. In a sense, this represents the completion of a circle, as indicated by the movements undergone by the word *liturgy*. The word derives from the Greek λειτουργία, *leitourgia*, meaning public service, from λεώς, λαός, *leos, laos,* people + -εργος, *ergos*, that which works. *Leitourgia* could include the provision by private citizens with a substantial income of entertainments and festivals, as well as the contribution to works of public construction. In Greek-speaking Christianity, *leitourgia* gradually acquired a more specifically cultic sense, partly because of the decision made by the translators of the Hebrew Bible into Greek to use the term to translate Hebrew *šeret*, service.[11] *Liturgy* entered English from Latin in the 1560s to refer specifically to the service of the Mass but was generalized by the beginning of the seventeenth century to the full complement of religious services encompassed by the *Book of Common Prayer*. The simultaneous diffusion and integration of such functions, ending after many transformations in the Adornian notion of the administered society, or society of administration, may be said to have put the idea of liturgy back, as it were, into the general service in which it began in Greece.

But even where work does not feature in specifically religious ideas, and even in vocabulary from which cultic force and significance may seem to have been evacuated altogether, it tends to have what might be called a religious force or operation. By religious here, I do not suggest reference to particular forms of belief, doctrine or ritual, but rather the suggestion of some magical dimension of the immeasurable or ineffable, which is both stronger and larger than the powers of thought and language, and yet itself derives entirely from the powers of thought, infected and inflected by the capacities of language, the apparatus that thought must use to think with, and nowhere more than in signifying what exceeds its powers. Religious thinking and other forms of cognitive operation are the conception of things believed to be beyond human power to conceive, in a strange but characteristic blend of self-reproach and self-laudation. Magical thinking is not just 'omnipotence of thoughts', in Freud's formulation – the sense that certain possibilities represented in thought (one's rival meeting with an accident, Auntie Una telephoning out of the blue) might be made to occur in actuality through the act of thinking them – but the thought of the omnipotence of thought as such, the thought of thought's excessiveness to itself, once it is set to work on the world.[12] The thought of work has a religious tonality in being the thought of the work that thought itself can do. It is in this sense that work has moved progressively from being an ingredient of religious belief to being a form of faith-operation in itself, something that calls upon us to exert ourselves in believing in it, faith being the name we give to beliefs that require to be worked at.[13] Work, as transformative exertion upon the world, is always in part a work of magic, in the thought that work will always be able to fulfil what thought projects.

The relation between magic and work is an ironic one, though. Magic is of course the opposite of work, as the name for something that does not really work, but something we pretend has been made to work through the pure exercise of our wishes. At the same time, magic is essentially to be understood as a magical form of work, full of ergonomic apparatus and procedure, operations that one must perform in order for the magic to work – turning round three times, washing one's hands for twenty seconds, scrying, assaying, measuring, eye of newt and wing of bat, and the rest. Although magic always requires some kind of imaginary work to be performed in order to work, it is also crucially the case that magic is believed to be able to work on its own, by accident and without being meant, in a sorceror's-apprentice kind of way, that can run beyond one's intent: 'Die ich rief, als Geister,/ Werd' ich nun nicht los' (The spirits that I called up,/ I can no more call off) in Goethe's poem.[14] Not that magic is in any sense spontaneous or arbitrary, for the involuntary accidents that set it off are always mechanical accidents that follow a logic of cause and effect.

It has often been thought that technology moves towards a condition of refinement, complexity and obscurity that seems to make it less and less distinguishable from magic, as we lose the understanding of how our cars and computers and radios might work. This makes magic both the deceitful parody of work and its ideal form, or apotheosis. Magic is the promise of a work redeemed from physics, from having laboriously to work things through in the real world: magic operates in the search engine succeeding upon the steam engine. But, as work that works without any need for work, beyond the work of wishing, magic performs and partakes of the phantasmatic operation of willing that is in fact at work in all work, for without it there would be no work at all, only aimless action. Nothing is more real and substantial than the magical thinking at work in all work, and especially in the work performed upon work to redeem it.

Genesis gives us a lot of detail about the creative work performed by God during the first six days, as well of course as the information that he rested on the seventh. It does not go into equivalent detail about what he did on the eighth day, that second Monday morning, as it were, and thereafter. The conviction has nevertheless grown among Christian writers that, in the words of the hymn written for the boys of Eton in 1894 by Arthur Campbell Ainger, 'God is working His purpose out as year succeeds to year:/ God is working His purpose out, and the time is drawing near.'[15] Jonathan Edwards reads the whole of history as a strenuous completion by God of the work begun in that first week, arguing that 'The work of redemption is a work that God carries on from the fall of man to the end of the world.'[16]

In a collection of sermons entitled *The Redemption of Work*, Francis Paget, the Bishop of Oxford, articulated a vision of God and his incarnated Son as examples of transcendent and joyous work. Beginning by noting the 'stubborn fact of *overwork*', he went on to observe that 'the life of Jesus Christ was what we should call a life of overwork,' but at the same time 'glorified the lot of overwork' in that 'the actual consequences of His willing death are the conclusive illustration of a power which may brought to sanctify, and invigorate even the most incessant, the most thankless toil'.[17] The means of this transfiguration is said to be sacrifice, since 'he who loseth his life does save it.' So part of Christ's incarnation is the fact of the suffering imposed by the necessity for work, even as work is at the heart of the transfiguration:

> His perfect joy goes forth with the resistless energy whereby He created and upholds the universe: the song of the morning stars was but the echo of His gladness when He laid the corner-stone of the earth, and made the cloud the garment thereof: all this vast throng of unnumbered worlds into whose millions upon millions of miles the

> mind of science travels still and finds no end: all the huge and ceaseless force which in every moment drives on the mysterious whirl of life, passing nothing by, knowing no resistance . . . all this is the Work of God, and the perfect joy of His Eternal Being.[18]

What Christ's incarnation enacts is both the suffering of work and the reuniting of work and joy which had been severed by the Fall.

Marie-Dominique Chenu particularizes this perspective in *The Theology of Work*, which argues that 'theology can base itself, in a human and Christian economy, on the physical density of work as part of the fabric of the world, and, religiously speaking, of divine government.'[19] Chenu understands work as domination, the most general form of which is the domination of man, as God's proxy, over Nature, for 'God has appointed him lord of creation' (*Theology of Work*, 10). Consequently, the dominion over nature (work) is a divine participation (*Theology of Work*, 23). Denouncing the immiserating and spirit-starving rise of mechanical industrialization, and the godless communism that arose as its image, Chenu nevertheless sees industrialization as part of a historical process whereby, perfecting himself, Man doubles and completes God's work of incarnation: 'The continuing incarnation; the Mystical Body of Christ; such will be the future classic theme of a spirituality in which the world of work will find its level and its place in Christianity' (*Theology of Work*, 24).

As is customary, in both theological accounts of work and well beyond them, work is seen as a means of redemption and a process of redeeming work itself: 'work, like everything else, including love, must be redeemed' (*Theology of Work*, 17). Much of Chenu's argument seems to draw on Marx's sense of the self-perfecting nature of work, with a Hegelian narrative of history as a striving towards the actualization of spirit as the bridge between them:

> Finally, since this social progress of man, spiritual as well as economic, determines the laws of his history, we see work becoming, in man's consciousness, one of the factors of this history, through the interaction of free will and the determinism of matter. Time is effectively the field and measure of its transformations, its efficacy, its purposes. Just as in the evolution of the cosmos man is physically perfected, so in the evolution of society, man is completed socially. Here work plays a primordial role. The impassable gulf between matter and spirit does not destroy this historical unity, in which the Creator has made man his agent. Man is precisely the being who, indissolubly and consubstantially matter and spirit, is fitted thereby to carry into history the mystery of the spirit. Angels have no history. (*Theology of Work*, 18)

Indeed, Chenu's argument suggests strongly that Marx provides a theology of work, complete in all respects but the little matter of the absence in it of anything divine:

> Marx, on the other hand, built up his own metaphysic of work, communal sociology and dialectic of history. This, as we have seen, was revolutionary material. He even – as his messianic imagery attests – elaborated his own religion and his own 'theology.' But it was the work of an atheist. (*Theology of Work*, 57)

It is in this sense that work may be regarded as sacramental, both in a specifically Catholic sense and in the more general omnipotence-imaginary of transvaluation. More recently, Stephan van Erp has recruited this idea of the potential holiness of work to the work of social criticism, emphasizing not the fulfilment of incarnation in work, but the aching, yet energizing, gap between actuality and divine tendency. It is the embarrassing and appalling chasm between human work and God's work, the latter being 'creating purely for the sake of the thing being created, gratuitously, out of sheer joy', that provides the theological leverage for social criticism:

> This sacramental aspect makes manifest that human work does not necessarily lead to injustice, but has the intrinsic opportunity to become a sign of God's work. And wherever human work has become instrumental to the opposite of divine work, it calls for criticism.[20]

The symbolic act of consecration to which work is subject consecrates the forms of political striving practised in its name and on its account. The work of work turns out to be self-consecration, which must busy itself in disguising the fact that the consecration simply *works*, like a charm.

It is customary to assume that work is required for survival and flourishing. One must sow, and sew, if one is to eat and be arrayed. And yet there are many philosophical systems that dispute this necessity, including that of a certain first-century Jewish preacher, who exhorted his followers to compare the condition of human beings to those of birds and flowers:

> Consider the lilies of the field, how they grow; they toil not, neither do they spin: And yet I say unto you, That even Solomon in all his glory was not arrayed like one of these. Wherefore, if God so clothe the grass of the field, which to day is, and to morrow is cast into the oven, shall he not much more clothe you, O ye of little faith? (Matthew 6:28–30)

Most people have answered Jesus's question with a round, if respectful, 'No, He probably won't.' Almost all humans have opted for the lifestyle of the ant over the grasshopper, the householder over the parasite, the one who, as we say, makes a living, over the one who lives off others, or scrapes a living from whatever lies to hand. John Gay's poem 'The Man, the Cat, the Dog, and the Fly: To My Native Country' conducts an interrogation in turn of a cat, a dog and a fly: the cat and the dog succeed in showing their utility, but the fly responds to the challenge 'From you/ What publick service can accrue?' with the declaration:

From me! the flutt'ring insect said;
I thought you knew me better bred.
Sir, I'm a gentleman. Is't fit
That I to industry submit?
Let mean mechanicks, to be fed,
By bus'ness earn ignoble bread:
Lost in excess of daily joys,
No thought, no care my life annoys.
At noon (the lady's matin hour)
I sip the tea's delicious flower:
On cates luxuriously I dine,
And drink the fragrance of the vine.
Studious of elegance and ease,
Myself alone I seek to please.[21]

The Man is disgusted by the fly's selfishness. But though 'with a sudden blow/ He laid the noxious vagrant low,' his condemnation of the insect's fluttering inutility accidentally betrays its working purpose:

Consider, sot, what would ensue,
Were all such worthless things as you:
You'd soon be forc'd (by hunger stung)
To make your dirty meals on dung.[22]

Work of God

This Diogenean strain remains the most indigestible, even revolutionary doctrine of Christianity, and other religions. States and authorities of all kinds have their work cut out to get sages and mystics such as Mohan Das, the 'rolling saint' from Madhya Pradesh, who rolls on average eight miles a day, to give up their arduous ergo-parodic performance art, in order to hold down a job. It affects even the work of miracles performed by Christ, as becomes apparent in the story told by John of the healing of the man blind from birth:

> And as Jesus passed by, he saw a man which was blind from his birth. And his disciples asked him, saying, Master, who did sin, this man, or his parents, that he was born blind? Jesus answered, Neither hath this man sinned, nor his parents: but that the works of God [τὰ ἔργα τοῦ Θεοῦ] should be made manifest in him. I must work the works [ἐργάζεσθαι τὰ ἔργα] of him that sent me, while it is day: the night cometh, when no man can work. As long as I am in the world, I am the light of the world. (John 9:1–4)

Jesus here seems to play on, and with, the idea that, as the incarnate form of God, he is the ergological aspect of divinity. The work he works is both actual and symbolic, since it is the work of manifestation, which depends more on information than on thermodynamics, and so is more soft than hard, in Michel Serres's formulation.[23] He then proves his point by embarking on a bit of magico-symbolic business, spitting on the ground and applying the clay paste to the eyes of the blind man. The work he performs is a sort of pantomime of working that nevertheless performs the real work of working the works (ἐργάζεσθαι τὰ ἔργα), or showing the workings of God in action, or, in this case, 'action'. In all this, the source of the action is strangely concealed, being apparent only in the fact of making apparent that makes of them a work of appearing, 'the works of the one having sent me' (ἔργα τοῦ πέμψαντός με).

It is John who articulates most openly at the beginning of his Gospel the meaning of Christ, not merely as a prophet, or witness, but as the very incarnation of the operative principle, the creating or gerund-instance of creation. At the beginning of John's Gospel, repeating the Ur-beginning of all things in Genesis 1:1, or its Ur-saying, in the inaugural word of the Bible, בְּרֵאשִׁית, *bereshit*, in the beginning, we are told that 'in the beginning', ἐν ἀρχῇ, *en arche*, was the word, the *logos*, the law, the truth, but also the power of the law to make good its law. In the beginning, therefore, and thereafter from the beginning onwards, there was an indwelling potential (the *logos*) of the *logos* to go out from itself, and to get to work on the world, or rather, as the world. For creation to exist, the splendid but inert self-identity of the *logos* dwelling with and within itself has, so to speak, to be put into operation, to get going, or put itself about in an unfolding of potential and purpose, which takes place in time but in the process is also the taking place of time. The OED suggests that in English the aphetic form *gan* of the past participle *began* associates it with the word *can* and other words that signify being able. In the beginning of all things, some being began to be able, able to make a beginning and therefore, in a sense, make a beginning of its own being.

So in the figure of Christ there is the incarnation – the exact parallel to the theological word *information*, the taking on of or entering into some form – of the power of incarnation itself, as the entering into actuality of God's word, considered as a mode of magic working through its jussive imperative: 'let there be'. This is the kind of verbal spell that, when uttered by a deity exerting itself in this manner, does exactly what it says. Gerard Manley Hopkins does better than most of the many others who have toiled to articulate this principle of dynamic self-actualization:

Each mortal thing does one thing and the same:
Deals out that being indoors each one dwells;
Selves – goes itself; *myself* it speaks and spells,
Crying *What I do is me: for that I came.*[24]

All this may explain the ambivalence attached to the idea of work in Christianity and some other religions. In one sense, productive work, as traditionally conceived, the effort to transform nature or bring about new potentialities in it, is a laudatory prolongation of the creative work of the uncreated God. David Graeber cheerfully bases his critique of useless or unproductive labour on the argument that

> our concept of 'production,' and our assumption that work is defined by its 'productivity,' is essentially theological. The Judeo-Christian God created the universe out of nothing ... His latter-day worshippers, and their descendants, have come to think of themselves as cursed to imitate God in this regard.[25]

This is an understandable view to take, for it is easy to verify by any number of religious and religiose urgings of the Gospel of Work. But it passes over the fact that there is, in Judaism and Christianity, and perhaps other religions beside, a deep uneasiness about this imitation. For work is a potentially blasphemous parody or appropriation of the primary work of Creation, as the self-working of the divine through all things, since earthly work is finite, instrumental and aimed not at free flourishing but local adjustment or advantage.

Work is at once the centre of religious belief, and deeply antagonistic to it. This is why Satan is the embodiment of the spirit of industry, who makes work for idle hands and does not simply cause pandemonium, but raises the city of Pandemonium in order to do it, wrenching from Milton horrified but irresistible admiration:

> greatest Monuments of Fame
> And Strength and Art are easily outdone
> By Spirits reprobate, and in an hour
> What in an age they with incessant toil
> And hands innumerable scarce perform . . .
> Anon out of the earth a Fabrick huge
> Rose like an Exhalation, with the sound
> Of Dulcet Symphonies and voices sweet.[26]

Blake's notoriously misunderstood satanic mills are a similar mixture of horror and aweing energy. Those who withdraw from the workaday world into monasteries, caves and deserts are pledged to some work, even if it is just the challenge of the circus feat, as by the self-starver, the mute, the stylite or the holy-roller, with their various projects of self-subjection. What makes work serious is its formalized agon, the strife against the intolerability of the merely given or passive subjection to whatever may come.

Christianity is riven by the division between the doctrines of faith and works, which are supposed to set Protestants and Catholics apart from each other. The division perhaps arises in part through the Protestant recoil against the decay of Catholic good works into commercialization – the buying and selling of salvation. The hiring of people to put in mouse-time by contemporary game-players, in order to accelerate their movement through levels of the game, parallels the practice of building monasteries and populating them with monks employed to pray for the souls of their founders. In fact, for all the bloody ferocity with which the doctrines of faith and works were counterposed, neither Catholics nor Protestants were really able to do for long without the principle of purposive and striving labour, if only because religious worship is constituted in the form of duties, services and observances, of which the structure of the calendar, with its cohering alternation between regulated times of industry and holiday, is a residue. Sneering at the idea of buying your salvation with good works, Protestants nevertheless flung themselves into soul-making through labour.

Even when work seems to be developed far in the other direction from religious belief, there remains what Simone Weil calls a 'mysticism of work'. In *The Need for Roots*, written as a practical guide to the social and political transformations that would be required in France following the Second World War, Weil laid out a programme that would redeem the practice of work from the palsied condition of toil and tedium into which it had withered. The goal of the transformation she lays out

> would be, not, according to the expression now inclined to become popular, the interest of the consumer – such an interest can only be a grossly material one – but Man's dignity in his work, which is a value of a spiritual order.[27]

Weil had no time for the doctrine that work is a curse or punishment, making an explicit claim that work is sacramental in nature. Work is not, therefore, the consequence of the Fall, but the victim itself of a fall from grace which must be reversed:

> If on the one hand the whole spiritual life of the soul, and on the other hand all the scientific knowledge acquired concerning the material universe are made to converge upon the act of work, work occupies its rightful place in a man's thoughts. Instead of being a kind of prison, it becomes a point of contact between this world and the world beyond . . . Thus only would the dignity of work be fully established. For, if we go to the heart of things, there is no true

> dignity without a spiritual root and consequently one of a supernatural order.[28]

Weil proclaimed that 'The contemporary form of true greatness lies in a civilization founded upon the spirituality of work,' which would heal the wounded division between man and nature that work itself had opened up:

> A civilization based upon the spirituality of work would give to Man the very strongest possible roots in the wide universe, and would consequently be the opposite of that state in which we find ourselves now, characterized by an almost total uprootedness.[29]

Weil devoted herself to a great deal of manual work, and insisted on its necessity even within the work of understanding and intelligence. Even reading required some quotient of physical labour:

> The world is a text with several meanings, and we pass from one meaning to another by a process of work. It must be work in which the body constantly bears a part, as, for example, when we learn the alphabet of a foreign language: this alphabet has to enter into our hand by dint of forming the letters. If this condition is not fulfilled, every change in our way of thinking is illusory.[30]

Weil's work is unfolded in the space between what she calls gravity and grace, the principles that, in her admirer Michel Serres, modulate into the 'hard' and the 'soft'. Unlike those who see the point of work in its production and transformation of the self, Weil, who deliberately spent time working in factories to understand the conditions of manual labour, found a transcendent principle simply in the 'fullness of attention' that is made possible in work – manual work as a preference, but intellectual work too, when it approximates to the absorptiveness of manual work.[31] Work, for Weil, provides the condition for attention. The worst kind of oppression, she wrote, is 'the crime against the attention of the workers' through Taylorized production which 'empties the soul of everything unconnected with speed' and so 'deserves to be likened to the crime against the Spirit'.[32] The point of school work, she writes, wisely enough perhaps, is simply 'the formation of attention'.[33] Indeed, one may say that, for Weil, work is really just a form of attention, though an attention which is not fixed on a problem, or the overcoming of a difficulty for some end: such an attention without ends or what Weil calls 'finality' allows the recognition that 'Absolutely unmixed attention is prayer' (*Gravity and Grace*, 117). Attention is the capacity for an absorption that resembles the simple obliteration of all freedom in the slave, yet is miraculously transfigured.

At times, Weil comes close to a redemptive idea of work as that by which humans both suffer and overcome the faultiness of their relation to the world.

> The secret of the human condition is that there is no equilibrium between man and the surrounding forces of nature, which infinitely exceed him when in action; there is only equilibrium in action by which man recreates his own life through work.
>
> Man's greatness is to recreate his life, to recreate what is given to him, to fashion the very thing that he undergoes. (*Gravity and Grace*, 178)

Like many others, Weil regards slavery as a revolting offence against human dignity because it reduces being to mere subsistence, in 'finality rebounding like a ball; to work in order to eat, to eat in order to work' (*Gravity and Grace*, 179). Accordingly, 'the slave is he to whom no good is proposed as the object of his labour except mere existence' (*Gravity and Grace*, 180). But Weil's recreation of life through labour is not a Hegelian idea of self-production forged through striving and overcoming, and the negation of negation. For Weil, in fact, the mysticism of work lies in the negation of that very relation. Just as the atheist is closer to God than the believer, because 'Religion in so far as it is a source of consolation is a hindrance to true faith' (*Gravity and Grace*, 115), and the atheist grasps the essential unapproachability and inconceivability of God, so the slave is close to God in the very fact of his life of 'effort without finality' (*Gravity and Grace*, 180) being accepted as one becomes 'submissive to time as matter is' (*Gravity and Grace*, 181). This will likely appear to many, as it certainly does to me, more revolting than revolutionary. And yet Weil's mysticism, or mystification of the nothingness of work, also offers a clue to the Hegelian mystification of work as heroic self-production.

In 'The First Condition of Work for a Free Person', written towards the end of her life in 1942, Weil provides an image for this mystification in the operations of the lever, of which she had previously written 'The upward movement in us is vain (and less than vain) if it does not come from a downward movement' (*Gravity and Grace*, 93):

> The image of the cross compared to a balance in the Good Friday hymn could be an inexhaustible inspiration for those who carry loads or handle levers and are tired in the evening from the weight of things. In a balance, a considerable weight near the point of application can be lifted by a very light weight placed at a great distance. The body of Christ was a very light weight, but, because of the distance between the earth and the sky, it makes for a counterweight to the universe. In a manner infinitely different, but analogous

> enough to serve as an image, whoever is working, or lifting loads, or handling levers, should also make of his weak body a counterweight to the universe. It is too heavy, and often the universe makes the body and the soul bend with heaviness. But he who clings to the heavens will easily make a counterweight.[34]

Gravity, for Weil, is the world of physical process, in which things work indifferently on each other according to the laws of physics. The opposite principle, light or grace, is dependent on it, since 'Creation is composed of the descending movement of gravity, the ascending movement of grace, and the descending movement of the second degree of grace' (*Gravity and Grace*, 4). The most important kind of work is that which provides sacramental symbols from the heart of, and in the midst of, corporeality, meaning that 'The point of unity of intellectual work and manual labour is contemplation, which is not work.'[35]

This is just a rhetorical trick, no doubt. And yet the cracked and paradoxical idea that one might weight the very lightness of grace against the ponderousness of physics may reveal something essential about work, or rather 'work', and the work performed by the idea of work. There is indeed a well-established tradition that sees light and lightness as not just set against weight and the realm of physical forces in general that it summarizes, but also as an active and operative principle within that realm. Where there is gravity, it was reasoned, there must be levity, considered not only as a disposition but as a counterforce in the world. Assuming that the action of combustion must consist in driving something out or off, investigators were puzzled that the ashes of a burned log in fact gained weight. Their solution to the puzzle was that combustion must drive off some of the material's levity, identified with the principle known as phlogiston. Pliny reported that the absconding of the soul at death led to a gain in weight in the abandoned body. It would eventually turn out that the amount of lightness lost was exactly equivalent to (because it was actually nothing but) the weight gained by the oxidation of burning.[36]

What must strike us again and again in Weil's impassioned evocations of the spirituality of work is their empty circularity. There is really no content to them except the yearning sense of transcendence, the principle in work that seems to strive to go beyond itself, and where the striving is the only beyondness possible. This motion is avowedly and specifically religious for Weil, but it is strongly comparable to many apparently more secular kinds of work-mysticism.

Meaningful

At least since Aristotle, philosophers have reflected on the nature and function of work in human life. Religious thinkers have often construed work as a means of redemption, for example, from the inherited burden of sin. Seemingly non-religious thinkers, like Marx, may nevertheless give to work a virtue that still seems redemptive, as the price paid for purifying the soul. But over the last two centuries that concern with redemption through work has shifted to a growing concern with the redemption of work itself. This has involved a shift from reflections on what the meaning of work might be, in the sense of its purpose or intention, to reflections on how to make work meaningful.

We live nowadays in a period in which the concern with the meaning – and more especially the meaningfulness – of work is conspicuous. This concern is much older than the phrase 'meaningful work', which carries and encodes it. Not only is this meaningfulness a leading feature of the phantasmatics of work, the second-order concern, among sociologists, occupational psychologists, managers and Human Resources departments, with the meaningfulness in general of other people's work, is an exercise in social phantasmatics, a collectively formed and transmitted set of willings-to-belief regarding the nature of work and the work of refurbishment we encourage ourselves to feel should be performed on it. Given the religious cast of much of the psychological writing about the ways in which people are supposed to find meaning in their work, nobody should be amazed at the existence of a 'workplace spirituality literature' within which '"spirit-friendly" work units were found to out-perform those that were less spirit-friendly since they tap into individual's [*sic*] fundamental need for meaningful work.'[37] The reported assumption that 'experienced meaningfulness is a state of mind that organizations can actively create or manage at least to some degree' seems to make it clear that there exist professional groups who, in a quite literal way, make it their business to perform this kind of performative enhancement of work.[38] It also seems clear that a large part of this work consists in the building and normalization of a psychosemantics relating to work practices and work attitudes, work, therefore, on establishing the concept of 'meaningful work' rather than in any obvious or straightforward way making work more meaningful, in whatever sense may be allowed to that phrase. This may be called a disciplinary endeavour in the primary sense that it is pedagogic and designed not so much to discipline as to create discipleship. One should not be surprised to find a concept like 'servant leadership' at work in this discourse.

This gives a newly precise meaning to terms like 'performance measures', though it cannot be said that employees who see assuming these idioms and attitudes as just another chore are simply performing in contrast to employees who genuinely feel that they make positive sense of their work experience. Both must act out. And, as Catherine Bailey et al. freely acknowledge, the 'meaningfulness displays' of those who play along with the game themselves constitute 'existential labor'.[39] Whether the work of displaying the meaningfulness of work could ever itself be regarded as meaningful is as yet unclear.

In the apparently minimal clinamen, or click of the dial, through which standard-issue meaning turns into intellectually glamourized meaningfulness lies a considerable outlay of phantasmatic work – imaginary work and work of imagining. Of course, different varieties of work and work scenarios may have different kinds of meaning, banal and exotic. I may work because it earns me money, which may therefore qualify as its meaning for me, but I am not likely to say or have it said in such a case that this makes it meaningful work. Plainly, only certain kinds of meaning count in accounting for meaningfulness. This is because for work to be regarded as 'meaningful' it must seem to contribute to some grander or more general purpose, beyond its local intentions and effects. Sometimes all it takes is a small expansion of reference: working to earn money may not seem very meaningful, but working to earn money in order to be able to afford medical care for my disabled daughter sounds like it could easily qualify as meaningful. It is not just that meaningful work should not be merely instrumental, as is sometimes said by people who are also liable to maintain that in order to be meaningful, work must be pursued for its own sake. There are many forms of instrumentality, or working for the sake of something other than the work – improving healthcare in the aged, building schools in remote regions or working for world peace, as aspiring beauty queens used to assure interviewers – which would plausibly under the right circumstances be described as meaningful.

Part of the explanation for what meaningful work might mean lies in the fact that it tends to be regarded as having existential meaning for the one performing it. That is, it has to be the kind of work that can be thought to give fulfilment to the whole life of the one performing it, rather than just making the time spent working worthwhile. Meaningful work therefore means not only that the work means something, in the sense that it has some creditable purpose, but also that by doing it workers themselves come to mean something. But this tends to be a specifically sacrificial understanding of fulfilment, which is distinguished sharply from the kind of fulfilment of impulse presumably enjoyed by Genghis Khan, say, or Casanova. The kind of fulfilment which work is thought to provide requires one to confirm the purpose and value of one's life by giving it away to work. In the absence of an afterlife in which to pick up one's pay packet for a lifetime of steady occupation, it is the very fact of labouring without reward that seems to allow one instantaneously to gather in what one has given away. Redemption, from the Latin *redimere*, *re-* + *emere*, to buy, seems apt for this kind of symbolic exchange, which really does seem to function as a phantasmal bargain or buying back.

Efforts by employers and corporate managers to inculcate meaningfulness or encourage workplace spirituality are not necessarily muddled, fudged or knavish, and they are bound sometimes to be able to bring about effects that people find valuable. But they are unlikely to bring about the transvaluation of work practices and work experiences at which they seem to aim. This is not, I think, for the reason of which Shoaib Ul-Haq complains, in an article that suggests that 'workplace spirituality cannot be separated from the prevailing power relations in the economic sphere', such that the efforts to 'deliver meaningfulness' through workplace spirituality are being employed 'to gain performative dividends instead of making work morally worthy'.[40] Ul-Haq concludes that

> we can understand WPS [workplace spirituality] as a broader response of the system to assuage the feelings of spiritual emptiness in employees. However, since WPS is system-generated, therefore, it is totally cut off from its roots in the lifeworld in the form of lived traditions and religions.[41]

It is easy indeed to see the rhetoric of spirituality as part of a Habermasian colonization of the lifeworld, but we are entitled to doubt whether the lifeworld – or, less glamorously, just life – has ever been capable of providing experiences of spontaneously meaningful work. The proceduralizing efforts attached to the idea of meaningful work are not a new round of alienation, or, if they are, they are profoundly of a piece with the redemptive agon which is essential from the beginning in the imaginary economy of work, even if their conceptual lexicon may appear new. Work cannot be redeemed, not because it is irredeemably corrupt, but rather because it is itself the engine-room of redemption. Work could not be the mysteriously, because hollowly, hallowed kind of thing it is without the assumption that it should itself be able to perform soteriological work, forging meaning from meaninglessness and life from death. Work is employed to maintain in being the human as 'A wonder tortur'd in the space/ Betwixt this world and that of grace'.[42] Most of all, work cannot be purged of alienation, because the redemption of work must make alienation its own for its sacrificial economy of redemption to function. We colonize ourselves through the conviction that *Arbeit macht frei*.

The sacrificial ambivalence that often attaches to work should also dent the assurance that meaningful work can be counterposed in a simple way to meaningless work, an assurance evident for example in the work of Catherine Bailey and Adrian Madden, who set out to solicit from their interviewees 'stories about incidents or times when they found their work to be meaningful and, conversely, times when they asked themselves, "What's the point of doing this job?"'[43] It is not just because the sense of meaningfulness is fragile and episodic, as the authors predictably detected, but because the meaningful and the meaningless can depend on each other (it is the burden of this book that they usually in fact do). That is, one's work can be regarded as meaningful precisely because of the sacrificial logic which transvaluates what might otherwise be merely futile and inconsequential effort into significance, a significance that it would not have without the kenosis of surrender to the meaningless, or the willingness to 'in the destructive element immerse', as Stein puts it in Joseph Conrad's *Lord Jim*.[44] Alternatively, one can readily imagine the ironic or tragicomic viewpoint of one who, like Conrad, Beckett or Larkin, can simultaneously apprehend the emptiness of work and appreciate the ways its very anaesthetic inanity can keep ultimate meaninglessness at bay: *laboro quia absurdum*. With those who will want to maintain that there is no ambivalence in such a case, because providing calming distraction is itself a way of being meaningful, I will offer to reason no longer. However, the importance of the always-present possibility of the sense of meaninglessness in and perhaps of work is in fact suggested by Bailey and Madden's finding, in the face of a vast amount of boosterish work in the area of management studies and workplace ethics, that 'meaningfulness is largely something that individuals find for themselves in their work, but meaninglessness is something that organizations and leaders can actively cause.'[45] The best that may be hoped for from management strategy, it seems, is to create a 'meaningfulness ecosystem' that keeps meaninglessness from asserting itself.[46]

The somewhat inconvenient fact is that any kind of work might be construed by the one doing it as meaningful. Despite appearances, and despite the tendency of most of the many discussions of it over the last three or four decades, meaningful work does not really refer to specific kinds of work, but rather to relations assumed, affirmed or promised between workers and their work. This has sometimes led to explicit worries. Unsatisfied by what he sees as the arbitrary subjectivism of what people say they find meaningful, Christopher Michaelson thinks that the idea of meaningful work can be given normative definition and justification on the grounds that there is substantial convergence between the different understandings of meaningful work entertained by different people. But this falls woefully short of being any kind of demonstration of 'an independent standard of meaningfulness'.[47]

All it demonstrates is that there can often be conformity between different standards of meaningfulness, which should not be surprising: it would be more astonishing if there were not. There can be consensual as well as individual hallucinations, with proclamations of objective moral truths and independent standards of 'Normatively Meaningful Work' being among the most potent hallucinogens.[48] Such ideas may well be just 'Meaningful Work Subjectivism' collectivized.[49] Michaelson promises soothingly that a normative definition of meaningful work 'transcends not only our individual preferences and social agreements to something universally and/or intersubjectively shared and sanctioned', but the 'and/or' coupling of universal and intersubjective is unearned, or earned only by its utterance.[50] Social phantasmatics are no less phantasmatic, in the sense of being things we urgently and systematically wish to believe, with wishing providing its own warranty, for being socialized, and are probably for this reason more phantasmatic. Michaelson does not want a watertight definition of meaningful work just for the sake of it. Braced with such a normative account, he believes, we will be able to embark on projects to improve the kinds of work we make available and the choices made by work. We will, in short, be able to make such a definition of meaningful work do all kinds of meaningful work. Somewhere along the line, 'meaningfulness' has become a self-levitating hovercraft.

But this does not mean that meaningfulness is entirely 'subjective', for the (not so) simple reason that subjectivity is not itself subjective. For a full understanding of meaningfulness requires acknowledgement of the meaning of that term, or, more precisely, in Wittgenstein's sense of 'meaning', the kind of work which the term does, or is capable of doing, when it is used. This is because, though all of us are capable of having idiosyncratic ideas of what counts as meaningful for us, we have to have in common a shared acceptation of what the idea of meaningfulness is. The information here is kept, as it were, on a shared drive, rather than locally.

In their introduction to a special issue of the *Journal of Management Studies* on meaningful work, Catherine Bailey et al. propose that 'meaningfulness is characterized by non-resolvable paradoxes, or intricate tensional knots' and distinguish five paradoxes that arise in relation to meaningful work:

- The drive to self-fulfilment through meaningful work can lead to harmful effects
- The self-fulfilment of meaningful work depends on others for its realisation
- Subjective shaping of meaningful work is dependent on objective frameworks
- Meaningful work is subjectively understood yet subject to external influence
- Meaningfulness is a sense of pervasive value but is dependent on impermanent conditions[51]

It is abundantly and gapingly obvious, however, that these are all versions of the same paradox, if it even is a paradox, namely, that meaningful work is supposed to be self-fulfilling yet can never be self-determining. This ought not to be surprising, at least not to anyone with a nodding acquaintance with philosophical reflections on the nature of subjective experience. But it also suggests a very late arrival at an apprehension of the fact that the experience of work is always saturated with ideas about what that experience could and should be – that not only 'meaningful work', but the meaning and therefore the experience of work in general and as such are projectively and vicariously constituted. When it comes to work, phantasmatics prevent us, in the seventeenth-century sense, everywhere.

Meaningfulness is to meaning as *veritatis* is to *verum* in Latin, as illustrated in J. L. Austin's '*In vino*, possibly, "*veritas*", but in a sober symposium "*verum*"'.[52] Here, *veritas* is the abstract condition of truthfulness or the general value as such of Truth, the kind of thing one might make a statue or institutional motto out of, like Harvard and Yale, while *verum* refers to the local truth or simple condition of being true, of some proposition or other. The two kinds of truth need not be identical: is it in fact true (*verum*) that 'beauty is truth' (*veritas*)? Nope. The elevation or magnification of common-or-garden meaning to meaningfulness is equivalent to taking a particular true thing (an accurate and up-to-date estimate of the population of Vladivostok) as exemplary of Truth. An important concomitant of this exaltation is a degree of obscurity: it is an important part of the notion of meaningfulness that to a certain degree it passeth understanding. But such semantic inflation can also lead to blur and erosion. So, as Truth can easily nowadays degrade into the automasquerade of 'truthiness', evoked first by Stephen Colbert in an episode of *The Colbert Report* of 17 October 2005, so the sublimation of meaning into meaningfulness can dissolve it into little more than a sanctifying odour: 'meaningful' can therefore become something like 'meaningish', employing the adaptably vague suffix *-ish*, which the OED defines so admirably as 'of the nature of, approaching the quality of, somewhat'. And it is perhaps in order to combat this stepwise evaporation of act into idea into aroma that the purveyors and partisans of meaningfulness must work so hard to secure the gravitational pull, forceful but formless, it is meant to exert.

Strangely, the somewhatish inflection of meaningfulness does not prevent it from usually being applied in an absolute(ish) or all-or-nothing way. One might easily feel that one was occasionally of some use as a shop assistant or shelf-stacker even if one were nevertheless disinclined to rate the job as meaningful. To say that such an occupation was somewhat meaningful or meaningful in parts would be logically quite coherent but, as with the fractional goodness of the curate's egg, would seem to strain against the holistic usage of the term 'meaningful', which implies some threshold that must be crossed in order to be really meaningful, which is to say fully meaningful, full of meaning in full. This perhaps has something to do with the assumption that meaningful work is a way of bringing wholeness to the worker's life, for we do not on the whole think of wholeness as partial or episodic (it can certainly be gradual, though, and perhaps always must be). As Adina Schwartz maintains, in one of the inaugural arguments in favour of the idea of meaningful work, jobs should be part of the process whereby citizens are given autonomy, which involves

> a process of integrating one's personality: of coming to see all one's pursuits as subject to one's activity of planning and to view all one's experiences as providing a basis for evaluating and adjusting one's beliefs, methods, and aims.[53]

There are some ways in which the paradoxical evacuation of specificity that comes with the addition of the suffix *-ful* (*wonderful*, *beautiful*, *powerful*, even, for a few centuries following the fourteenth century, *allmightiful*, crammed with almightiness) can in fact assist the imaginative hypostasis of the feeling of meaning. For, in circumstances in which one might be hard pressed to characterize precisely what kind of meaning one's particular occupation, as lecturer, losel or loblolly-man, might embody, it can be helpful to have the hum of reassurance given by a term like 'meaningful work' that the work is, or should be, or perhaps might be, meaningful because it is a kind of work, making it thereby comparable to all the other kinds of work that people do insofar as they participate in however small a degree in the assumed, alleged or projected meaningfulness of work as such.

It is odd to find so much of the critical literature relating to meaningful work in the trade journals of human resource and management studies taking their departure from Marx's account of alienated labour, as concentrated especially in his *Economic and*

Philosophical Manuscripts of 1844. The idea of alienation is important because it is what meaningful work is supposed to resist, transform or redeem. In the course of a dozen or so pages, Marx offers a subtle and encompassing analysis of the various kinds of alienation embodied in industrial labour, as typified by the factory worker. Alienation in English does the work of the two terms that Marx employs: *Entfremdung*, or estrangement, and *Entäusserung*, externalization, abandonment or relinquishment. The worker, he says, is alienated in four respects. First of all, he is alienated from the products of his labour, which are made for the benefit of another, or many others. Then, as a result of this, he is also alienated from his own labour, because, 'if the product of labor is alienation, production itself must be active alienation.' The logic here is not absolutely shipshape, not least because of the striking inversion to which it leads Marx, in which labour is described as 'the alienation of activity, the activity of alienation'. This leads to the grandest part of Marx's conception, that labour alienates man from his essential 'species being'. And finally, all the other forms of alienation produce 'an *estrangement of man* from *man*'.[54]

Marx's analysis is subtle, concentrated, far-reaching and powerfully encompassing. The problem, at least for those, and they have obviously been legion, who would like to use his analysis as a means of critique and path to revolutionary or other remedy, is that it is so encompassing that it leaves nothing over. Marx is massively right about all the ways in which a worker can be alienated from the practice or products of their work, but miserably wrong to suggest that there could ever be such a thing as unalienated work. What has been taken to be a howl of outrage at the terrible distortions wrought upon labour is in fact a sober account of the conditions attaching to anything, ever, that could have qualified as work. For something to be work, there must be some effort against a resistance, and a co-constituted resistance to one's effort, if only that of gravity, and that resistance can only be exercised upon me from some outside, from some form or aspect of the not-me. Obviously, I can work against myself, through Canadian Air Force exercises, or interior philosophical dialogue, but only by means of interior self-distribution. Though work can seem to represent a cooperation of subject and object to produce a product, which is then separate from me but suffused with my labour, it can only be a product, whether I use it for myself or exchange it for other goods or services, if it is no longer identical with the labour of forming it. Indeed, one might say that alienation should be seen as identical to growth, multiplication and propagation themselves, and therefore the cardinal value of all conceivable kinds of work. Look at a fair field full of flowers, or for that matter full of folk, and you will see splitting off, self-estrangement and self-outering as far as the eye can see. If existence is, as Heidegger observes, to be understood as *ex-sistere*, a standing out or placing outside, then alienation is inalienable. It is only a pathologically locked and appropriative sense of originary self-inherence that makes the processes of outering the inward seem like a crime against nature.

It may readily be objected that there are different kinds of alienation, some of which are just much more unpleasant than others. It is true that I must subject myself to the realm of objects to hit a tennis ball, but it is also true that it would not be much fun to be employed twelve hours a day as a human target for somebody practising their service. This can readily be granted, but at less cost to my argument than might be thought. What matters, it seems, is who is doing the alienating. If I willingly make myself an object, says Marx, then I am not alienated, or at a distance from my work, but rather somehow absorb that distance or objecthood into myself. I may well feel better about this than I would about being treated like a chattel, but Marx is rightly not usually thought of as a utilitarian philosopher of well-being, so how I feel about things is not really the issue. Marx wants us to accept that we can actually overcome the subject–object dichotomy in work, not just feel happier about it. But we can only do this with the cooperation of magical misrecognition. That there are undeniably certain kinds of labour conditions that seem more desirable than others has little to do with how much or how little alienation they involve. It has to do rather with what we make of that alienation, which is to say, the kind and degree of phantasmatic work we perform on it. It is not alienation that must be removed or reduced but alienation from one's alienation.

If this seems like the most offensively vacuous form of idealism, let us think of the situation of the classically alienated worker, toiling in a factory for twelve hours a day for tuppence a week, just about enough to keep them alive enough to stagger dazedly back to work each morning. When one compares this situation to that of the factory owner, dressing his wife in silks on the profits of the factory and sipping fine wines as he glories in his status as a self-made man, it seems unarguable that something is being ripped off from somebody. But now consider exactly the same situation, the factory just as dark and satanic, the hours as long, industrial accidents just as frequent, except that the factory is owned by a collectivist state in which all property is held in common, and all are expected to work according to their capacities for the common good. Our exhausted factory-hand has in fact been a hero of the revolution which has brought about the current state of affairs and is absolutely committed to the value of their sacrifice, and their privilege in being able to work for the good of their fellow beings. It is plain to them that their work conditions are starkly opposed to that of their benighted predecessor, though an outsider might wonder in what way they differ. It will be obvious to the one who believes that alienation is something in the world, rather than a relation to that something, that the worker is simply being deceived: the magical word 'material' will likely be produced to prove that the alienation is just there, needing to be transformed.

In fact, Marx helps us see what he strives to avoid seeing, or at least saying, himself, namely that alienation must be intrinsic to whatever operation it is that constitutes something as work. In fact, we are about to see that work deploys and depends on the prospect of the greatest and most absolute alienation of all.

Living Work

For work irresistibly precipitates thoughts of life and death. This is partly because work has often been thought of as itself a matter of ensuring life, or staving off death, and partly because our lifetimes are supposed to be given purpose and definition by our working occupations. The porch of All Saints Church in Bakewell, Derbyshire, displays a number of medieval tombstones found on the site which record not the names of those buried beneath them, but rather their occupations, indicated by carvings of emblematic objects like swords for soldiers or shears for weavers, as though it was the work that had expired and not the workers. Because it has itself represented the extreme possibilities of life and death, work has been subjected to a sort of mythical animation, such that it can itself be represented in dead or living forms.

This thinking, for all its intense hold on the work of imagining work, is paradoxical, and perhaps all the more intense for this tension of paradox. The central paradox is this: work is living when it is productive, which is to say aimed at some goal or outcome. Work without purpose is not merely not work, but a kind of dead simulation of work. However, the products precipitated by work cannot be as alive as the work itself. If, on the one hand, they are so suffused with the activity of work that we give them the same name, as though the work resulting from work were still the working that produced them, on the other hand we know that, as symbols of work accomplished, they must always also be dead residues of work that has ceased. The epic poem, well-wrought urn or soaring cathedral may seem lifelike, but that life will always be fetishistic or phantasmal. In Jacques Derrida's neat formulation, 'as soon as there is production, there is fetishism.'[55] What issues from work must always represent the death of work, for the purpose of anything that could count as work, that is, purposeful striving, is to put itself to death, the death of its consummation.

Of course, there are always ways in which these objectifications of the labour process can themselves form the basis of new kinds of purposeful striving. One may, for example, work at shaping tools and instruments of work. One's work may also generate different kinds of surplus, whether of grain or coin, which can be put to work in new enterprises, such as planting fields and hiring workers to till them. For Marx, who went further than anyone in formalizing ideas about life and death in work, these forms of surplus are seen as crystallized or dead labour. However, the real meaning of these forms of dead labour is that they are never really or finally dead, for they awaken, and are capable of being awakened by, the Gothic imagination of the undead or the living dead, as in Marx's famous, creepy formulation: 'Capital is dead labour, that, vampire-like, only lives by sucking living labour, and lives the more, the more labour it sucks.'[56] Vampires, succubi and other kinds of viral vitality-swigging abominations are never far away when Marx thinks about the nature of work. They are dead, but dead with a strangely vigorous, diabolically attributive life. It is not the fact that capital kills labour that makes Marx's flesh creep, it is that it impersonates and threatens to outdo labour in crypto-living productivity. In as comradely a way as he can manage, Derrida points to the 'ordeal of undecidability' that assails the labour-vitalism of Marxism:

> All the grave stakes we have just named in a few words would come down to the question of what one understands, with Marx and after Marx, by effectivity, effect, operativity, work,

> labor [*Wirklichkeit*, *Wirkung*, work, operation], living work, in their supposed opposition to the spectral logic that also governs the effects of virtuality, of simulacrum, of 'mourning work,' of ghost, *revenant*, and so forth.[57]

The cult of living labour is the attempt to disentangle the living and dead, to purge death, or rather deathliness, from the purely living. This attempt must fail, for abjuring always works by conjuration. Capital is dead labour which, vampire-like, lives only by sucking living labour, and lives all the more the more labour it sucks, insofar as all work engenders new life-in-death chimerae.

But in fact the problem begins much earlier, before it is any question of what work is to be done with the products of living work, and whether or not those products and what is done with them are living or dead. The problem begins to churn at the moment at which one starts to think of work as the proof and perfected form of living being, as the essence of the species being. Because the essence of living being for the kinds of being that humans are is to be a creature that works, and thereby produces, not only objects in the world but itself; its essence cannot lie in itself, it must be brought into being. The indwelling essence of human being therefore lies in prospect, either ahead of or outside itself. Human beings live by simply existing, but they have lives only through the work they perform. This means that that which gives them life is in fact not itself already alive, in any simple fashion. Considered in this way, the life or livingness of humans, as a making good of a potential for work that must be lived out in order to be actualized, is itself a surplus value, never simply given, but always an affair, that is to be worked out in work.

Life as actualized potential is therefore itself a kind of parasitical outgrowth of simple existence, the necessity fangled out of the non-necessary. The idea of a life is itself the virus, the life-in-waiting, or life-time that sustains itself by siphoning off the life from its living host, who is merely existent until animated by the life-idea. The life-idea, which is supposed to be both actualized and subject to assault by the conditions of work, meaning that work itself has to be redeemed, brought to life or brought back to life, is a product, material and philosophical, of the work that human beings do on their own being. Work, as the phantasmatic form of what transforms the mere workings of nature into an action of work, is the life-blood of this transformation of being into life. Through work, 'life' ghosts and haunts itself.

All of this seems mystical, in ways that might be anticipated, given the notorious difficulty of providing any nonmystical definition of life, as something distinctively apart from and in addition to all the processes that are held to be at work in living creatures. The odd incursions of the mystico-phantasmal in the works of Marx and the styles of thought bequeathed by the tradition in which he works to the forms of political economics that thrive today in the factories of discourse on work serve by their very outlandishness to reassure the technicians of work that what they are really about is something for the most part much more non-metaphysical and workaday, a work of positive analysis and engineering of what seem like material processes. It may be this very materialism that allows the mysticism of work to insinuate itself most universally in the work of reform and perfecting that we persuade ourselves we are performing on our work. It is the work of realism in keeping far hence the thought of the phantasmatic nature of our own thought about work that constitutes its mysticism.

This mysticism is at the heart of the strangely stubborn duality whereby we must be condemned, and indeed must condemn ourselves, to work and in that very process be condemned to the work of redemption that would transform that condemnation into acquittal. The necessity of work is the necessity of the work of redeeming it, but dissolving its necessity. And yet work must be unredeemable, and for a strange reason. The reason that work is not to be redeemed is just because work is the *to-be-redeemed*. Work cannot be redeemed, because it is itself the work of redemption. That is what work is for. Why, or how, might that work of redemption ever itself be redeemable?

Drudgery is important because, like the suffering that belongs to toil, it secures the value of sacrifice, or the sacralization of loss. It is necessary that work should enact a cost. Typically, of course, this cost is represented as an investment, in the interest of delayed gratification, but what matters most is that the payoff can never be certain, or certain to be enough. This means that, however much work may be caught up in systems of calculation, contract and compensation, it represents a magical rather than a logical kind of bargain. This principle of sacrifice makes work devotional. This is why work can be experienced as self-rewarding, in just the same way as prayers are thought of as self-fulfilling. Indeed, there is a tradition of seeing *orare* as a representative form of *laborare*. This not because prayer is seen as utilitarian, but because work is seen as magico-symbolic observance.

If this were not the case, we should be at a loss to explain the persistent idealization of work, the sense that to work simply as a trade-off for the necessities of life is a degradation, not just of life but of work itself. And yet, of course, there is degradation in work, and indeed this is part of its esoteric necessity: degradation is part of sacrifice. The logical or utilitarian form of exchange operates according to a single logic of equivalence, but magical exchange works through transfiguration, based upon radical ambivalence, the principle of the spontaneous communication and convertibility of opposites, as promised in the Christian second coming, when the poor shall inherit the earth, or in the dictatorship of the proletariat. This is why Hegel's 'labour of the negative' in fact encompasses all labour, in which negativity must always play a leading role. This is different from simply putting negativity to work: it is rather the principle of unrecuperable negativity embodied in the slow suicide of work, a cool, careful orgy of self-immolation, at once lucid and hallucinogenic, perpetuated by being maintained life-long, permitting the idea that a working life is building towards some kind of life's work, rather than being an extended opening of the veins.

Georges Bataille's theory of a general economy based upon sacrifice and dissipation sets productive and accumulative work against luxury, obscenity and sacrifice: 'There is taking possession through work; work is human activity in general, intellectual, political, or economic; to which is opposed sacrifice, laughter, poetry, ecstasy, etc.'[58] Bataille is never more charmingly adolescent than when he protests that 'work goes against erotic freedom, hampers it; and, conversely, erotic excess develops to the detriment of work.'[59] His view of class society, a compound of Hegel and Sade, sees workers as simply building the bonfires the combustion of which proves the sovereignty of their aristocratic masters: workers are 'so many slaves working like cowards to prepare the beautiful blustering eruptions that alone are capable of answering the needs that torment the bowels of most men'.[60] And, to be sure, nothing could resemble Bataille's spectacles of conspicuous waste – the bullfight, the public execution, the riotous carnival – less than the unremitting toil of the peasant or the slave in the fields, or the prudential, pension-piling accumulations of the working week and workaday world. Bataille's own life and career, as a librarian in the Bibliothèque nationale pursuing a literary career at the weekends as an occult pornographer and Sadeian prophet of violence, seems to act out this split with comic literalness: no wonder the editors of *The Bataille Reader* can insist that the very notion of a cumulative work cannot be applied to Bataille's writings without absurdity, so that

> it may be advisable to speak not of the work, or oeuvre, of Georges Bataille, but of the unworking performed by his

> writing in and against all discourse: it is not an *oeuvre* but a *désoeuvre*, in the sense that its negativity is unemployed, in the service of nothing and no one, inoperative in respect of specified and useful goals.[61]

But in fact, work operates just those principles of wasteful expenditure, albeit at a speed, and a temperature just about freezing point, that make it seem like the opposite of a strike or a week in Tenerife. The difference between accumulation and expenditure is a matter of speed for Bataille: where accumulation depends on delay and a steady, regularly accretive rhythm, expenditure is convulsive and explosive, the sudden release of energies long in the gathering, as in an earthquake or a volcanic eruption. But this contrast is an optical illusion, from a chronically parochial perspective, a product of the disproportion between cosmic and human timescales. The sun, the very epitome of ecstatic squandering in Bataille's system, is characterized, episodes of flaring apart, not by intermittence but by steady and continuous effusion, even if we prefer to imagine it building towards a final conflagration. The sun is the image of a slow, sustained self-extinguishing, in the strange, splendid futility in which work shares. The drudgery that must form a part of all work is the principle of sacrifice secreted through its profane opposite. It is figured best not in the explosive form of spontaneous human combustion rumoured for so many centuries, but in the ignominious melting into igneous ooze and soot of the smouldering pig in a blanket, used to demonstrate experimentally the 'wick effect', which allows an insensible large mammal to burn down like a candle over many hours. The horror and glory of the life-sacrifice made irrecuperably through work are enacted through a comparable slow-motion autophagous haemorrhage. Disguised within the citizenly straight-and-narrow of production and accumulation is the mysticism of work so scandalously and astonishingly embodied in the pure negativity of the slave, 'he to whom no good is proposed as the object of his labour except mere existence' as imagined by Simone Weil.[62] Speed up the cumulated self sacrifices without return of the work of humans over epochs and you would be confronted, like Benjamin's Angel of History, with a savagely and gloriously roaring auto-da-fé of waste. The point of work rhythms and work disciplines, scoring toil into the music of time, is to spread out the incineration anaesthetically across a lifetime.

In fact, however, neither work-as-investment nor work-as-sacrifice constitute its reality, overshadowing the merely phantasmatic value of the other. For both investment and sacrifice are functions of the phantasmatics of work, defining the work that the idea of work is required to do in the lives of individuals and epochs. There is nothing that constitutes the ultimate meaning of work, unless it is the work in progress of this very inultimacy, or ongoing penultimacy.

The dream of the real is so commanding that those in its grip are not well equipped to appreciate the reality of their dream, and the work involved in dreaming it onward. I have written this book during the last few months of my employment in the University of Cambridge, as I was faced with the involuntary ending of the kind of ambivalent occupation I have been fortunate to have had since the day I stopped, to all appearances, being a student in September 1979. It has felt like two different kinds of awakening. First of all, there is an awakening from what seems in retrospect to have been a dream, of needs, aims and responsibilities that have suddenly melted away. The arbitrary ending of this manner of life makes the whole of the life lived through in this manner itself seem figmental and adventitious. But this means it is also an awakening, not only *from* a kind of dreamwork, but, more importantly, *into* it, as it currently – but perhaps only momentarily – seems to me. As such, it is less like a sudden opening of eyes than the abating of a life-long inadvertence. Like Bottom, I must affirm, scarcely sure whether I yet wake or sleep, that I have had a dream past the wit of man to say what dream it was. And so I cannot yet know what kind of work the work I have gone about to expound this dream will have amounted to, or how close I will have got to getting to the bottom of it.

References

1 Dreamworks

1 Steven Connor, 'Professing', *Critical Quarterly*, LXI (2019), p. 46.

2 Sigmund Freud, *The Interpretation of Dreams*, in *The Standard Edition of the Complete Psychological Works of Sigmund Freud*, 24 vols, trans. James Strachey et al. (London, 1953–74), vol. IV, pp. 276–508.

3 Charles Madge, *Society in the Mind: Elements of Social Eidos* (New York, 1964); Gregory Bateson, *Naven: A Survey of the Problems Suggested by a Composite Picture of the Culture of a New Guinea Tribe Drawn from Three Points of View*, 2nd edn (Stanford, CA, 1958), pp. 218–56; Charles W. Nickolls, 'The Misplaced Legacy of Gregory Bateson: Toward a Cultural Dialectic of Knowledge and Desire', *Cultural Anthropology*, X (1995), pp. 367–94.

4 Joanne B. Ciulla, *The Working Life: The Promise and Betrayal of Working Life* (New York, 2000), pp. xvi–xvii.

5 Ibid., p. 7.

6 Giorgio Agamben, *Potentialities: Collected Essays in Philosophy*, ed. and trans. Daniel Heller-Roazen (Stanford, CA, 1999), p. 182.

7 Anon., *Cursor mundi: [The Cursor of the World]: A Northumbrian Poem of the XIVth Century*, 3 vols, ed. Richard Morris, Heinrich Hupe, Hugo Carl Wilhelm Haenisch and Mark Kaluza (London and Toronto, 1874–93), vol. I, p. 69.

8 Nicholas H. Smith, 'Work and the Struggle for Recognition', *European Journal of Political Theory*, VIII (2009), pp. 46–60.

9 Steven Connor, *A Philosophy of Sport* (London, 2011), p. 173.

10 Aristotle, *Nicomachean Ethics*, trans. H. Rackham (Cambridge, MA, and London, 1934), pp. 89, 91.

11 Ibid., p. 89.

12 Ibid., p. 327.

13 Thomas Carlyle, *Past and Present* (Oxford, 1927), p. 206.

14 J. L. Austin, *Philosophical Papers*, 3rd edn, ed. J. O. Urmson and G. J. Warnock (Oxford, 1979), p. 259.
15 Ibid., p. 271.
16 Hannah Arendt, *The Human Condition*, 2nd edn (Chicago, IL, 1958), pp. 80–81.
17 Olivier Frayssé, 'Work and Labour as Metonymy and Metaphor', *tripleC*, XII (2014), pp. 468–85.
18 George Puttenham, *The Arte of English Poesie* (London, 1589), p. 150.
19 Ludwig Wittgenstein, *Philosophical Investigations*, trans. G. E. Anscombe (Oxford, 1972), 32e.
20 Nicholas H. Smith and Jean-Philippe Deranty, eds, *New Philosophies of Labour: Work and the Social Bond* (Leiden and Boston, MA, 2012), pp. 26–7.
21 Steven Connor, 'Polyphiloprogenitive: Towards a General Performativity' (2013), http://stevenconnor.com.
22 Daniel Lagache, 'Symposium on Fantasy – Fantasy, Reality and Truth', *International Journal of Psychoanalysis*, XLV (1964), p. 186.
23 Ibid., p. 187.
24 Jean Laplanche and Jean-Bertrand Pontalis, *The Language of Psycho-Analysis*, trans. Donald Nicholson-Smith (London, 1983), p. 317.
25 Didier Anzieu, *Freud's Self-Analysis*, trans. Peter Graham (London, 1986), p. 98.
26 Madeleine Baranger, Willy Baranger and Jorge Mario Mom, 'The Infantile Psychic Trauma from Us to Freud: Pure Trauma, Retroactivity and Reconstruction', *International Journal of Psycho-Analysis*, LXIX (1988), p. 119.
27 Parisa Dashtipour and Bénédicte Vidaillet, 'Work as Affective Experience: The Contribution of Christophe Dejours' "Psychodynamics of Work"', *Organization*, XXIV (2017), pp. 18–35.
28 Christophe Dejours, ed., *Psychopathology of Work: Clinical Observations*, trans. Caroline Williamson (London, 2015).
29 Jürgen Habermas, *The Theory of Communicative Action*, vol. I: *Reason and the Rationalization of Society*, trans. Thomas A. McCarthy (Boston, MA, 1984), p. 25.
30 Rodrigo Ventura, 'The Concept of Work in the Psychoanalytic Experience', *Psicologia USP*, XXVII (2016), p. 282.
31 Ibid., p. 287.
32 Ives Hendrick, 'Work and the Pleasure Principle', *Psychoanalytic Quarterly*, XII (1943), p. 314.
33 W. H. Auden, *Collected Poems*, ed. Edward Mendelson (London, 1976), p. 134.

34 Bertrand Russell, *Mysticism and Logic, and Other Essays* (London, 1917), pp. 59–60.
35 Steven Connor, *The Madness of Knowledge: On Wisdom, Ignorance and Fantasies of Knowing* (London, 2019), pp. 10–17.
36 *Toronto Daily Star* (5 April 1947), p. 6.
37 Philip Larkin, *Collected Poems*, ed. Anthony Thwaite (London, 1988), p. 89.
38 Freud, *Standard Edition*, vol. XVIII, p. 30
39 Bernard Stiegler, *Technics and Time*, vol. I: *The Fault of Epimethus*, trans. Richard Beardsworth and George Collins (Stanford, CA, 1998), p. 141.
40 Ibid.
41 Ibid.
42 Connor, *Madness of Knowledge*, pp. 136–7.

2 Hard Work

1 Fredric Jameson, *The Political Unconscious: Narrative as a Socially Symbolic Act* (Ithaca, NY, 1981), p. 102.
2 James Boswell, *The Life of Samuel Johnson*, ed. Christopher Hibbert (London, 1986), p. 122.
3 Thomas Reid, *An Inquiry into the Human Mind: On the Principles of Common Sense: A Critical Edition*, ed. Derek R. Brookes (University Park, PA, 1997), p. 55.
4 Ibid., pp. 55–6.
5 Ibid., pp. 56–7.
6 Ibid., p. 58.
7 Lorne Falkenstein, 'Hume and Reid on the Perception of Hardness', *Hume Studies*, XXVIII (2002), pp. 27–48; Adam Weiler Gur Arye, 'Reid, Hardness and Developmental Psychology', *Journal of Scottish Philosophy*, XII (2014), pp. 145–62.
8 Thomas Reid, *Essays on the Intellectual Powers of Man*, ed. A. Z. Woozley (London, 1941), p. 163.
9 James Boswell, *James Boswell's Life of Johnson: An Edition of the Original Manuscript, in Four Volumes*, vol. I: *1709–1765*, ed. Marshall Waingrow (Edinburgh and New Haven, CT, 1994), p. 332.
10 Gaston Bachelard, *La Terre et les rêveries de la volonté* (Paris, 1948), p. 78 (my translation).
11 Jean-Paul Sartre, *Critique of Dialectical Reason*, vol. I: *Theory of Practical Ensembles*, trans. Alan Sheridan Smith, ed. Jonathan Rée (London, 1982), p. 67.

12 William Empson, *Argufying: Essays on Literature and Culture*, ed. John Haffenden (Iowa City, IA, 1987), p. 113.
13 Ibid., p. 160.
14 Ibid., p. 115.
15 G.W.F. Hegel, *The Phenomenology of Spirit*, trans. Michael Inwood (Oxford, 2018), p. 11.
16 Arthur Little, 'The Philosophy of Work', *Irish Monthly*, LXXVI (1948), p. 57.
17 George Orwell, *The Collected Essays, Journalism and Letters of George Orwell*, vol. IV: *In Front of Your Nose, 1945–1950*, ed. Sonia Orwell and Ian Angus (London, 1968), p. 42.
18 Harold Weiss, 'The Sabbath in the Writings of Josephus', *Journal for the Study of Judaism in the Persian, Hellenistic, and Roman Period*, XXIX (1998), pp. 363–90; Sigve K. Tonstad, 'To Fight or Not to Fight: The Sabbath and the Maccabean Revolt', *Andrews University Seminary Studies*, LIV (2016), pp. 135–46.
19 Sartre, *Critique of Dialectical Reason*, p. 90.
20 Ibid., p. 91.
21 Alfred Lord Tennyson, *In Memoriam*, ed. Susan Shatto and Marion Shaw (Oxford, 1982), p. 133.
22 G.W.F. Hegel, *Hegel's Philosophy of Mind*, trans. William Wallace (Oxford, 1894), p. 43.
23 Gaston Bachelard, *The Right to Dream*, trans. J. A. Underwood (Dallas, TX, 1988), p. 39.
24 Ibid., p. 40.
25 Karl Marx, *Capital: A Critique of Political Economy*, vol. I, in *Marx/Engels, Collected Works*, XXXV, trans. Samuel Moore and Edward Aveling (New York, 1996), p. 188.
26 Ibid.
27 Ibid.
28 Bertrand Russell, 'In Praise of Idleness', in *In Praise of Idleness and Other Essays* (London, 1935), p. 12.
29 William Shakespeare, *Complete Works*, ed. Richard Proudfoot, Ann Thompson and David Scott Kastan (London, 2011), p. 157.
30 Thomas Khurana, 'Force and Form: An Essay on the Dialectic of the Living', *Constellations*, XVIII (2011), p. 23.
31 Ibid., p. 30.
32 Sigmund Freud, 'Notes Upon a Case of Obsessional Neurosis', in *The Standard Edition of the Complete Psychological Works of Sigmund Freud*, 24 vols, ed. and trans. James Strachey et al. (London, 1953–74), vol. X, pp. 232–3.
33 Baptista Gurarini, *Il Pastor Fido: The Faithfull Shepherd: A Pastorall* (London, 1647), p. 163.

34 Michel Serres, *The Five Senses: A Philosophy of Mingled Bodies*, trans. Margaret Sankey and Peter Cowley (London, 2008), p. 112; Stevan Harnad, 'On the Virtues of Theft Over Honest Toil: Grounding Language and Thought in Sensorimotor Categories' (1996), http://cogprints.org.
35 Harnad, 'On the Virtues of Theft'.
36 Stevan Harnad and Silvia Coradeschi, 'Interview with Prof. Stevan Harnad', *Künstliche Intelligenz*, XXVII (2013), p. 170.
37 At www.honest-toil.eu, accessed 11 January 2022.
38 Steven Connor, *The Book of Skin* (London, 2004), p. 188.
39 Shakespeare, *Complete Works*, p. 637.
40 J. L. Austin, *Philosophical Papers*, ed. J. O. Urmson and G. J. Warnock, 3rd edn (Oxford, 1979), p. 271.
41 J. P. Mallory and D. Q. Adams, eds, *Encyclopaedia of Indo-European Culture* (London and Chicago, IL, 1997), p. 362.
42 Stephen Wren, *Parentalia; or, Memoirs of the Family of the Wrens* (London, 1750), p. 281.
43 Vilém Flusser, *The Shape of Things: A Philosophy of Design*, trans. Anthony Mathews (London, 1999), p. 21.
44 Ibid.
45 Vilém Flusser, *Vom Stand der Dinge: Eine kleine Philosophie des Designs* (Göttingen, 1993).
46 Ranulph Higden, *Polychronicon Ranulphi Higden Monachi Cestrensis; Together with the English Translations of John Trevisa*, 10 vols, ed. Churchill Babington and Joseph Rawson Lumby (London, 1865–86), vol. VI, p. 83.
47 John Lydgate, *The Lyf of Our Lady* (London, 1484), sig. k1r.
48 Thomas Carlyle, *Past and Present* (Oxford, 1927), pp. 206–7.
49 Michel Serres, *Hermes: Literature, Science, Philosophy*, ed. Josué V. Harari and David F. Bell (Baltimore, MD, 1982), p. 44.
50 David Graeber, *Bullshit Jobs: A Theory* (London, 2019), p. 8.
51 Charles Dickens, *Great Expectations*, ed. Margaret Cardwell (Oxford, 1994), pp. 93–4.
52 George Bernard Shaw, *Mrs Warren's Profession* (London, 1905), p. 235.
53 Keith Hearne, 'A "Light-Switch Phenomenon" in Lucid Dreams', *Journal of Mental Imagery*, V (1981), p. 98.
54 Graeber, *Bullshit Jobs*, p. 145.
55 Anon., 'Mr. Froude on Landed Gentry', *Saturday Review*, XLII (1876), p. 592; J. A. Froude, 'On the Uses of a Landed Gentry', *Fraser's Magazine*, XIV (1876), pp. 671–85.
56 John Carey, *What Good Are the Arts?* (London, 2005), pp. 46–7.

57 Sol LeWitt, 'Paragraphs on Conceptual Art', in *Conceptual Art: A Critical Anthology*, ed. Alexander Alberro and Blake Stimson (Cambridge, MA, and London, 1999), p. 12.
58 Ibid.
59 Ibid., p. 16.

3 At Work

1 Franklin Becker and Fritz Steele, *Workplace by Design: Mapping the High-Performance Workscape* (San Francisco, CA, 1995), p. 13.
2 Charles Dickens, *Great Expectations*, ed. Margaret Cardwell (Oxford, 1993), p. 208.
3 Ibid., p. 209.
4 Nikil Saval, *Cubed: A Secret History of the Workplace* (New York, 2014), p. 27.
5 Alison Light, *Mrs Woolf and the Servants: An Intimate History of Domestic Life in Bloomsbury* (New York, 2008), p. 67.
6 Virginia Woolf, *Collected Essays*, 2 vols (London, 1966), vol. I, p. 320.
7 Richard Hooker, *Of the Lavves of Ecclesiasticall Politie Eight Bookes* (London, 1604), p. 52.
8 Frederick Winslow Taylor, *The Principles of Scientific Management* (New York and London, 1911), p. 10.
9 Peter Sloterdijk, *Schäume: Sphären*, vol. III: *Plurale Sphärologie* (Frankfurt, 2004), p. 87.
10 W. H. Auden, *Collected Shorter Poems, 1930–1944* (London, 1950), p. 75.
11 Saval, *Cubed*, p. 96.
12 Tim Ingold, 'The Temporality of the Landscape', *World Archaeology*, XXV (2000), p. 158.
13 Ibid., p. 159.
14 Ibid., p. 154.
15 Gillian Darley, *Factory* (London, 2003), pp. 55–73.
16 Benjamin Disraeli, *Coningsby; or, The New Generation*, ed. B. N. Langdon-Davies (London, 1963), p. 133.
17 Ibid., pp. 133–4.
18 Peter J. T. Morris, *The Matter Factory: A History of the Chemistry Laboratory* (London, 2015).
19 Ben Jonson, *Works*, vol. V: *Volpone; Epicoene; The Alchemist; Catiline*, ed. C. H. Herford and Percy Simpson (Oxford, 1937), p. 296. References to *Alchemist* in the text hereafter.
20 George Ripley, *The Compound of Alchymy* (London, 1591), p. 24.
21 Morris, *The Matter Factory*, p. 72.

22 Robert Neville, *An English Inquisition for a Heretick; or, The Punishment Due to Hereticks* (London, 1673), p. 13.
23 Walter Charleton, *Physiologia Epicuro-Gassendo-Charltoniana; or, A Fabrick of Science Natural, upon the Hypothesis of Atoms Founded by Epicurus* (London, 1654), p. 342.
24 *Engineering Magazine*, XV (1898), p. 243.
25 Clive Wilkinson, *The Theatre of Work* (Amsterdam, 2019), pp. 280, 8.
26 Ibid., p. 10.
27 Terry Eagleton, *Against the Grain: Essays 1975–1985* (London, 1986), p. 132.
28 F. W. Moorman, *Songs of the Ridings* (London, 1918), pp. 23, 24.
29 Christopher Marlowe, *Complete Works*, vol. II: *Dr Faustus*, ed. Roma Gill (Oxford, 1990), p. 12.
30 Darley, *Factory*, p. 157.
31 Simone de Beauvoir, *The Second Sex*, ed. and trans. H. M. Parshley (New York, 1953), p. 451.
32 Hannah Arendt, *The Human Condition*, ed. Margaret Canovan, 2nd edn (Chicago, IL, 1958), p. 135.
33 Susan Strasser, *Never Done: A History of American Housework* (New York, 1982), pp. 8–9.
34 Laura Humphreys, *Globalizing Housework: Domestic Labour in Middle-Class London Homes, 1850–1914* (London, 2021), p. 122.
35 William R. Beer, *Househusbands: Men and Housework in American Families* (New York, 1983), pp. 93, 112.
36 Silvia Federici, *Revolution at Point Zero: Housework, Reproduction, and Feminist Struggle*, 2nd edn (Oakland, CA, 2012), p. 14.
37 Charlotte Perkins Gilman, *The Home: Its Work and Influence*, ed. William L. O'Neill (Urbana, Chicago, IL, and London, 1972), p. 117.
38 Federici, *Revolution at Point Zero*, p. 15.
39 Beauvoir, *Second Sex*, p. 450.
40 Sigmund Freud, 'Fragments of an Analysis of a Case of Hysteria', in *The Standard Edition of the Complete Psychological Works of Sigmund Freud*, 24 vols, ed. and trans. James Strachey et al. (London, 1953–74), vol. VII, p. 19.
41 Michel Serres, *Malfeasance: Appropriation through Pollution?*, trans. Anne-Marie Feenberg-Dibon (Stanford, CA, 2011), pp. 3–4.
42 Sándor Ferenczi, *Further Contributions to the Theory and Technique of Psycho-Analysis*, ed. John Rickman, trans. Jane Isabel Suttie et al. (London, 1926), p. 257; *Bausteine zur Psychoanalyse. Band II Praxis* (Leipzig, Vienna and Zürich, 1927), p. 234.
43 Ferenczi, *Further Contributions*, p. 257.

44 Sándor Ferenczi, *Contributions to Psycho-Analysis*, trans. Ernest Jones (Boston, MA, and Toronto, 1916), p. 278.
45 Ibid., n.1.
46 Ibid.
47 Samuel Beckett, *Collected Poems in English and French* (London, 1977), p. 129.
48 Mary Townsend, 'Housework', *Hedgehog Review*, XVIII (2016), pp. 122–3.
49 Ibid., p. 123.
50 Kathryn Allen Rabuzzi, *The Sacred and the Feminine: Toward a Theology of Housework* (New York, 1982).
51 D. H. Lawrence, *The Rainbow*, ed. Kate Flint (Oxford, 1997), pp. 6, 7.
52 Freud, *The Psychopathology of Everyday Life*, in *Standard Edition*, vol. VI, p. 39.
53 Beauvoir, *Second Sex*, p. 165.

4 Off Work

1 Christophe Dejours, Jean-Philippe Deranty, Emmanuel Renault and Nicholas H. Smith, *The Return of Work in Critical Theory: Self, Society, Politics* (New York, 2018), p. 4.
2 Jean de Cartigny, *The Voyage of the Wandering Knight*, trans. William Goodyear (London, 1581), p. 51.
3 Thomas Lodge, *An Alarum against Usurers* (London, 1584), p. 6.
4 Anon., *The Protestatyon of Martin Marprelat* (Wolston, 1589), p. 25.
5 Ben Jonson, *Works*, vol. VI: *Bartholomew Fair; The Devil Is an Ass; The Staple of News; The New Inn; The Magnetic Lady*, ed. C. H. Hertford, Percy Simpson and Evelyn Simpson (Oxford, 1938), p. 83.
6 Ibid., p. 11.
7 Laurence Sterne, *The Florida Edition of the Works of Laurence Sterne*, vol. I: *The Life and Opinions of Tristram Shandy, Gentleman: The Text*, ed. Melvyn New and Joan New (Gainesville, FL, 1978), p. 86.
8 Flann O'Brien, *The Third Policeman* (London, 1974), pp. 72–8.
9 Samuel Beckett, *Company* (London, 1980), p. 45
10 Theodor W. Adorno and Max Horkheimer, *Dialectic of Enlightenment*, trans. John Cumming (New York, 1989), p. 144.
11 Theodor W. Adorno, 'Free Time', trans. Gordon Finlayson and Nicholas Walker, in *The Culture Industry: Selected Essays on Mass Culture*, ed. J. M. Bernstein (London, 1991), pp. 188–9.
12 Ibid., p. 189.
13 H. P. Horne, 'A Preface', *Hobby Horse*, XIII (1889), p. 1.
14 Arthur H. Mackmurdo, 'The Guild Flag's Unfurling', *Hobby Horse*, I (1884), p. 2.

15 Robert A. Stebbins and Jenna Hartel, 'Concepts', *Serious Leisure Perspective*, www.seriousleisure.net, accessed 14 September 2022.
16 Robert A. Stebbins, *The Serious Leisure Perspective: A Synthesis* (Cham, 2020), p. 29.
17 Steven Connor, *Giving Way: Thoughts on Unappreciated Dispositions* (Stanford, CA, 2019), pp. 95–6.
18 Amy Sue Bix, '"Remember the Sabbath": A History of Technological Decisions and Innovation in Orthodox Jewish Communities', *History and Technology*, XXXVI (2020), pp. 212–13.
19 Alan Dundes, *The Shabbat Elevator and Other Sabbath Subterfuges: An Unorthodox Essay on Circumventing Custom and Jewish Character* (Lanham, Boulder, New York and Oxford, 2002), p. vii.
20 Pinchas H. Peli, *The Jewish Sabbath: A Renewed Encounter* (New York, 1988), p. 37.
21 Erich Fromm, *The Forgotten Language: An Introduction to the Understanding of Dreams, Fairy Tales, and Myths* (New York, 1976), p. 245.
22 Michel Serres, *Malfeasance: Appropriation through Pollution?*, trans. Anne-Marie Feenberg-Dibon (Stanford, CA, 2011).
23 Barry Smith, 'On Place and Space: The Ontology of the Eruv', in *Cultures: Conflict – Analysis – Dialogue*, ed. Christian Kanzian and Edmund Runggaldier (Frankfurt, 2007), p. 417.
24 Michel Serres, 'The Origin of Language: Biology, Information Theory, and Thermodynamics', in *Hermes: Literature, Science, Philosophy*, ed. Josué V. Harari and David F. Bell (Baltimore, MD, 1982), p. 73.
25 Joseph Livni and Lewi Stone, 'The Stabilizing Role of the Sabbath in Pre-Monarchic Israel: A Mathematical Model', *Journal of Biological Physics*, XLI (2015), pp. 215, 214.
26 Bernard J. Bamberger, *The Story of Judaism* (New York, 1957), p. 9.
27 Abraham Joshua Heschel, *The Sabbath: Its Meaning for Modern Man* (New York, 2005), pp. 14–15.
28 Giorgio Agamben, *The Omnibus Homo Sacer*, various translators (Stanford, CA, 2017), p. 594.
29 Ibid.
30 Samuel Beckett, *Complete Dramatic Works* (London, 1986), pp. 193, 194.
31 Sylvia Plath, *Complete Poems*, ed. Ted Hughes (London, 1981), p. 222.
32 Beckett, *Complete Dramatic Works*, p. 84.
33 Michel Serres, *Geometry: The Third Book of Foundations*, trans. Randolph Burks (London, 2017), p. xxxiii.
34 Emmanuel Levinas, *The Levinas Reader*, ed. Seán Hand (Oxford, 1989), p. 31.
35 Steven Connor, *Living By Numbers: In Defence of Quantity* (London, 2016), pp. 155–8.

36 Henry, Prince of Orange, *The Prince of Orange, His Royall Entertainment to the Qveen of England* (London, 1641), sig. A4r.
37 Steven Connor, 'The Poorest Things Superfluous: On Redundancy' (2011), http://stevenconnor.com.
38 George Bernard Shaw, *Man and Superman: A Comedy and a Philosophy* (London, 1903), pp. 37–8.
39 Ibid., p. xxxii.
40 Geoffrey Chaucer, *Works*, ed. F. N. Robinson (Boston, MA, 1961), p. 182.
41 Isaac Watts, *Divine Songs Attempted in Easy Language for the Use of Children* (London, 1716), p. 29.
42 William Shakespeare, *Complete Works*, ed. Richard Proudfoot, Ann Thompson and David Scott Kastan (London, New York, New Delhi and Sydney, 2011), p. 1014.
43 Robert Greene, *Greenes Groats-Worth of Witte, Bought with a Million of Repentance* (London, 1592), sig. F3r.
44 Steven Connor, *Beyond Words: Sobs, Hums, Stutters and Other Vocalizations* (London, 2014), pp. 148–53.
45 Shakespeare, *Complete Works*, p. 421.
46 Jeremy Taylor, *The Rule and Exercises of Holy Living* (London, 1650), p. 12.
47 Shakespeare, *Complete Works*, pp. 660, 669.
48 Ibid., p. 896.
49 John Wycliffe, *The Holy Bible, Containing the Old and New Testaments, with the Apocryphal Books, in the Earliest English Versions Made from the Latin Vulgate by John Wycliffe and His Followers*, ed. Josiah Forshall and Frederic Madden (Oxford, 1850), p. 79.
50 Bob Black, *The Abolition of Work and Other Essays* (Port Townsend, WA, 1985), pp. 18, 20.
51 Ibid., p. 17.
52 Bertrand Russell, 'In Praise of Idleness', in *In Praise of Idleness and Other Essays* (London, 1935), p. 14.
53 Ibid., p. 15.
54 Daniel Bell, *Work and Its Discontents* (Boston, MA, 1956), p. 55.
55 Ibid., p. 56.
56 Samuel Noah Kramer, *History Begins at Sumer* (Garden City, NY, 1959), pp. 13, 14.
57 Ibid., p. 15.
58 Serres, *Hermes*, ed. Harari and Bell, p. 76 n.6.
59 William Morris, *News from Nowhere and Other Writings*, ed. Clive Wilmer (London, 2004), p. 51.
60 Georges Jean-Aubry, *Joseph Conrad: Life and Letters* (London, 1927), vol. II, p. 47.

61 William Blake, *William Blake's Writings*, vol. I: *Engraved and Etched Writings*, ed. G. E. Bentley (Oxford, 1978), p. 83.
62 William Stirling-Hamilton, *The Cloister Life of the Emperor Charles the Fifth* (London, 1852), p. 173.

5 Working Out

1 Hannah Arendt, *The Human Condition*, ed. Margaret Canovan, 2nd edn (Chicago, IL, and London, 1998), pp. 126–7.
2 Michel Foucault, *The History of Sexuality*, vol. I: *An Introduction*, trans. Robert Hurley (New York, 1978), p. 136.
3 Ibid., p. 6.
4 Ibid., p. 69.
5 Christophe Dejours, *Travail vivant 1: Sexualité et travail* (Paris, 2009); *Travail vivant 2: Travail et émancipation* (Paris, 2013).
6 Nicholas H. Smith and Jean-Philippe Deranty, eds, *New Philosophies of Labour: Work and the Social Bond* (Leiden and Boston, MA, 2012).
7 Glen U. Cleeton, *Making Work Human* (Yellow Springs, OH, 1949).
8 Asma Afsaruddin, *Striving in the Path of God: Jihād and Martyrdom in Islamic Thought* (Oxford, 2013), p. 2.
9 P. Kopiec, 'The Idea of the Biblical Economics: Utopia or Chance in the Face of the Contemporary Transformations of the Sphere of Work', *HTS Teologiese Studies/Theological Studies*, LXXV (2019), a5164, https://doi.org/10.4102/hts.v75i4.5164.
10 Giorgio Agamben, *The Omnibus Homo Sacer*, various translators (Stanford, CA, 2017), p. 720.
11 Ibid., p. 654.
12 Sigmund Freud, *Totem and Taboo: Some Points of Agreement between the Mental Lives of Savages and Neurotics*, in *The Standard Edition of the Complete Psychological Works of Sigmund Freud*, 24 vols, ed. and trans. James Strachey et al. (London, 1953–74), vol. XIII, p. 84.
13 Steven Connor, 'Religion Beyond Belief' (2012), http://stevenconnor.com.
14 Johann Wilhem Goethe, *Goethes Werke, Band 1: Gedichte und Epen*, ed. Erich Trunz (Munich, 1981), p. 279 (my translation).
15 Anon., *The Church Missionary Hymn Book* (London, 1899), p. 8.
16 Jonathan Edwards, *A History of the Work of Redemption* (Boston, MA, 1782), p. 9.
17 Francis Paget, *The Redemption of Work* (Oxford and London, 1882), pp. 18, 19.
18 Ibid., pp. 20, 29–30.
19 Marie-Dominique Chenu, *The Theology of Work: An Exploration*, trans. Lillian Soiron (Dublin, 1963), p. 14. References to *Theology of Work* in the text hereafter.

20 Stephan van Erp, 'Holiness in the Making: Labor and Sacrament in Catholic Theology', *Journal of Religious Ethics*, XLV (2017), pp. 288–9.
21 John Gay, *Poetical Works*, ed. G. C. Faber (London, 1926), pp. 292–3.
22 Ibid., p. 293.
23 Steven Connor, 'Michel Serres: The Hard and the Soft' (2009), http://stevenconnor.com.
24 Gerard Manley Hopkins, *The Poems of Gerard Manley Hopkins*, ed. W. H. Gardner and N. H. Mackenzie, 4th edn (London, New York and Toronto, 1970), p. 90.
25 David Graeber, *Bullshit Jobs: A Theory* (London, 2019), p. 221.
26 John Milton, *Poetical Works*, vol. I: *Paradise Lost*, ed. Helen Darbishire (Oxford, 1963), p. 23.
27 Simone Weil, *The Need for Roots: Prelude to a Declaration of Duties toward Mankind*, trans. Arthur Wills (New York, Evanston, IL, San Francisco, CA, and London, 1971), p. 78.
28 Ibid., p. 94.
29 Ibid., pp. 97, 98–9.
30 Simone Weil, *Gravity and Grace*, trans. Emma Crawford and Mario von der Ruhr, ed. Gustave Thibon (London and New York, 2002), pp. 130–31. References to *Gravity and Grace* in the text hereafter.
31 Simone Weil, *Late Philosophical Writings*, trans. Eric O. Springsted and Lawrence E. Schmidt, ed. Eric O. Springsted (Notre Dame, IN, 2015), p. 137.
32 Ibid., p. 142.
33 Ibid., p. 140.
34 Ibid., p. 137.
35 Ibid., p. 140.
36 Steven Connor, 'Absolute Levity', *Comparative Critical Studies*, VI (2009), p. 415.
37 Catherine Bailey, Adrian Madden, Kerstin Alfes, Amanda Shantz and Emma Soane, 'The Mismanaged Soul: Existential Labor and the Erosion of Meaningful Work', *Human Resource Management Review*, XXVII (2017), p. 418.
38 Ibid.
39 Ibid., p. 423.
40 Shoaib Ul-Haq, 'Spiritual Development and Meaningful Work: A Habermasian Critique', *Human Resource Development International*, XXIII (2020), p. 126.
41 Ibid., p. 136.
42 George Herbert, *The Works of George Herbert*, ed. F. H. Hutchinson (Oxford, 1941), p. 90.

43 Catherine Bailey and Adrian Madden, 'What Makes Work Meaningful – Or Meaningless', *MIT Sloan Management Review*, LVII (2016), p. 53.
44 Joseph Conrad, *Lord Jim: A Tale*, ed. John Batchelor (Oxford, 1983), p. 214.
45 Bailey and Madden, 'What Makes Work Meaningful', p. 58.
46 Ibid., p. 60.
47 Christopher Michaelson, 'A Normative Meaning of Meaningful Work', *Journal of Business Ethics*, CLXX (2021), p. 421.
48 Ibid., p. 422.
49 Ibid., p. 216.
50 Ibid., p. 424.
51 Catherine Bailey, Marjolein Lips-Wiersma, Adrian Madden, Ruth Yeoman, Marc Thompson and Neal Chalofsky, 'The Five Paradoxes of Meaningful Work', *Journal of Management Studies*, LVI (2019), pp. 489–95.
52 J. L. Austin, *Philosophical Papers*, ed. J. O. Urmson and G. J. Warnock, 3rd edn (Oxford, 1979), p. 117.
53 Adina Schwartz, 'Meaningful Work', *Ethics*, XCII (1982), p. 638.
54 Karl Marx, *Economic and Philosophical Manuscripts of 1844*, trans. Martin Milligan, ed. Dirk J. Struik (New York, 1964), pp. 110, 114.
55 Jacques Derrida, *Specters of Marx: The State of the Debt, the Work of Mourning, and the New International*, trans. Peggy Kamuf (New York and London, 1994), p. 166.
56 Karl Marx, *Capital: A Critique of Political Economy*, vol. I, in *Marx/Engels, Collected Works*, XXXV, trans. Samuel Moore and Edward Aveling (New York, 1996), p. 241.
57 Derrida, *Specters of Marx*, p. 75.
58 Georges Bataille, *The Bataille Reader*, ed. Fred Botting and Scott Wilson (Oxford, 1997), p. 56.
59 Ibid., p. 245.
60 Ibid., p. 149.
61 Ibid., p. 4.
62 Weil, *Gravity and Grace*, p. 180.

Further Reading

Adorno, Theodor W., 'Free Time', trans. Gordon Finlayson and Nicholas Walker, in *The Culture Industry: Selected Essays on Mass Culture*, ed. J. M. Bernstein (London, 1991), pp. 187–97

Agamben, Giorgio, *Opus Dei: An Archaeology of Duty*, trans. Adam Kotsko, in *The Omnibus Homo Sacer* (Stanford, CA, 2017), pp. 643–758

Arendt, Hannah, *The Human Condition*, ed. Margaret Canovan, 2nd edn (Chicago, IL, and London, 1998)

Bailey, Catherine, and Adrian Madden, 'What Makes Work Meaningful – Or Meaningless', *MIT Sloan Management Review*, LVII (2016), pp. 53–61

Beer, William R., *Househusbands: Men and Housework in American Families* (New York, 1983)

Bell, Daniel, *Work and Its Discontents* (Boston, MA, 1956)

Black, Bob, *The Abolition of Work and Other Essays* (Port Townsend, WA, 1985)

Chenu, Marie-Dominique, *The Theology of Work: An Exploration*, trans. Lillian Soiron (Dublin, 1963)

Ciulla, Joanne B., *The Working Life: The Promise and Betrayal of Modern Work* (New York, 2000)

Cleeton, Glen U., *Making Work Human* (Yellow Springs, OH, 1949)

Darley, Gillian, *Factory* (London, 2003)

Dejours, Christophe, *Travail vivant: Tome 1 – Sexuality et travail* (Paris, 2009)

—, *Travail vivant: Tome 2 – Travail et émancipation* (Paris, 2013)

—, ed., *Psychopathology of Work: Clinical Observations*, trans. Caroline Williamson (London, 2015)

—, Jean-Philippe Deranty, Emmanuel Renault and Nicholas H. Smith, *The Return of Work in Critical Theory: Self, Society, Politics* (New York, 2018)

Dundes, Alan, *The Shabbat Elevator and Other Sabbath Subterfuges: An Unorthodox Essay on Circumventing Custom and Jewish Character* (Lanham, MD, Boulder, CO, New York and Oxford, 2002)

Federici, Silvia, *Revolution at Point Zero: Housework, Reproduction, and Feminist Struggle*, 2nd edn (Oakland, CA, 2020)
Graeber, David, *Bullshit Jobs: A Theory* (London, 2019)
Harnad, Stevan, 'On the Virtues of Theft Over Honest Toil: Grounding Language and Thought in Sensorimotor Categories' (1996), http://cogprints.org
Hendrick, Ives, 'Work and the Pleasure Principle', *Psychoanalytic Quarterly*, XII (1943), pp. 311–29
Heschel, Abraham Joshua, *The Sabbath: Its Meaning for Modern Man* (New York, 2005)
Humphreys, Laura, *Globalizing Housework: Domestic Labour in Middle-Class London Homes, 1850–1914* (London, 2021)
Little, Arthur, 'The Philosophy of Work', *Irish Monthly*, LXXVI (1948), pp. 56–65
Morris, Peter J. T., *The Matter Factory: A History of the Chemistry Laboratory* (London, 2015)
O'Connor, Brian, *Idleness: A Philosophical Essay* (Princeton, NJ, 2018)
Rabuzzi, Kathryn Allen, *The Sacred and the Feminine: Toward a Theology of Housework* (New York, 1982)
Russell, Bertrand, 'In Praise of Idleness', in *In Praise of Idleness and Other Essays* (London, 1935), pp. 9–29
Saval, Nikil, *Cubed: A Secret History of the Workplace* (New York, 2014)
Schwartz, Adina, 'Meaningful Work', *Ethics*, XCII (1982), pp. 634–46
Smith, Nicholas H., and Jean-Philippe Deranty, eds, *New Philosophies of Labour: Work and the Social Bond* (Leiden and Boston, MA, 2012)
Stebbins, Robert A., *The Serious Leisure Perspective: A Synthesis* (Cham, 2020)
Strasser, Susan, *Never Done: A History of American Housework* (New York, 1982)
Suzman, James, *Work: A History of How We Spend Our Time* (London, 2020)
Taylor, Frederick Winslow, *The Principles of Scientific Management* (New York and London, 1911)
Ventura, Rodrigo, 'The Concept of Work in the Psychoanalytic Experience', *Psicologia USP*, XXVI (2016), pp. 282–8
Weil, Simone, *Gravity and Grace*, trans. Emma Crawford and Mario von der Ruhr, ed. Gustave Thibon (London and New York, 2002)
Wilkinson, Clive, *The Theatre of Work* (Amsterdam, 2019)

Index